STATE RESPONSIBILITY, CLIMATE CHANGE AND HUMAN RIGHTS UNDER INTERNATIONAL LAW

The last decade has witnessed an increasing focus on the relationship between climate change and human rights. Several international human rights bodies have expressed concern about the negative implications of climate change for the enjoyment of human rights, and the Paris Agreement is the first multilateral climate agreement to refer explicitly to states' human rights obligations in connection with climate change. Yet despite this, there are still significant gaps in our understanding of the role of international human rights law in enhancing accountability for climate action or inaction. As the Paris Agreement has shifted the focus of the climate change regime towards voluntary action, and the humanitarian impacts of climate change are increasingly being felt around the world, accountability for climate change has become an increasingly salient issue. This book offers a timely and comprehensive analysis of the legal issues related to accountability for the human rights impact of climate change, drawing on the state responsibility regime. It explains when and where state action relating to climate change may amount to a violation of human rights, and evaluates various avenues of legal redress available to victims. The overall analysis offers a perceptive insight into the potential of innovative rights-based climate actions to shape climate and energy policies around the world.

State Responsibility, Climate Change and Human Rights under International Law

Margaretha Wewerinke-Singh

•HART•
OXFORD • LONDON • NEW YORK • NEW DELHI • SYDNEY

HART PUBLISHING

Bloomsbury Publishing Plc

Kemp House, Chawley Park, Cumnor Hill, Oxford, OX2 9PH, UK

HART PUBLISHING, the Hart/Stag logo, BLOOMSBURY and the Diana logo are trademarks of Bloomsbury Publishing Plc

First published in Great Britain 2019

A catalogue record for this book is available from the British Library.

Library of Congress Cataloging-in-Publication data

Names: Wewerinke-Singh, Margaretha, author.

Title: State responsibility, climate change and human rights under international law / Margaretha Wewerinke-Singh.

Description: Oxford, UK ; Portland, Oregon : Hart Publishing, 2019. | Based on author's thesis (doctoral - European University Institute, Florence, 2015). | Includes bibliographical references and index.

Identifiers: LCCN 2018049672 (print) | LCCN 2018051100 (ebook) | ISBN 9781509918454 (Epub) | ISBN 9781509918447 (hardback)

Subjects: LCSH: Liability for climatic change damages. | Liability for human rights violations. | Government liability (International law) | Environmental law, International. | BISAC: LAW / Environmental. | LAW / Civil Rights. | LAW / International.

Classification: LCC K955 (ebook) | LCC K955 .W49 2019 (print) | DDC 344.04/633—dc23

LC record available at https://lccn.loc.gov/2018049672

ISBN: HB: 978-1-50991-844-7
ePDF: 978-1-50991-846-1
ePub: 978-1-50991-845-4

Typeset by Compuscript Ltd, Shannon

To find out more about our authors and books visit www.hartpublishing.co.uk. Here you will find extracts, author information, details of forthcoming events and the option to sign up for our newsletters.

ACKNOWLEDGEMENTS

The journey of this research project started at the European University Institute (EUI) in Florence, where I had the opportunity to complete a PhD. I owe a debt of gratitude to my supervisors, Martin Scheinin and Markus Gehring, for their rigorous feedback, ever-useful criticism, trust and encouragement. I am also grateful to Marise Cremona and Frédéric Mégret for their critical engagement with my PhD as members of the Examination Board, and to Francesco Francioni, Dennis Patterson and Robert Howse for rich discussions. Marina Aksenova, Alice Margaria, Wim Muller and many other colleagues at the EUI provided intellectual input and extended friendship and support. Valerio del Piccolo and the members of the EUI choir and orchestra enriched my life in Florence, and a co-coaching arrangement with Emmanuelle Mathieu had a tremendously positive impact on my writing and well-being throughout the process.

I carried out most of the second part of the research project at the University of Cambridge, first as a visiting scholar at the Lauterpacht Centre for International Law (LCIL) and later as an affiliated researcher at the Centre for Climate Change Mitigation Research (4CMR). At LCIL, James Crawford was always available for a discussion and generous with his time, and Philip Allott helped me to develop and question my ideas at multiple occasions. I am also grateful to Sarah Nouwen, Surabhi Ranganathan, Jessie Hohmann, Alexia Solomou, Sheng Zhang, Kae Oyama, Anita Rutherford, Karen Fachechi and many other members of the staff and visiting fellows at LCIL for their support and friendship. Very special thanks to Katarzyna Galka for reading, criticising and correcting several versions of the initial manuscript. At 4CMR, I am particularly grateful to Douglas Crawford-Brown, Jean-François Mercure, Louise Segar and Pablo Salas for enlightening discussions and good times.

Outside the academic realm, I have had the opportunity to work with some of the most brilliant and dedicated climate justice activists, advisors, lawyers and negotiators from around the world. Their insights have informed the writing of this book at critical junctures. I would particularly like to thank Matthew Stilwell, Lim Li Lin, Asad Rehman, Meena Raman, Martin Khor, Vicente Paolo Yu, Doreen Stabinsky, Kate Dooley, Mithika Mwenda, Augustine Njamnshi, Sivan Kartha, Yves Lador, Alyssa Johl, Gita Parihar, Martin Wagner, Sébastien Duyck and Christoph Schwarte. I thank Dawda Saine and Roxana Castellon for the opportunity to learn about and witness the adverse effects of climate change on the livelihoods of communities in the Gambia and Bolivia. It has also been, and still is, a privilege to work with many members of the Pan African Climate Justice Alliance.

While completing the manuscript for this book, I had the privilege of joining the University of the South Pacific (USP)'s School of Law in Port Vila, Vanuatu. Numerous colleagues at USP have provided me with invaluable advice and support, especially Eric Colvin, Elisabeth Holland, Justin Rose, Wesley Morgan, Joseph Foukona, Anita Jowitt, Donald Paterson, Howard Van Trease, Wesley Kendall, Darryn Jensen, Angileeta Devi and Fane Rai. I also learnt much from my students, and would especially like to mention Fitilagi Fa'anunu, Calvy Aonima, Shivanal Kumar, Kate Donnelly, Litia Baleilevuka, Tommie Lui, Howard Lapo and Leerick Riimana. Anne Pakoa, Willy Missack, Priscilla Samson, Matisse Walkden-Brown, Emele Duituturaga, Makereta Waqavonovono and Christopher Bartlett were amongst the many inspiring civil society colleagues who helped me to gain much-needed grounding in the realities of climate change experienced in the Pacific Island countries. I also learnt tremendously from advising the Vanuatu Ministry of Climate Change at the international climate change negotiations, and would particularly like to thank Jesse Benjamin for his trust and leadership.

This book would not have been written without the financial support provided by the Netherlands Organisation for International Cooperation in Higher Education (NUFFIC); the EUI; the Prins Bernhard Cultuurfonds and the Hendrik Müller Vaderlandsch Fonds. I would also like to record my sincere gratitude to Sinead Moloney and the dedicated staff of Hart Publishing. The feedback I received from two anonymous peer reviewers helped me to improve the final manuscript. I am also very grateful to Ashleigh McCoach and Tess Van Geelen for editing the final version of the manuscript. There are many others who contributed to this project, in various ways. I would particularly like to express my deep gratitude to Curtis Doebbler, John Dernbach and Jan Pronk for their mentorship. My deepest thanks as well to Michael Onyebuchi Eze, Tshepo Madlingozi, Lama Jbarah-Tarbush, Naji Haraj, Cyril Kuttiyanikkal, Agata Pacho, Jane and John Henson and other friends around the world for their friendship and support.

Finally, I am grateful to my family for supporting me and my endeavours in all possible ways. I remember my grandfather Nicolaas van Etten, whose lust for life and eagerness to learn continue to be inspiring, and wish to express special thanks to my beloved grandmother Margaretha van Etten-van der Meer, who was the first to encourage my interest in law and legal studies. Dorieke, Thijs, Sem, Finn, Lente, Lara, Josine, Hjalmar and Floran for their love, endless support and sense of humour. Very special thanks to my parents Florens and Jolanda. Words fall short to express my thanks and love to my husband Sanjeev and our daughter Adira.

CONTENTS

ABBREVIATIONS

ACHPR	African Charter on Human and Peoples' Rights
ACHR	American Convention on Human Rights
ADRDM	American Declaration of the Rights and Duties of Man
Annex I Parties	Australia, Austria, Belarus, Belgium, Bulgaria, Canada, Croatia, Czech Republic, Denmark, Estonia, European Union, Finland, France, Germany, Greece, Hungary, Iceland, Ireland, Italy, Japan, Latvia, Liechtenstein, Lithuania, Luxembourg, Malta, Monaco, Netherlands, New Zealand, Norway, Poland, Portugal, Romania, Russian Federation, Slovakia, Slovenia, Spain, Sweden, Switzerland, Turkey, Ukraine, United Kingdom and the United States of America
AOSIS	Alliance of Small Island States
Arab CHR	Arab Charter on Human Rights
ARIO	ILC Articles on the Responsibility of International Organisations
ARS	ILC Articles on the Responsibility of States for Internationally Wrongful Acts
AU	African Union
AWG-KP	Ad Hoc Working Group on Further Commitments for Annex I Parties under the Kyoto Protocol
AWG-LCA	Ad Hoc Working Group on Long Term Co-operative Action under the Framework Convention on Climate Change
CAT	Committee Against Torture
CBDR	Common But Differentiated Responsibilities
CBDRRC	Common But Differentiated Responsibilities and Respective Capabilities
CDM	Clean Development Mechanism
CEDAW	Convention on the Elimination of All Forms of Discrimination Against Women
CERD	Committee on the Elimination of Racial Discrimination
CESCR	Committee on Economic, Social and Cultural Rights

CFR	Charter of Fundamental Rights of the EU
CHR	UN Commission on Human Rights
CJEU	Court of Justice of the European Union
CMA	Conference of the Parties serving as the Meeting of the Parties to the Paris Agreement
CMP	Conference of the Parties serving as the Meeting of the Parties to the Kyoto Protocol
CMW	International Convention on the Protection of the Rights of All Migrant Workers and Members of Their Families
COP	Conference of the Parties to the United Nations Framework Convention on Climate Change
CRC	Convention on the Rights of the Child
CRPD	Convention on the Rights of Persons with Disabilities
DRC	Democratic Republic of Congo
EC	European Community
ECHR	European Convention on Human Rights
ECJ	European Court of Justice
ECOSOC	UN Economic and Social Council
ECSR	European Committee of Social Rights
ECtHR	European Court of Human Rights
EEZ	Exclusive Economic Zone
EIA	Environmental Impact Assessment
EIT	Countries with Economies in Transition
EU	European Union
EPA	US Environmental Protection Agency
ETS	Emissions Trading Scheme
EU ETS	European Union ETS
GA	General Assembly of the UN
GDP	Gross domestic product
GEF	Global Environmental Facility
GHG	Greenhouse Gas
HRC	Human Rights Committee
IACtHR	Inter-American Court of Human Rights
IACHR	Inter-American Commission on Human Rights
ICAO	International Civil Aviation Organisation

ICCPR	International Covenant on Civil and Political Rights
ICERD	International Convention on the Elimination of All Forms of Racial Discrimination
ICESCR	International Covenant on Economic, Social and Cultural Rights
ICJ	International Court of Justice
IEA	International Energy Agency
ILA	International Law Association
ILC	International Law Commission
ILM	International Legal Materials
ILO	International Labour Organisation
INC	Intergovernmental Negotiation Committee for the UNFCCC
IPCC	Intergovernmental Panel on Climate Change
ITLOS	International Tribunal for the Law of the See
JI	Joint Implementation
LDCs	Least Developed Country Parties
NAMAs	Nationally Appropriate Mitigation Action
NAPAs	National Adaptation Programmes of Action (for LDCs)
NATO	North Atlantic Treaty Organisation
NGO	Non-Governmental Organisation
OAS	Organisation of American States
ODA	Official Development Assistance
OECD	Organisation for Economic Co-operation and Development
OHCHR	Office of the UN High Commissioner for Human Rights
OIC	Organisation of Islamic States
OP-ICCPR	First Optional Protocol to the ICCPR
OP-ICESCR	Optional Protocol to the ICESCR
PCIJ	Permanent Court of International Justice
QELRC	Quantified Emissions Limitation or Reduction Commitments
REDD+	Reducing Emissions from Deforestation and Forest Degradation in developing countries
Res	Resolution
SBI	Subsidiary Body for Implementation
SBSTA	Subsidiary Body for Scientific and Technological Advice
SC	Security Council

SIDS	Small Island Developing States
UDHR	Universal Declaration of Human Rights
UK	United Kingdom
UN	United Nations
UNCED	United Nations Conference on Environment and Development
UNCLOS	United Nations Convention on the Law of the Sea
UNDRIP	United Nations Declaration on the Rights of Indigenous Peoples
UNDP	United Nations Development Programme
UNEP	United Nations Environment Programme
UNFCCC	United Nations Framework Convention on Climate Change
UNTS	United Nations Treaty Series
USA	United States of America
VCLT	Vienna Convention on the Law of Treaties
WCED	(UN) Word Commission on Environment and Development
WHO	World Health Organisation
WMO	World Meteorological Organisation

LEGAL MATERIALS

Treaties

UN Resolutions and Other Official Documents

Cases

PCIJ, International Court of Justice, ITLOS and International Arbitration

International and Regional Human Rights Cases, Concluding Observations and General Comments

National and European Union Cases

PART I

Legal and Conceptual Foundations

1

Introduction

Introduction: Climate Change as a Human Rights Issue

Climate change has been characterised as one of the defining challenges of our time.[1] The Nobel Prize winning Intergovernmental Panel on Climate Change (IPCC) has stated unequivocally in numerous reports that greenhouse gas-emitting human activities are causing global warming and associated damage to natural and human systems.[2] The Earth has now warmed by about 1.1°C since pre-industrialisation, and this is mostly attributable to the fossil fuel combustion that facilitated the economic development of what are now high-income countries from around 1750 onwards.[3] Carbon dioxide stocked in the atmosphere were at an approximated level of 1,900 billion tonnes in 2013, a level unprecedented in at least 800,000 years, and one that continues to rise.[4] The IPCC has indicated that as a result of these existing stocks, many aspects of climate change and associated impacts will continue for centuries even if anthropogenic emissions of greenhouse gases are stopped today.[5] However, greenhouse gases have not been stopped and instead the flow of global emissions is expanding, partly as a result of increasing contributions from countries that have relatively recently embarked on carbon-intensive pathways of economic growth. This expansion leads to an accelerating increase of the atmospheric stocks of greenhouse gases which, if it continues, could have catastrophic consequences for human populations.

The IPCC's reports make it clear that the adverse effects of climate change are already posing significant threats to human life, livelihoods and traditional

[1] United Nations Secretary General, Ban Ki-Moon, 'Address to High-Level Event on Climate Change' (2007). See also United Nations Development Programme, 'Fighting Climate Change: Human Solidarity in a Divided World' (Human Development Report 2007/2008) 8.

[2] See Intergovernmental Panel on Climate Change (IPCC), 'Contribution of Working Group I to the IPCC Fifth Assessment Report' in Thomas F Stocker et al (eds), *Climate Change 2013: The Physical Science Basis* (Cambridge, Cambridge University Press, 2013) Section D.3, 2.2, 6.3, 10.3–6, 10.9 (finding that 'It is *extremely likely* that human influence has been the dominant cause of the observed warming since the mid-20th century').

[3] Ibid 12; NASA, 'Climate Change: Vital Signs of the Planet: Evidence' available at www.climate.nasa.gov/evidence/.

[4] IPCC, 'Contribution of Working Group I to the IPCC Fifth Assessment Report' (n 2) 5.

[5] Ibid.

cultures, especially in developing countries with a limited capacity to adapt.[6] For example, inhabitants of low-lying coastal zones and small islands are facing an increased risk of death, injury, ill health and disrupted livelihoods due to storm surges, coastal flooding and rising sea levels. Poor populations in rural and urban areas face the risk that continuing rises in temperature, changing precipitation patterns and the increased occurrence of drought, extreme weather events and flooding will cause the breakdown of food systems on which they rely for sustenance. Urban populations are exposed to an increased risk of mortality and morbidity during periods of extreme heat; and fishing communities in the tropics and the Arctic are already facing climate change-induced water scarcity and irreversible degradation of marine and coastal ecosystems, all of which puts their traditional livelihoods at risk.[7] It has been established with a relatively high degree of certainty that these specific impacts are attributable to climate change. An important premise of this book is that this attribution has normative consequences under existing international human rights law.

It is also significant that existing evidence provides insight into the consequences of various emission scenarios and the sort of actions needed to alleviate the risks of future climate change. The IPCC's latest Physical Science Report carries a strong warning that without additional mitigation efforts, and even with adaptation, by the end of the twenty-first century warming will lead to a 'high to very high risk of severe, widespread and irreversible impacts globally'.[8] Pathways that are likely to limit warming to below 2°C relative to pre-industrial levels would require substantial emission reductions over the next few decades and near zero emissions by the end of the century, while pathways to limit warming to lower levels associated with lower risks to human life, health and traditional cultures will require deeper and more rapid cuts.[9] In relation to emission pathways, the IPCC's Mitigation Report stresses that mitigation and adaptation capacity differ immensely between countries, and that mitigation pathways that impose too heavy a burden on developing countries could reduce the resilience of populations to the impact of climate change and other causes of environmental stress.[10] The International Energy Agency's finding that 1.3 billion people are still without access to electricity and 2.6 billion people are without clean cooking facilities

[6] IPCC, 'Contribution of Working Group II to the IPCC Fifth Assessment Report' in Vicente R Barros et al (eds), *Climate Change 2014: Impacts, Adaptation and Vulnerability* (Cambridge, Cambridge University Press, 2014) 13. See also United Nations Development Programme (n 2) 8 (pointing out that of the 262 million people affected by climate disasters annually in the period 2000–2004, over 98 per cent lived in developing countries).

[7] See IPCC, 'Contribution of Working Group II to the IPCC Fifth Assessment Report' (n 6) 13.

[8] IPCC, 'Contribution of Working Group I to the IPCC Fifth Assessment Report' (n 2) 5 (stating that 'most greenhouse gases (GHGs) accumulate over time and mix globally, and emissions by any agent (e.g., individual, community, company, country) affect other agents').

[9] Ibid.

[10] IPCC, 'Contribution of Working Group III to the IPCC Fifth Assessment Report' in Ottmar Edenhofer et al (eds), *Climate Change 2014: Mitigation of Climate Change* (Cambridge, Cambridge University Press, 2014) 5.

(over 95 per cent of them in sub-Saharan African or developing Asia) illustrates the IPCC's recommendation that effective global mitigation pathways must involve international cooperation to create or facilitate sustainable development pathways in all regions.[11]

International human rights law is prima facie relevant to climate change because its impacts, as well as measures to respond to climate change, have consequences for the enjoyment of internationally recognised human rights. Indeed, the link between climate change and human rights has been articulated in multilateral forums, by various human rights treaty bodies,[12] and by the Conference of the Parties (COP) to the United Nations Framework Convention on Climate Change (UNFCCC).[13] The first attempt to link human rights and climate change in an international agreement was made in November 2007, when several Small Island Developing States (SIDS) convened a conference on the human impact of climate change in order to stimulate concern about the human rights impacts of climate change at the international level. The Small Island Conference led to the adoption of a document that outlined the 'clear and immediate impacts' of climate change on human rights.[14] Several months later the UN Human Rights Council adopted Resolution 7/23 on human rights and climate change, initiated by a 'core group' composed of the Maldives, Costa Rica and Switzerland. The resolution recognises that climate change 'poses an immediate and far-reaching threat to people and

[11] Ibid 5.

[12] See, eg, UN Convention on the Elimination of All Forms of Discrimination Against Women (CEDAW), Statement of the CEDAW Committee on Gender and Climate Change, adopted at 44th Sess held in New York, USA, from 20 July to 7 August 2009; African Commission on Human and Peoples' Rights (ACHPR), 'Climate Change and the Need to Study Its Impacts on Africa', ACHPR/ Res153 (XLVI)09, adopted at the 46th Ordinary Session (25 November 2009); ACHPR, 'Climate Change in Africa', ACHPR/ Res271, adopted at the 55th Ordinary Session (12 May 2014); ACHPR, 'Climate Change and Human Rights in Africa', ACHPR/Res342 (LVIII), adopted at the 58th Ordinary Session (20 April 2016); Inter-American Commission for Human Rights, 'IACHR Concludes Its 141st Regular Session' available at www.cidh.oas.org/Comunicados/English/2011/28-11eng.htm; 'Petition to the Inter American Commission on Human Rights Seeking Relief from Violations Resulting from Global Warming Caused by Acts and Omissions of the United States' available at www.earthjustice.org. For a detailed discussion see ch 9.

[13] United Nations Framework Convention on Climate Change (UNFCCC), 'Paris Agreement' (adopted 12 December 2015, entered into force 4 November 2016) UN Doc FCCC/CP/2015/L.9/Rev.1 (Paris Agreement), preambular para 11 (stating that that Parties 'should, when taking action to address climate change, respect, promote and consider their respective obligations on human rights, the right to health, the rights of indigenous peoples, local communities, migrants, children, persons with disabilities and people in vulnerable situations and the right to development') and UNFCCC, *Decision 1/CP.16*, UN Doc FCCC/CP/2010/7/Add.1 (15 March 2011) preambular para 7 (quoting from UN HRC Res. 10/4) and ch I, para 8 (stating that 'States should, in all climate change-related actions, fully respect human rights'). For a general overview of international discussions on climate change and human rights, see Siobhán McInerney-Lankford, Mac Darrow and Lavanya Rajamani, 'Human Rights and Climate Change: a Review of the International Legal Dimensions' (World Bank Study no 61308, 2011); for an account of the role of human rights law in international climate negotiations see Lavanya Rajamani, 'The Increasing Currency and Relevance of Rights-Based Perspectives in the International Negotiations on Climate Change' (2010) 22 *Journal of Environmental Law* 391.

[14] Small Island Conference, Malé, Maldives, 13–14 November 20007, Malé Declaration on the Human Dimension of Global Climate Change (14 November 2007) para 2.

communities around the world and has implications for the full enjoyment of human rights'.[15] It also requested the Office of the United Nations High Commissioner on Human Rights (OHCHR) to undertake a detailed analytical study of the relationship between climate change and human rights.[16] The OHCHR replied to the request from the Council by submitting a thirty-two page report to the Council's 10th Regular Session.[17] This report was based on OHCHR research and submissions from more than thirty States, thirteen inter-governmental organisations and seventeen non-governmental organisations.[18] The report details the implications of climate change impacts and risks for the enjoyment of a range of human rights, including the rights to life, adequate food, safe drinking water and sanitation, the highest attainable standard of health, adequate housing and self-determination.[19] In addition, it notes that 'Industrialized countries, defined as Annex I countries under the UN Framework Convention on Climate Change, have historically contributed most to manmade greenhouse gas emissions' while the impacts of climate change 'disproportionally [affect] poorer regions and countries, that is, those who have generally contributed the least to human-induced climate change'.[20] It states that human rights standards and principles can 'inform debates on equity and fair distribution of mitigation and adaptation burdens' by '[focusing] attention on how a given distribution of burden affects the enjoyment of human rights',[21] and also explicitly mentions that States' obligations to address climate change include obligations owed to non-nationals located outside a State's territory.[22] Another key finding is that 'International human rights law complements the [UNFCCC] by underlining that international cooperation is not only expedient but also a human rights obligation and that its central objective is the realization of human rights'.[23] Yet the report fails to take these points to their

[15] Human Rights Council Resolution 7/23, Human Rights and Climate Change (UN Doc A/HRC/7/78, 14 July 2008) preambular para 1.

[16] Ibid.

[17] UN Office of the High Commissioner for Human Rights (UN OHCHR), 'Report of the Office of the United Nations High Commissioner for Human Rights on the Relationship between Climate Change and Human Rights' (15 January 2009) UN Doc A/HRC/10/61. The report comments on five thematic areas: (a) the relationship between the environment and human rights; (b) implications of the effects of climate change for the enjoyment of specific rights; (c) vulnerabilities of specific groups; (d) human rights implications of climate change-induced displacement and conflict; and (e) human rights implications of measures to address climate change.

[18] For discussions of the report, see John H Knox, 'Linking Human Rights and Climate Change at the United Nations' (2009) 33 *Harvard Environmental Law Review* 1 and R Dudai, 'Climate Change and Human Rights Practice: Observations on and around the Report of the Office of the High Commissioner for Human Rights on the Relationship between Climate Change and Human Rights' (2009) 1 *Journal of Human Rights Practice* 294.

[19] UN OHCHR, 'Report of the Office of the United Nations High Commissioner for Human Rights on the Relationship between Climate Change and Human Rights' (n 17) paras 20–41.

[20] Ibid para 10.

[21] Ibid para 88.

[22] Ibid paras 27, 33, 41, 74.

[23] Ibid para 99.

logical conclusion, stating that 'The physical impacts of global warming cannot easily be classified as human rights violations, not least because climate change-related harm often cannot clearly be attributed to acts or omissions of specific States'.[24] The report also suggests that it is difficult to establish climate change-related human rights violations because it is 'virtually impossible to disentangle the complex causal relationships linking historical greenhouse gas emissions of a particular country with a specific climate change-related effect, let alone with the range of direct and indirect implications for human rights'.[25] Unfortunately these two claims confuse questions of evidence with legal issues of State responsibility: it is the conduct of States, and not the occurrence of weather-related impacts or the existence of causal relationships per se, which has the potential to produce legal consequences under existing international law.[26]

Despite these shortcomings, the report appears to have consolidated a political consensus about the existence of a link between climate change and enjoyment of human rights.[27] This consensus is reflected in Resolution 10/4, adopted by the Council at its 10th Regular Session held in March 2009. Here too it was initiated by the Maldives, Costa Rica and Switzerland. The resolution lists specific rights that are implicated by climate change, building on the first OHCHR report: '*inter alia*, the right to life, the right to adequate food, the right to the highest attainable standard of health, the right to adequate housing, the right to self-determination and human rights obligations related to access to safe drinking water and sanitation'.[28] The Council also acknowledged that 'human rights obligations and commitments have the potential to inform and strengthen international and national policy-making in the area of climate change, promoting policy coherence, legitimacy and sustainable outcomes'.[29] Climate change has since remained on the Council's agenda: it has now adopted a total of eight resolutions on human rights and climate change[30] and held several seminars and panel discussions on the topic. The Human Rights Council has also encouraged its Special Procedures mandate-holders to consider climate change as part of their respective mandates.[31] Several of them have since published reports on issues relating to climate change, and a

[24] Ibid para 96.

[25] Ibid para 70.

[26] See also Knox (n 18) 5 (stating that 'The greatest shortcoming of the OHCHR report is that it says very little about the content of states' duties concerning climate change').

[27] Consolidating this consensus seems to have been the main objective of the initiators of the resolution. For a discussion, see Marc Limon, 'Human Rights and Climate Change: Constructing a Case for Political Action' (2009) 33 *Harvard Environmental Law Review* 1, 445.

[28] Human Rights Council Resolution 10/4, Human Rights and Climate Change (UN Doc A/HRC/10/L.11, 12 May 2009) preambular para 7.

[29] Ibid preambular para 10.

[30] Human Rights Council Resolutions 7/23 (n 15); 10/4 (n 28); 18/22 (UN Doc A/HRC/18/22, 28 September 2011); 26/27 (UN Doc A/HRC/26/27, 23 June 2014); 29/15 (UN Doc A/HRC/29/15, 30 June 2015); 32/33 (UN Doc HRC/32/33, 28 June 2016); 35/20 (UN Doc A/HRC/35/20, 19 June 2017) and 38/4 (UN Doc A/HRC/38/4, 2 July 2018), all titled 'Human Rights and Climate Change'.

[31] See resolutions 10/4 para 3; 26/27 para 8; 29/15 para 7.

group of mandate-holders issued a joint letter, statements and a report to highlight the importance of integrating human rights into climate action.[32] The Special Rapporteur on Human Rights and the Environment in particular has actively engaged with the international climate change negotiations to encourage States to integrate human rights into climate action. The Human Rights Council now also regularly discusses the nexus between climate change and human rights under its Universal Periodic Review (UPR) process.[33] In sum, climate change has become a recurring feature on the Council's agenda, and advocacy around the nexus can be expected to continue in years to come.

Climate Change, Human Rights and State Responsibility

It is worth noting that in the increasingly voluminous body of statements of international bodies linking climate change with human rights, no reference has, as yet, been made to 'violations' of human rights. Nevertheless, it has been suggested in the literature that climate change as such violates human rights.[34] This proposition undoubtedly has some rhetorical force. However, it disregards the doctrinal point that human rights violations result from the actions of States. This doctrinal point would seem to underpin much of the scepticism regarding human rights and climate change which characterises a significant part of the legal literature on the topic: Bodansky, for example, maintains that despite the overwhelming body of evidence about the man-made causes of climate change and its adverse effects on the enjoyment of human rights, 'Legally, climate change no more violates human rights than does a hurricane, earthquake, volcanic eruption, or meteor impact'.[35] However, Bodansky's conclusion, although legally accurate, sits uncomfortably with the premise that the purpose of human rights law is, to quote the European Court of Human Rights (ECtHR), '[to guarantee] not rights that are theoretical

[32] These reports, letters and statements are available at www.ohchr.org/EN/Issues/Environment/SREnvironment/Pages/ClimateChange.aspx.

[33] See further ch 9.

[34] Simon Caney states, 'it is clear that anthropogenic climate change violates [the right to life]', citing factual evidence of severe weather events and heatwaves that will lead to loss of life. Simon Caney, 'Climate Change, Human Rights and Moral Thresholds' in Stephen Humphreys (ed), *Human Rights and Climate Change* (Cambridge, Cambridge University Press, 2009) 77. See also Sumudu Atapattu, 'Global Climate Change: Can Human Rights (and Human Beings) Survive this Onslaught?' (2008) 20 *Colorado Journal of International Environmental Law and Policy* 35, 47 (similarly basing her conclusion on factual evidence).

[35] Daniel Bodansky, 'Climate Change and Human Rights: Unpacking the Issues' (2010) 38 *Georgia Journal of International & Comparative Law* 511, 519. See also, Siobhán McInerney-Lankford, 'Human Rights and Climate Change' in Michael B Gerrard and Gregory E Wannier (eds), *Threatened Island Nations: Legal Implications of Rising Seas and a Changing Climate* (Cambridge, Cambridge University Press, 2012) 232.

or illusory but rights that are practical and effective'.[36] To achieve this purpose in the context of climate change, legal consequences must be drawn from the fact that climate change is caused or exacerbated by human behaviour. At the very least, a critical examination of substantive human rights norms is needed to test the presumption that international human rights law allows States to permit or perform greenhouse gas-emitting activities without legal consequences.

In pursuing this examination, the methodology used in this book differs significantly from the methodology that is most commonly used in the scholarship on human rights and climate change. This book uses the Vienna Rules of Interpretation to address what is perhaps the greatest methodological challenge connected with the application of human rights law to climate change, namely the absence of international jurisprudence dealing with climate change and human rights (or transnational human rights problems with similar features).[37] This jurisprudential gap means that it is not clear how open-textured provisions of human rights treaties must be interpreted in the context of climate change. Most legal research on human rights and climate change has dealt with this challenge by analysing existing human rights jurisprudence resulting from claims brought by individuals against their national State, followed by an analysis to establish to what extent States' obligations are limited by a presumed 'territorial scope' of human rights obligations.[38] This territorial scope is often explored by reference to human rights

[36] See, eg, *Airey v Republic of Ireland* (1979) Series A no 32, 2 EHRR, 305. See also Stephen Humphreys, 'Introduction: Human Rights and Climate Change' in Stephen Humphreys (ed), *Human Rights and Climate Change* (Cambridge, Cambridge University Press, 2010) 11 (suggesting that the absence of a remedy for victims of climate change would significantly undermine the hegemonic status (or aspiration) of human rights law).

[37] See however ch 9, which discusses recent developments in rights-based climate change litigation at the domestic and regional levels.

[38] See, eg, John H. Knox, 'Climate Change and Human Rights Law' (2009) 50 *Virginia Journal of International Law* 198, 202, and McInerney-Lankford, Darrow and Rajamani (n 13) 41. This approach reflects the approach taken in a significant body of human rights scholarship that has concerned itself with the identification of a supposed territorial scope of human rights obligations. See, eg, Marko Milanovic, 'From Compromise to Principle: Clarifying the Concept of State Jurisdiction in Human Rights Treaties' (2008) 8 *Human Rights Law Review* 411, 26 and Maarten Den Heijer and Rick Lawson, 'Extraterritorial Human Rights and the Concept of "Jurisdiction"' in Malcolm Langford et al (eds), *Global Justice, State Duties: The Extraterritorial Scope of Economic, Social and Cultural Rights in International Law* (Cambride, Cambridge University Press, 2012). On climate change specifically, see, eg, Edward Cameron and Marc Limon, 'Restoring the Climate by Realizing Rights: The Role of the International Human Rights System' (2012) 21 *Review of European, Comparative & International Environmental Law* 204 (stating that 'the possible extraterritorial application of human rights … has always been a core, contestable and contentious issue at the heart of the international human rights system and its capacity to address climate change' and that 'Clarifying the extraterritorial dimension of human rights obligations in the context of climate change is especially important for vulnerable countries and communities'. Cf Barbara Frey, 'Obligations to Protect the Right to Life: Constructing a Rule of Transfer Regarding Small Arms and Light Weapons' in Mark Gibney and Sigrid Skogly (eds), *Universal Human Rights and Extraterritorial Obligations* (Philadelphia, University of Pennsylvania Press, 2010) 50 ('When a state party has the means to prevent the violation of core human rights treaty obligations outside its territory and fails to do so, it is acting contrary to the object and purpose of the treaty and violates the principle of *pacta sunt servanda*').

jurisprudence concerning extraterritorial conduct of States. The problem with this approach is that it misses an important point: emission-producing activities that are known to cause climate change occur primarily, if not solely, *within* the territories and jurisdictions of States. The picture becomes even more blurred where reference is made to admissibility decisions to clarify the content of substantive human rights obligations. For example, some scholars try to explain the content of States' obligations in addressing climate change by reference to the ECtHR's admissibility decision in *Bankovic et al v Belgium and 16 Other Contracting States*,[39] concerned with the alleged responsibility of members of the North Atlantic Treaty Organisation (NATO) for violations of the ECHR resulting from NATO bombing in Belgrade in 1999. The analysis leads to an unusual line of reasoning: the scope of States' obligations to address climate change would be narrow because 'if dropping bombs on a city does not amount to "effective control" of its occupants, the less immediate and drastic measure of allowing pollution to move across an international border would be unlikely to constitute such control'.[40] Subsequent jurisprudence indicates that the ECtHR's reasoning on 'extraterritorial' obligations in the *Bankovic* case was flawed.[41] All this emphasises the need for a methodology that is more firmly rooted in existing rules and principles of international law, including the Vienna Rules of Interpretation, whereby jurisprudence can serve as additional material for analysis.

Based on this methodology, this book is able to demonstrate that reconciling the lofty principles of international human rights law with the realities of climate change is, in principle, possible. The doctrinal analysis perused in the book shows that existing norms of international law are sufficient to establish State responsibility for acts and omissions that lead to dangerous climate change and associated violations of human rights. As part of this analysis, the book tackles a range of doctrinal issues that are often understood to be obstacles to successful climate change litigation: the implications of existing *lex specialis* on climate change for the applicability of human rights law to climate change; the implications of the open-texturedness of human rights treaties for the substantive scope of human rights obligations; the territorial or extraterritorial scope of human rights obligations; the correct approach to remedies in the absence of a principle of joint and several liability for human rights violations; and questions related to causation and proof of damages. The book also addresses the overarching question of whether existing rules of international law can be applied to climate change and associated human

[39] *Bankovic et al v Belgium and 16 Other Contracting States (Admissibility)*, App no 52207/99 (ECtHR, 12 December 2001). For discussions see Fons Coomans and Menno T Kamminga, *Extraterritorial Application of Human Rights Treaties* (Antwerp, Intersentia, 2004) and Marko Milanovic, *Extraterritorial Application of Human Rights Treaties* (Oxford, Oxford University Press, 2011).

[40] McInerney-Lankford, Darrow and Rajamani (n 13) 41. For a similar line of argument with a less definite conclusion see Knox (n 38) 202.

[41] See *Al-Skeini v United Kingdom* App no 55721/07 (ECtHR, 7 July 2011), paras 136–37 and *Al-Jedda v United Kingdom* App no 27021/08 (ECtHR, 7 July 2011). See further Marko Milanovic, 'Al-Skeini and Al-Jedda in Strasbourg' (2012) 23 *European Journal of International Law* 121.

rights harm without producing absurd or unjust results, whether in a specific case or through spill-over effects on the international legal system.

The book tackles these issues systematically through an analysis of three frameworks of international law and the way they are interrelated: international human rights law, the *lex specialis* of the UNFCCC,[42] and the general law of State responsibility. The relevance of the UNFCCC *lex specialis* for interpreting human rights norms follows from the observation that this law not only has significant limits on States' discretion to permit or perform activities that contribute to climate change, but also requires action that reflects States' differing historical responsibilities for climate change and their capabilities to respond to it. As will be noted, a potential for 'systemic integration' of rules derived from the UNFCCC, the Kyoto Protocol and the Paris Agreement into other fields of law is already apparent from recent cases brought before national and regional courts.[43] Actual and potential synergies between the two respective frameworks and the general law of State responsibility are also explored,[44] ultimately illuminating how international human rights law and the law of State responsibility can function as 'adjoining fields'[45] to the international climate change regime.

The argument presented in the book has important implications for those involved in or considering climate change-related legal action under international law. It follows from the doctrinal analysis in this book that human action and inaction leading to climate change can be attributed to States under the general rule of attribution. Conceptually, this approach builds on the idea that international

[42] United Nations Framework Convention on Climate Change (adopted 9 May 1992, entered into force 19 June 1993) 1771 UNTS 107 (UNFCCC).

[43] The Court of Justice of the European Union (CJEU)'s decision in the 2011 case that resulted from a challenge to the EU's emission trading scheme brought jointly by the Air Transport Association of America and several North American airlines shows that a Catch-22 might result from a lack of clarity: the Court considered itself unable to apply provisions of international law (here, the Kyoto Protocol) on the basis that the provisions relied upon were insufficiently clear and precise. See *Case C-366/10, Air Transport Association of America, American Airlines Inc., Continental Airlines Inc., United Airlines Inc. v Secretary of State for Energy and Climate Change* CJEU [2011] OJ C 260/9. It should be pointed out, however, that this restriction follows from the CJEU's interpretation of EU law and is not related to international law as such. Indeed, neither Art 31(3)(c) of the VCLT nor any other international rule of interpretation requires rules to be clear and precise in order to fulfil an interpretative function.

[44] On State responsibility and climate change generally see Christina Voigt, 'State Responsibility for Climate Change Damages' (2008) 77 *Nordic Journal of International Law* 1, 2 (considering that the relevance of the law of State responsibility for climate change consists for a significant part in 'providing injured States with a right to restitution and compensation'). See also Roda Verheyen, *Climate Change Damage and International Law: Prevention Duties and State Responsibility* (Leiden, Martinus Nijhoff, 2005); Richard SJ Tol and Roda Verheyen, 'State Responsibility and Compensation for Climate Change Damages: A Legal and Economic Assessment' (2009) 32 *Energy Policy* 1109; Christian Tomuschat, 'Global Warming and State Responsibility' in Holger Hestermeyer et al (eds), *Law of the Sea in Dialogue* (Saint Paul, Springer, 2011); and René Lefeber, 'Climate Change and State Responsibility' in Rosemary Rayfuse and Shirley V Scott (eds), *International Law in the Era of Climate Change* (Portland, Elgar, 2012).

[45] To borrow from Tawhida Ahmed and Duncan French, 'Competing Narratives in Climate Change Law' in Stephen Farrall, Tawhida Ahmed and Duncan French (eds), *Criminological and Legal Consequences of Climate Change* (Oxford, Hart Publishing, 2012) 254–55.

human rights law has always been, and remains, intrinsically linked to the concept of State sovereignty; a 'key organising concept' in general international law[46] that is incorporated into the *lex specialis* of climate change.[47] Although human rights lawyers have often considered it to be a potential shield against human rights accountability, the book focuses on its potential to function as 'a common denominator for the world's manifold cultures and traditions'.[48] More specifically, State sovereignty may be understood in terms of international law that 'not only [serves] to place certain limits on the nature and scope of governmental authority but also [contributes] to the development of a justifiable basis for that authority'.[49] In the context of human rights, it is the State's sovereign power, including its capacity to legislate, that makes the State best suited to create the conditions for the enjoyment of internationally protected human rights.[50] Moreover, States' sovereign capacity to regulate public and private actors' emission-producing activities provides a potential basis for obligations to protect the human rights of those affected by climate change. As emission-producing activities affect human beings everywhere, it is worth noting that the limits of a State's territory are not the limits of its legal power: as the Permanent Court of International Justice found in the *Lotus* case, States have 'a wide measure of discretion ... to extend the application of their laws and the jurisdiction of their courts to persons, property and acts outside their territory'.[51] This does not mean that sovereignty entitles a State to do as it pleases: it was implicit in *Lotus* that the sovereignty of other States and international law itself must be respected.[52]

Sovereignty not only underpins States' obligations to protect the human rights of people at home and abroad, but also entitles them to cooperate internationally

[46] James R Crawford, 'Responsibility to the International Community as a Whole' (2001) 8 *Indiana Journal of Global Legal Studies* 303, 12. See also Benedict Kingsbury, 'Sovereignty and Inequality' (1998) 9 *European Journal of International Law* 599; and Christopher G Weeramantry, *Universalising International Law* (Leiden, Martinus Nijhoff, 2004) 38 ('Whether we like it or not, the sovereign state system provides the basis of current international law').

[47] UNFCCC, Preamble ('Reaffirming the principle of sovereignty of States in international cooperation to address climate change').

[48] Crawford (n 46) 308. See also Weeramantry (n 46) 112, 138 ('The old view of sovereignty held that the manner in which a sovereign dealt with his own subjects was that sovereign's exclusive concern. No longer can any sovereign state plausibly take up such a position, and no longer is the world public opinion prepared to accept such an attitude. [The] breach of the walls of sovereignty which human rights doctrine has thus effected is a major factor conditioning both states and peoples into the frame of mind that sovereignty is not absolute but must yield to certain universally accepted norms and standards' ... If state sovereignty is to continue into the indefinite future it can only be on the basis of a progressive enlargement of the obligations attendant on sovereignty').

[49] Matthew Craven, 'Legal Differentiation and the Concept of the Human Rights Treaty in International Law' (2000) 11 *European Journal of International Law* 489, 519.

[50] See, eg, Brigit Toebes, 'The Right to Health' in Asbjørn Eide, Catarina Krause and Allan Rosas (eds), *Economic, Social and Cultural Rights: A Textbook* (Leiden, Martinus Nijhoff, 2001) 169 (noting that States' obligations related to the right to health result from the States' sovereign capacity to provide 'the basic conditions under which the health of the individual is protected and possibly even enhanced').

[51] *The Case of the S.S. Lotus (France v Turkey)* [1927] PCIJ Reports, Ser A, No. 10.

[52] See also Crawford (n 46) 308 (describing how international law has moved away from freedom from law or *legibus solutes*).

as equals and to invoke the responsibility of other States for breaches of their international obligations for injury caused to its nationals,[53] in accordance with Vattel's doctrine where: 'Whoever uses a citizen ill, indirectly offends the state, which is bound to protect his citizen'.[54] Today the law of State responsibility reflects this doctrine, but recognises that peoples and individuals, and not States, are the ultimate beneficiaries of human rights obligations.[55] An example of how sovereignty may function as a vehicle for the protection of human beings against climate change and associated impacts is provided by the landmark climate change case *Massachusetts v EPA*.[56] Here the United States Supreme Court upheld the argument submitted by a dozen states in the US, American Samoa, the District of Columbia, the cities of New York and Baltimore and several NGOs that the regulation of greenhouse gas emissions from motor vehicles fell within the mandate of the United States Environmental Protection Agency (EPA). The most significant part of the Court's decision sets out the basis for standing against the defendants: standing was recognised based on the states' sovereign capacity 'to have the last word as to whether its mountains shall be stripped of their forests and its inhabitants shall breathe pure air'.[57] This book demonstrates that at the international level, States can, in a similar vein, invoke the international responsibility of other States that act in breach of their international obligations with regard to climate change to protect the right of their people. It is relevant to recall here that some Small Island Developing States have at various occasions in the past expressed their desire to raise the issue of climate change with the International Court of Justice.[58] It is hoped that the analysis in this book will inform further discussions about climate change liability, as well as alternatives to litigation.

The potential of human rights law as a tool to address climate change is apparent from the book's in-depth analysis of substantive human rights norms in connection with climate change. This analysis focuses on the scope of States'

[53] Articles on Diplomatic Protection, Report of the International Law Commission on the Work of its 58th Session, Official Records of the General Assembly, UN Doc A/61/10, 2006, Art 1 (referring to 'diplomatic protection [consisting] of the invocation by a State, through diplomatic action or other means of peaceful settlement, of the responsibility of another State for an injury caused by an internationally wrongful act of that State to a natural or legal person that is a national of the former State with a view to the implementation of such responsibility', ibid 24). This definition was recognised as reflecting customary international law in *Ahmadou Sadio Diallo (Guinea v Democratic Republic of the Congo) (Preliminary Objections)*, [2007] ICJ Rep 582, para 39.

[54] Vattel, *Le Droit des Gens*, vol II (1758, Anon. tr 1797) para 71. See also James Crawford, *Brownlie's Principles of Public International Law*, 8th edn (Oxford, Oxford University Press, 2012) 607 (noting that there is no widespread recognition in general international law that harm done to a State's citizens triggers an obligation, not just an entitlement, to take international action under the law of diplomatic protection).

[55] See generally Dinah L Shelton, 'Litigating a Rights-Based Approach to Climate Change' (International Conference on Human Rights and the Environment, Tehran, 2009).

[56] *Massachusetts v EPA* 549 US SC 497 (2007).

[57] Ibid 14 (quoting from another landmark environmental case, *Georgia v Tennessee Copper Co.* 206 US SC 230 (1907)).

[58] See ch 9.

obligations related to the exercise or non-exercise of their regulatory capacity and their capacity to cooperate with other States. Because States' obligations under international human rights law are to a large extent rights-specific,[59] obligations derived from four specific rights, each representing a different category of rights, are considered: the right of self-determination (a group right); the right to life (a civil and political right); the right to enjoy culture (a cultural right); and the right to the highest attainable standard of health (an economic and social right). This analysis highlights, first, in what circumstances States may be internationally responsible for human rights violations associated with climate change; and second, that international human rights law imposes standards of care on each State that can be ascertained through an analysis of facts and environmental standards that are already binding on the State. This opens the door to an analysis of the relevance of States' existing obligations under the UNFCCC for clarifying the content of human rights obligations of States with differing responsibilities for climate change and different capacities to address it.

To set the stage for the legal analysis, the remainder of this chapter provides a brief overview of the science that is most relevant to rights-based State responsibility claims connected with climate change. It concludes with a note on the increasing currency of climate change litigation as a tool to address climate change – a topic that is further discussed in chapter nine, which will outline the options for individuals, communities and States to bring rights-based climate cases before judicial and quasi-judicial tribunals at the national, regional and international levels. The conclusion in chapter ten elaborates on the potential role of the law of State responsibility in strengthening the legal protection offered by international law to peoples and individuals affected by climate change. This will illustrate the capacity of the international legal system to respond to the negative human rights impact of climate change.

The Science

The scientific evidence on climate change is partly interrelated with the international norms discussed in this book, and the role of the IPCC in the development of these norms requires closer examination. The function of the IPCC is to 'provide internationally coordinated scientific assessments of the magnitude, timing and potential environmental and socio-economic impact of climate change and realistic response strategies'.[60] This is achieved by reviewing and assessing 'the most recent scientific, technical and socio-economic information produced worldwide

[59] For a more detailed discussion see V Engström, 'Who Is Responsible for Corporate Human Rights Violations?' (Åbo Akademi University Institute for Human Rights, 2002) 18.

[60] UNFCCC, Preamble, para 5.

relevant to the understanding of climate change'.[61] The IPCC's first Assessment Report was published in 1990 and played a key role in the drafting and adoption of the UNFCCC: the treaty reflects recognition of a causal link between human activities that lead to the emission of certain greenhouse gases (primarily CO_2) and climatic changes which produce 'adverse effects'. It contains a legal definition of climate change (Article 1), which defines it as 'a change of climate which is attributed directly or indirectly to human activity that alters the composition of the global atmosphere and which is in addition to natural climate variability observed over comparable time periods'.[62] States' obligations under the treaty relate to an 'ultimate objective' of achieving, 'in accordance with the relevant provisions of the Convention, stabilization of greenhouse gas concentrations in the atmosphere at a level that would prevent dangerous anthropogenic interference with the climate system' (Article 2). Climate change and its 'adverse effects' are acknowledged as 'a common concern of humankind', and 'adverse effects' are defined as 'changes in the physical environment or biota resulting from climate change which have significant deleterious effects on the composition, resilience or productivity of natural and managed ecosystems or on the operation of socio-economic systems or on human health and welfare'.[63] The adequacy of States' obligations is subject to review by the Conference of the Parties 'in light of the best available scientific information and assessment on climate change and its impacts, as well as relevant technical social and economic information',[64] which in practice is provided by the IPCC.

The IPCC produced follow-up reports in 1996, 2004, 2007 and 2014 (the next one is due in 2021), and a large number of technical papers, meeting reports and regular conferences. In all these reports, the IPCC has confirmed that the observed phenomenon of climate change is largely man-made and caused by the excessive emission of anthropogenic greenhouse gases since industrialisation. In 1996 the IPCC found 'stronger evidence that most of the warming observed over the last fifty years is likely to be attributable to human activities'.[65] In its Fourth Assessment Report, the IPCC confirmed, based on observations of increases in global average air and ocean temperatures, widespread melting of snow and ice and rising global average sea level that 'Warming of the climate system is unequivocal'.[66] The Summary for Policymakers of the Fifth Assessment confirms again that 'Human influence on the climate system is clear' and 'evident from the increasing

[61] IPCC website, 'Organisation' available at www.ipcc.ch/organization/organization.shtml#.Us_UznnxbwI.

[62] UNFCCC, Art 1 (emphasis added).

[63] UNFCCC, Preamble and Art 1.

[64] UNFCCC, Art 4(2)(d).

[65] IPCC, 'Contribution of Working Group I to the IPCC Second Assessment Report (1996)' in John T Houghton et al (eds), *Climate Change 1995: The Science of Climate Change* (Cambridge, Cambridge University Press, 1996).

[66] Lenny Bernstein et al, 'Synthesis Report, adopted at IPCC Plenary XXVII, Valencia, Spain, 12–17 Nov 2007' in *Climate Change 2007* (Intergovernmental Panel on Climate Change, 2007) 30.

greenhouse gas concentrations in the atmosphere, positive radiative forcing [ie that has a warming effect on the climate], observed warming, and understanding of the climate system'.[67] It states that 'It is *extremely likely* that more than half of the observed increase in global average surface temperature from 1951 to 2010 was caused by the anthropogenic increase in greenhouse gas concentrations and other anthropogenic forcings together' and that 'Greenhouse gases contributed a global mean surface warming *likely* to be in the range of 0.5°C to 1.3°C over the period 1951 to 2010, with the contributions from other anthropogenic forcings, including the cooling effect of aerosols, *likely* to be in the range of −0.6°C to 0.1°C'. Thus anthropogenic influence on the climate system is plainly distinguishable from natural forcings: 'the contribution from natural forcings is *likely* to be in the range of −0.1°C to 0.1°C, and from natural internal variability is *likely* to be in the range of −0.1°C to 0.1°C'.[68] The Fifth Assessment Report also clarifies the influence of humans on specific adverse effects of climate change, finding that 'Anthropogenic influences have *very likely* contributed to Arctic sea ice loss since 1979'[69] and to the global mean sea level rise since the 1970s.[70]

The most recent IPCC report on Impacts, Adaptation and Vulnerability provides evidence of 'risks of climate change that warrant consideration', including 'potentially severe impacts relevant to "dangerous anthropogenic interference with the climate system" as described in Article 2 of the UN Framework Convention on Climate Change' which 'can involve potentially large or irreversible consequences, high probability of consequences, and/or limited adaptive capacity'.[71] The report expressed 'high confidence' that 'key risks that span sectors and regions' include the following:

i. Risk of death, injury, and disrupted livelihoods in low-lying coastal zones and Small Island Developing States, due to rising sea levels, coastal flooding and storm surges;
ii. Risk of food insecurity linked to warming, drought, flooding and precipitation variability, particularly for poorer populations;
iii. Risk of severe harm for large urban populations due to inland flooding;
iv. Risk of loss of rural livelihoods and income due to water scarcity and reduced agricultural productivity, particularly for farmers and herders with minimal capital in semi-arid regions;
v. Risk of breakdown of infrastructure networks and essential services (such as water, electricity and health services) as a result of extreme weather events;
vi. Risk of loss of marine ecosystems and consequent coastal livelihoods, especially for fishing communities in the tropics and the Arctic;

[67] IPCC, 'Contribution of Working Group I to the IPCC Fifth Assessment Report (2013)' (n 2) 13.

[68] Ibid (adding that 'Together these assessed contributions are consistent with the observed warming of approximately 0.6°C to 0.7°C over this period').

[69] Ibid 17.

[70] Ibid.

[71] Ibid 6–7.

vii. Risk of loss of terrestrial and inland water ecosystems and the services they provide for livelihoods;
viii. Risk of mortality, morbidity and other physical harm during periods of extreme heat, particularly for vulnerable urban populations and those working outdoors.[72]

The report notes that due to the time lapse between the emission of anthropogenic greenhouse gases and the effects on the climate system, 'Projected global temperature increase over the next few decades is similar across emission scenarios'.[73] However, it finds that 'Mitigation of greenhouse gas emissions over the next few decades can substantially reduce risks of climate change in the second half of the twenty-first century',[74] and provides a range of emission scenarios with associated likelihood of keeping temperature increases below 2°C.[75] It clarifies that, 'A lower warming target, or a higher likelihood of remaining below a specific warming target, will require lower cumulative CO_2 emissions'.[76] The IPCC pointed out earlier that, 'The array of potential adaptive responses available to human societies is very large', but that 'Adaptation alone is not expected to cope with all the projected effects of climate change, and especially not over the long term as most impacts increase in magnitude'.[77] It also found that 'the projected impacts of climate change can vary greatly due to the development pathway assumed' and that differences in regional population, income and technological development are often a strong determinant of the level of vulnerability to climate change.[78] It is likely that the pace of progress towards sustainable development in low-income countries is slowed down 'either directly through increased exposure to adverse impact or indirectly through erosion of the capacity to adapt'.[79]

[72] Ibid.
[73] Ibid 5.
[74] Ibid 7. An earlier report found that the continuation of the current rate of greenhouse gas emissions would make a rise of average global temperatures of more than 2°C within two or three decades nearly inevitable – a level of warming that would almost certainly cause rising sea levels, heatwaves, droughts and more extreme weather conditions.
[75] Ibid 25 (finding that 'Limiting the warming caused by anthropogenic CO_2 emissions alone with a probability of >33%, >50%, and >66% to less than 2°C since the period 1861–1880, will require cumulative CO_2 emissions from all anthropogenic sources to stay between 0 and about 1570 GtC (5760 $GtCO_2$), 0 and about 1210 GtC (4440 $GtCO_2$), and 0 and about 1000 GtC (3670 $GtCO_2$) since that period, respectively. An amount of 515 [445 to 585] GtC (1890 [1630–2150] $GtCO_2$), was already emitted by 2011').
[76] Ibid 26.
[77] IPCC, 'Contribution of Working Group II to the IPCC Fourth Assessment Report' in ML Parry et al (eds), *Climate Change 2007: Impacts, Adaptation and Vulnerability* (Cambridge, Cambridge University Press, 2007) 19. 'Adaptive capacity' is defined as 'the ability of a system to adjust to climate change (including climate variability and extremes) to moderate potential damages, to take advantage of opportunities, or to cope with the consequences' (21).
[78] Ibid 20. 'Vulnerability' is defined as 'the degree to which a system is susceptible to, and unable to cope with, adverse effects of climate change, including climate variability and extremes. Vulnerability is a function of the character, magnitude, and rate of climate change and variation to which a system is exposed, its sensitivity, and its adaptive capacity' (21).
[79] Ibid.

One of the most relevant questions regarding potential legal claims about climate change under international law is to what extent anthropogenic climate change can be traced back to State conduct. Here it is worth highlighting the range of potential evidence that could be used to establish attribution – either directly or in the context of an obligation to regulate or otherwise influence the conduct of private actors. For example, in his ground-breaking 'carbon major' study Richard Heede was able to demonstrate how 'nearly two-thirds, 63 per cent, of all industrial carbon dioxide and methane released into the atmosphere can be traced to fossil fuel and cement production by just ninety entities: investor-owned companies, such as Gazprom and Saudi Aramco; and solely government-run industries, such as in the former Soviet Union and China (for its coal production)'.[80] Other examples are studies that focus on the influence of States' energy policies on climate change, such as the International Energy Agency (IEA)'s World Energy Outlook 2013 which argued that the development and use of renewable forms of energy 'hinges on government support'.[81] The latest World Energy Outlook report includes a major new scenario – the Sustainable Development Scenario – that represents an integrated approach to the achievement of internationally agreed goals on climate change, air quality and universal access to modern energy.[82] It is evident from this and other sources that reducing the risks of dangerous climate change would require scaled-up international cooperation and assistance to States with limited technological or financial capacity to make the transition to low-carbon development pathways.

Another question of factual attribution that has received much attention in legal literature is the level of probability with which causation between climate change on the one hand, and specific harm or injury on the other, can be established. The general principle here seems to be that probabilities are higher when the harm is the result of long-term adverse effects (such as coastal erosion, rising sea levels and melting icecaps), and lower when it is the result of sudden-onset events (such as heatwaves, hurricanes, storm surges and very heavy rainfall).[83] However, the science of attribution is evolving rapidly and even for sudden-onset events it is sometimes possible to establish a link with anthropogenic climate change with high levels of probability and precision. One example is scientific research on the effect of climate change, in terms of probability, to the 2003 heatwave in Europe and the consequences of this event for human beings. It was established that approximately 22,000 to 35,000 deaths were attributable to the heat, and that 75 per cent of those who died would probably have survived for more than a year without

[80] Richard Heede, 'Tracing Anthropogenic Carbon Dioxide and Methane Emissions to Fossil Fuel and Cement Producers, 1854–2010' (2013) 122 *Climatic Change* 229.

[81] International Energy Agency, *World Energy Outlook 2013* (Paris, Organisation for Economic Co-Operation and Development and International Energy Agency, 2013) 197.

[82] Ibid.

[83] As pointed out by Michael B Gerrard, 'What Litigation of a Climate Nuisance Suit Might Look Like' (2011) 121 *The Yale Law Journal Online* 135, 139; and Knox (n 38) 240.

the heatwave.[84] Human activities had generated a tenfold increase in the risk of such weather.[85] Consequently, the argument that attributing specific weather events to greenhouse gas emissions is by definition impossible is no longer a 'truism'.[86] The IPCC report on Impacts, Adaptation and Vulnerability also reflects progress in the scientific understanding of attribution. It notes, for example, that 'Each degree of warming is projected to decrease renewable water resources by at least 20% for an additional 7% of the global population'.[87] Finally, a recent study that built on Heed's 'carbon major' research was able to calculate the contribution of major State-owned and private carbon producers to particular climate impacts.[88] Studies such as these allow us to estimate the contribution of anthropogenic climate change to the likelihood that specific human rights grievances occur, or were caused by, climate change.

While science is essential for dealing with legal questions related to climate change, it is also important to appreciate the limits of science when it comes to decision-making. These limits are evident from an innovative study by Elzen et al, which demonstrated how methodological choices that are ultimately normative can lead to extremely different conclusions regarding the links between climate change and specific States. For example, they point out that the relative contribution of developed States as a group to climate change can be 'as high as 80% when excluding recent emissions [which do not yet affect the climate], non-CO_2 GHGs, and changes in land use and forestry CO_2; or about 48% when including all these emissions and discounting historical emissions for technological progress'.[89] Elzen distinguishes between States' *contributions* to climate change and their *responsibility* for it, the latter being a broader concept that includes 'ethical aspects such as the "basic needs" principle'.[90] The methodology for calculating 'responsibility' involves discounting emissions that have been used to meet quantifiable basic needs, such as heating and cooking.[91] Because of the correlation between basic needs and a range of internationally recognised human rights, methodologies

[84] Myles Allen et al, 'Scientific Challenges in the Attribution of Harm to Human Influence on Climate' (2007) 155 *University of Pennsylvania Law Review* 1353.

[85] Ibid; and Peter A. Stott et al, 'Human Contribution to the European Heatwave of 2003' (2004) 432 *Nature* 610.

[86] Gerrard, 'What Litigation of a Climate Nuisance Suit Might Look Like' (n 83) 139 (suggesting that attributing specific weather events to GHG emissions is impossible because 'hurricanes, droughts, and heatwaves … occurred long before the industrial era; there has always been natural variability').

[87] IPCC, 'Contribution of Working Group I to the IPCC Fifth Assessment Report (2013)' (n 2) 8.

[88] See Brenda Ekwurzel and others, 'The Rise in Global Atmospheric CO2, Surface Temperature, and Sea Level from Emissions traced to Major Carbon Producers' (2017) 144(4) *Climatic Change* 579. According to the study, the carbon majors are responsible for 50 per cent of global surface temperature rise, 57 per cent of the increase in carbon dioxide in the atmosphere and between 26 and 32 per cent of global sea level rise.

[89] Michel GJ Elzen et al, 'Countries' Contributions to Climate Change: Effect of Accounting for all Greenhouse Gases, Recent Trends, Basic Needs and Technological Progress' (2013) 121 *Climatic Change* 397.

[90] Ibid 399 (footnote omitted).

[91] Ibid.

such as these could be used to produce evidence that sheds light on the limits of States' mitigation obligations under international human rights law and the extent to which there is a case of conflicting rights. Furthermore, it could be used to help determine appropriate contributions for reparations in cases of climate change-related damage where multiple States are responsible for the same internationally wrongful act. The remainder of this book aims to provide further insight into the normative framework of international law and the extent to which it requires certain choices when it is consistently applied to the evidence.

Finally, is important to note that conclusions have already been drawn from IPCC reports and other scientific evidence in a range of national court cases. These indicate that IPCC reports can be used as conclusive evidence for establishing a link between greenhouse gas-emitting activities on the one hand and damage or risks affecting human beings on the other. For example, in Australia a local government council was forced to consider the likely consequences of environmental impact of greenhouse gas emissions from a power plant when considering a planning application for its continued operation.[92] Pollution caused by the plant was considered a potential threat to the quality of life of human beings everywhere, including those in the locality of the council. Furthermore, the Verwaltungsgericht in Berlin, Germany, found that the government had a duty to publicly disclose government-supported projects which increase greenhouse gas emissions based in part on the argument that greenhouse gas emissions in due course threaten the lives of human beings.[93] In *Massachusetts v EPA*, the Supreme Court relied on the evidence contained in the IPCC's Fourth Assessment Report to establish that the risk of rising sea levels was sufficiently 'real' to grant the state of Massachusetts standing,[94] referring to the 'enormity of the potential consequences associated with man-made climate change'.[95] And in *Urgenda v the Netherlands*, the Hague District Court found the State of the Netherlands in breach of its constitutional duty of care 'in view of the latest scientific and technical knowledge' which, according to the court, indicated that it is 'the most efficient to mitigate and it is more cost-effective to take adequate action than to postpone measures in order to prevent hazardous climate change'.[96] More than 900 climate change related cases have now been brought before judicial and quasi-judicial bodies across the globe, and a small but increasing number of cases relies on human rights law as a basis for alleged liability.[97] However, no rights-based climate case has so far been brought at the international level. While this book does not purport to portray litigation as a

[92] *Australian Conservation Foundation v Minister for Planning* [2004] VCAT 2029 (29 October 2004).

[93] *Bundes fur Umwelt- und Naturschutz Deutschland et al, v Bundesrepublik Deutschland* Case No VG 10 A 21504 (10 January 2006) Verwaltungsgericht, Berlin.

[94] *Massachusetts v EPA* 549 US SC 497, 1438, 1455–56.

[95] Ibid.

[96] *The Urgenda Foundation v Kingdom of the Netherlands* [2015] District Court of the Hague, HAZA c/09/00456689, June 2015, para 4.73.

[97] United Nations Environment Programme (UNEP), '*The Status of Climate Change Litigation: a Global Review*' (UNEP, 2017).

panacea for all aspects of the climate change problem, it does build on the premise that a focus on State responsibility is valuable for addressing its human rights dimension. International-level litigation would be particularly valuable if climate change negotiations continue to leave victims of climate change without redress for human rights violations suffered – a scenario which seems increasingly likely since the COP decision adopted in Paris excluded liability and compensation from the scope of the Paris Agreement. The following chapters will demonstrate the legal basis for a human rights approach to climate change premised on State responsibility, with chapter nine explaining more concretely how this law can be invoked before judicial and quasi-judicial bodies by individuals, communities and States to get some recourse to justice for actual human rights violations resulting from climate change.

2

International Human Rights Law

Sources of International Human Rights Law

As part of international law, international human rights law is premised on the general theory of sources of international law. This theory builds on the premise that international legal norms, like any legal norms, are determined on the basis of widely shared criteria, which establish how rules become law. The common point of reference for these criteria in international law is Article 38 of the Statute of the Court of Justice – a provision that finds its origins in State practice, arbitral decisions and legal scholarship.[1] The lack of 'tertiary rules' that determine how rules relating to ascertaining norms are created or modified means that the sources of international law can be broad-based in character, influence each other in practice and often overlap.[2]

Understanding the way in which the sources of international law overlap and interact is important in the context of climate change for at least two distinct reasons. First, the scope of States' obligations under one source of law may be affected by another source of law. For example, general principles of law may fill gaps within the law and influence the interpretation and implementation of custom and treaties.[3] Human rights norms that become general principles of law can therefore modify custom and treaties, both within and outside the framework of international human rights law.[4] This will be illustrated below in relation to the territorial scope of human rights treaties, and in chapters three and five in relation to the international climate change regime.

Second, the interaction of sources affects the extent to which human rights norms are relevant outside the context of a particular treaty regime. Perhaps the most obvious example is the existence of human rights norms as norms of custom

[1] Statute of the International Court of Justice (adopted 26 June 1945, entered into force 24 October 1945) 892 UNTS 199. The provision identifies treaties, custom and general principles of law as the three main sources of international law, with judicial decisions and teachings of the most highly qualified jurists as subsidiary means for interpreting the rules of law.

[2] Hugh Thirlway, 'The Sources of International Law' in Malcolm D Evans (ed), *International Law*, 3rd edn (New York, Oxford University Press, 2010) 98–99, 115; James Crawford, *Brownlie's Principles of Public International Law*, 8th edn (Oxford, Oxford University Press, 2012) 20.

[3] Nina HB Jørgenson, *The Responsibility of States for International Crimes* (Oxford, Oxford University Press, 2003).

[4] Jane McAdam, *Climate Change, Forced Migration, and International Law* (Oxford, Oxford University Press, 2012) 263, fn 178.

and/or general principles of law, which extends the applicability of these norms to States that have not ratified relevant treaties. More broadly, the co-existence of human rights norms in multiple sources of law provides a method for reconciling value-based principles with a consensualist conception of international law.[5] The involvement of virtually all States in the causes of climate change, as well as in response measures, makes it important to identify human rights norms that have a universal or quasi-universal applicability. The general analysis below, and the analysis of specific rights in chapter seven, pays particular attention to the extent to which specific norms are embedded in multiple sources of law.

The International Human Rights System

The corpus of international human rights law has emerged primarily from a large number of treaties, and is continuously expanding, both normatively and institutionally. The UN Charter contains more than a dozen references to human rights, proclaims the realisation of human rights as one of the main purposes of the Organisation and provides that Member States shall cooperate to take joint and separate action with the UN to promote respect for and observance of human rights.[6] The Universal Declaration of Human Rights (UDHR) can be understood as an authoritative interpretation of the substantive rights referred to in the UN Charter, based on its preambular recital 'Whereas Member States have pledged themselves to achieve in co-operation with the United Nations the promotion of universal respect for and observance of human rights' and 'Whereas a common understanding of these rights and freedoms is of the greatest importance for the full realization of this pledge' and the proclamation of the UDHR as providing 'a common standard of achievement for all peoples and all nations'.[7] The UDHR

[5] Bruno Simma and Philip Alston, 'The Sources of Human Rights Law: Custom, Jus Cogens, and General Principles' (1988–1989) 12 *Australian Yearbook of International Law* 105 (referring to *South West Africa (Second Phase) (Judgment)* [1966] ICJ Reports 6, 34).

[6] United Nations, Charter of the United Nations (24 October 1945) 1 UNTS XVI. Art 1 of the Charter mentions the four purposes of the United Nations. According to Art 1(3) the purposes of the United Nations include 'To achieve international co-operation in solving international problems of an economic, social, cultural, or humanitarian character, and in promoting and encouraging respect for human rights and for fundamental freedoms for all without distinction as to race, sex, language, or religion'. In addition, Art 55 of the Charter provides: 'With a view to the creation of conditions of stability and well-being which are necessary for peaceful and friendly relations among nations based on respect for the principle of equal rights and self-determination of peoples, the United Nations shall promote: a. higher standards of living, full employment, and conditions of economic and social progress and development; b. solutions of international economic, social, health, and related problems, and c. universal respect for, and observance of, human rights and fundamental freedoms for all without distinction as to race, sex, language, or religion.' Art 56 of the Charter provides that 'All Members pledge themselves to take joint and separate action in cooperation with the Organization for the achievement of the purposes set forth in Article 55'.

[7] See also Proclamation of Teheran, Final Act of the International Conference on Human Rights, Teheran (22 April to 13 May 1968) UN Doc A/CONF. 32/41 3. See further Olivier de Schutter et al,

may also be understood as constituting 'subsequent agreement between the parties' to the Charter regarding its interpretation or the application of its provisions.[8] Furthermore, the parallel existence of human rights norms in a great number of national legal systems has the potential to make those norms binding under international law as general principles of law, and thus as a separate source of international law that can modify the application of treaty or custom.[9]

When considering States' obligations under international human rights law, it is important to recall that human rights obligations derived from the UN Charter include civil, political, economic, social and cultural rights. This reflects the axiom that human rights are universal, indivisible, interdependent, interrelated and inalienable rights of all human beings.[10] The specific human rights provided in the UDHR have also been codified in the two International Covenants adopted in 1966 which form, together with the UDHR, the International Bill of Human Rights. The International Covenant on Civil and Political Rights (ICCPR)[11] has 167 State Parties, which include all States listed in Annex I to the UN Framework Convention on Climate Change (UNFCCC), and dozens of States located in areas where climate change already has serious negative impacts on human life and livelihoods.[12] The vast majority of States have also ratified the International Covenant on Economic, Social and Cultural Rights (ICESCR),[13] with 160 State Parties.[14] There are many other widely ratified international human rights treaties, including conventions that protect rights of particular categories of people. The number of ratifications of human rights treaties has risen rapidly in recent years, with all UN Member States having ratified at least one core human rights treaty and 80 per cent having ratified four or more.[15] The effect of the consolidation of human rights norms through various sources of international law is that the norms contained in the UDHR are applicable across different fields of international law as customary

'Commentary to the Maastricht Principles on Extraterritorial Obligations of States in the Area of Economic, Social and Cultural Rights' (2012) 34 *Human Rights Quarterly* 1084, 1092.

[8] Vienna Convention on the Law of Treaties (adopted 23 May 1969, entered into force 27 January 1980) 1155 UNTS 331 (VCLT) Art 31(3)(b). See also Nihal Jayawickrama, *The Judicial Application of Human Rights Law: National, Regional and International Jurisprudence* (Cambridge, Cambridge University Press, 2002) 30.

[9] McAdam (n 4) 263.

[10] World Conference on Human Rights, *Vienna Declaration and Programme of Action*, 1(5), UN Doc A/CONF.157/23 (12 July 1993) Art 5.

[11] International Covenant on Civil and Political Rights (adopted 16 December 1966, entered into force 23 March 1976) 999 UNTS 171 (ICCPR).

[12] For ratification status, see 'Multilateral Treaties Deposited with the Secretary-General' available at treaties.un.org/Pages/Treaties.aspx?id=4&subid=A&lang=en.

[13] International Covenant on Economic, Social and Cultural Rights (adopted 16 December 1966, entered into force 3 January 1976) 993 UNTS 3 (ICESCR).

[14] For ratification status, see 'Multilateral Treaties Deposited with the Secretary-General' available at treaties.un.org/Pages/Treaties.aspx?id=4&subid=A&lang=en.

[15] See also website of the United Nations Office of the High Commissioner of Human Rights, 'Monitoring the Core International Human Rights Treaties' available at www.ohchr.org/EN/HRBodies/Pages/TreatyBodies.aspx.

norms binding on all States.[16] This was recognised by the International Court of Justice in its Advisory Opinion, *Legality of the Threat or Use of Nuclear Weapons*, where it noted the existence of many humanitarian law rules 'so fundamental to the respect of the human person' that all States must observe them 'whether or not they have ratified the conventions that contain them', because 'they constitute intransgressible principles of international customary law'.[17]

International human rights treaties are authoritatively interpreted by human rights treaty bodies with quasi-judicial functions. In the international human rights system there are ten such treaty bodies composed of independent experts, which monitor compliance with the nine core human rights conventions and optional protocols with reporting procedures. Eight acting human rights treaty bodies are currently reviewing individual complaints,[18] and one other body will soon follow suit.[19] Eight treaty bodies also possess a mandate to consider State-to-State complaints.[20] Yet to date these mandates have not been used. The interpretation of human rights treaties occurs as part of the State reporting procedures, through General Comments, or quasi-judicial litigation processes.[21]

The United Nations Human Rights Committee ('HRC' or 'Committee'), is the body of independent experts expressly mandated under the treaty to interpret the provisions of the ICCPR and monitor its implementation.[22] The interpretative

[16] See, eg, Margot E Salomon, 'Deprivation, Causation, and the Law of International Cooperation' in Malcolm Langford et al (eds), *Global Justice, State Duties: The Extraterritorial Scope of Economic, Social and Cultural Rights in International Law* (Cambridge; New York, Cambridge University Press, 2013) 304 (arguing that 'Today, the existence of a customary international law principle to respect and observe human rights in the main, which can be said to apply to basic socio-economic rights, is increasingly difficult to refute'); and ED Kinney, 'The International Human Right to Health: What Does This Mean For Our Nation and World?' (2001) 34 *Indiana Law Review* 1457, 1467. Cf Crawford (n 2) 21 (suggesting that some norms contained in the UDHR have obtained the status of customary international law). On the difficulty of distinguishing within a treaty between norms that are an expression of existing custom on the one hand and norms only created by the treaty on the other see Prosper Weil, 'Towards Relative Normativity in International Law?' (1983) 77 *The American Journal of International Law* 413, 428. See also Henry J Steiner, Philip Alston and Ryan Goodman, *International Human Rights in Context: Law, Politics, Morals*, 3rd edn (Oxford, Oxford University Press, 2008).

[17] *Legality of the Threat or Use of Nuclear Weapons (Advisory Opinion)* [1996] ICJ Reports 241, para 79.

[18] The Human Rights Committee, Committee Against Torture (CAT), Committee on the Elimination of Racial Discrimination (CERD), Committee on the Elimination of Discrimination Against Women (CEDAW), Committee on the Rights of Persons with Disabilities (CRPD), and the Committee on Enforced Disappearances (CED) and the Committee on Economic, Social and Cultural Rights (CESCR) and the Committee on the Rights of the Child (CRC).

[19] Committee on Migrant Workers (CMW).

[20] The Human Rights Committee, CERD, CAT, CMW, CED, CEDAW, CESCR and CRC.

[21] See, eg, Michael O'Flaherty, 'The Concluding Observations of United Nations Human Rights Treaty Bodies' (2006) 6 *Human Rights Law Review* 1 (on State reporting procedures); Nihal Jayawickrama, *The Judicial Application of Human Rights Law: National, Regional and International Jurisprudence* (Cambridge, Cambridge University Press, 2002) 131. See also Theodor Meron, *Human Rights Law-Making in the United Nations* (New York, Oxford University Press, 1986) 10 (pointing out that the interpretative practice of treaty bodies affects the reporting obligations of States as well as their domestic and international practice).

[22] ICCPR, Arts 28–45.

practice of the HRC consists of reviews of State reports submitted by State Parties in accordance with Article 40(1)(a) of the Covenant[23] and General Comments, which it is mandated to make under Article 40(4) of the Covenant, including on Article 6 (the right to life), Article 1 (the right to self-determination) and Article 27 (the rights of minorities). In addition, it interprets Covenant provisions when reviewing individual complaints under the Optional Protocol,[24] which has led to a significant body of jurisprudence that sheds light on the attributes of rights protected under the ICCPR and on States' obligations to respect and ensure those rights. The ICCPR provides for an inter-State complaint procedure under Articles 41 and 42, subject to the States involved having made a declaration recognising the competence of the Committee to consider inter-State complaints. As of today, only fifty States have made such a declaration[25] and, remarkably, no State has ever used the procedure.[26] This has led the HRC to stress the 'potential value' of the procedure in a recent General Comment.[27] As discussed in chapter nine, this potential value is particularly significant for States seeking to hold other States to account for human rights violations associated with the adverse effects of climate change.[28]

The compliance of State Parties with the ICESCR is monitored by the Committee on Economic, Social and Cultural Rights (CESCR). This is a body of independent experts established under ECOSOC Resolution 185/17 of

[23] Art 40(1)(a) requires an initial report to be submitted within one year of ratification of the Covenant and, in Art 40(1)(b), submission of further reports at the request of the Committee. The latter requirement has been interpreted as requiring submission of reports every five years. See: United Nations Human Rights Committee (HRC), 'Yearbook of the Human Rights Committee' (Vol 1, Documents of the 11th to 16th sessions, United Nations Human Rights Committee, 1981–82) para 2.

[24] Optional Protocol to the International Covenant on Civil and Political Rights (adopted 16 December 1966, entered into force 23 March 1976) 999 UNTS 302 (OP-ICCPR).

[25] See generally 'Multilateral Treaties Deposited with the Secretary-General' available at treaties.un.org/Pages/Treaties.aspx?id=4&subid=A&lang=en.

[26] For a discussion, see Manfred Nowak, *U.N. Covenant on Civil and Political Rights: CCPR Commentary*, 1st edn (Kehl; Arlington, NP Engel Publisher 1993) 585. See also *General Comment No. 31: The Nature of the General Legal Obligations Imposed on State Parties to the Covenant (para 2)* (29 March 2004), UN Doc CCPR/C/21/Rev.1/Add.13, HRC (General Comment No 31) (encouraging States to make a declaration under Art 41 and/or avail themselves of the procedure under Art 41).

[27] *General Comment No. 31*. In contrast with the individual complaint procedure established under the Optional Protocol, the inter-State procedure is aimed at the amicable settlement of disputes between the State Parties involved. The procedure becomes potentially quasi-judicial only in the second instance, when a so-called 'Ad hoc Conciliation Commission' has been appointed and the State Parties involved fail to reach an amicable solution (Art 42(1)(a)). At this stage, the Conciliation Commission would produce a report containing its findings on 'questions of fact' and 'its views on the possibilities of an amicable solution of the matter' (Art 42(7)(c)). This could presumably involve formulating views resembling judicial decisions on the merits, as the HRC has done under Art 5(4) of the Optional Protocol. See further Manfred Nowak, *U.N. Covenant on Civil and Political Rights: CCPR Commentary*, 2nd edn (Kehl, NP Engel Publisher, 2004) 613.

[28] For a hypothetical example, see Margaretha Wewerinke, 'Climate Change: Human Rights Committee, Ad Hoc Conciliation Commission' in Mark Gibney and Wouter Vandenhole (eds), *Litigating Transnational Human Rights Obligations: Alternative Judgments* (Abingdon, Routledge, 2014).

28 May 1985[29] to carry out the monitoring functions assigned to the UN Economic and Social Council (ECOSOC) in Part IV of the ICESCR.[30] Although it is not established under the treaty which it monitors, the CESCR has gradually developed into a quasi-judicial body resembling the HRC,[31] and eventually obtained a treaty basis for its work with the entry into force of the Optional Protocol to the ICESCR. The Protocol mandates the Committee to receive and consider communications,[32] and provides that these may be submitted 'by or on behalf of individuals or groups of individuals',[33] and also creates a procedure for inter-State communications.[34] The authoritative weight of the Committee's General Comments as interpretations of the Covenant provisions is supported by the fact that these General Comments are included in its annual reports to ECOSOC, which are in turn considered by the General Assembly.[35]

In addition to treaty bodies, the UN human rights system includes a Charter-based human rights body, the UN Human Rights Council, which is a subsidiary body of the UN General Assembly[36] consisting of forty-seven UN Member States elected by the General Assembly.[37] The Council holds a mandate to '[promote] universal respect for the protection of all human rights and fundamental freedoms for all'[38] and to 'promote the effective coordination and the mainstreaming of human rights within the United Nations system'.[39] The resolutions adopted by the Council are not legally binding and (due to the relatively small number of Council Members) probably not as relevant to the creation of customary international law as resolutions that are adopted by the General Assembly. It could nonetheless be argued that the Council, as the United Nations' primary human rights body, is in an ideal position to consider what is needed to address climate change in

[29] UN Economic and Social Council (ECOSOC), Res. 185/17 (28 May 1985), UN Doc E/1985/85, para 15.

[30] ICESCR, Arts 16–25.

[31] See generally ECOSOC, *International Covenant on Economic, Social and Cultural Rights*, Res 1987/5 (26 May 1987) [7]; *Indivisibility and Interdependence of Economic, Social, Cultural, Civil and Political Rights*, GA Res A/Res/42/102, 93rd mtg (7 December 1987) [5]; and UN Committee on Economic, Social and Cultural Rights, *Report of the 7th Session*, Supp 2, UN Doc E/1993/22, [264]–[265]. See also Matthew Craven, *The International Covenant on Economic, Social, and Cultural Rights: a Perspective on its Development* (Oxford, Oxford University Press, 1998) 91.

[32] See, eg, *Optional Protocol to the International Covenant on Economic, Social and Cultural Rights*, GA Res 832, UN GAOR, 63rd Sess, UN Doc A/RES/63/117 (10 December 2008) (OP-ICESCR). See also Arne Vandenbogaerde and Wouter Vandenhole, 'The Optional Protocol to the International Covenant on Economic, Social and Cultural Rights: An Ex Ante Assessment of its Effectiveness in Light of the Drafting Process' (2001) 10 *Human Rights Law Review* 207.

[33] OP-ICESCR, Art 2.

[34] OP-ICESCR, Art 10. This procedure is subject to declarations made by the relevant States under the article.

[35] ICESCR, Arts 16–25.

[36] The Council was created by the General Assembly on 15 March 2006 and replaced the former UN Commission on Human Rights. See: *Human Rights Council*, GA Res 60/251, 60th sess, UN Doc A/RES/60/215, (3 April 2006) para 1.

[37] Ibid para 7.

[38] Ibid para 2.

[39] Ibid para 3.

accordance with human rights obligations, and to promote compliance with States' obligations to prevent dangerous climate change in accordance with existing legal obligations.[40]

Interpretation

Given that international human rights treaties do not specifically address climate change, it is crucial to understand to what extent and how their provisions can be interpreted to address climate change-related harms. In the words of Rosenne, the provisions of human rights treaties are largely 'written in axiomatic or syllogistic form' and thus 'require significant interpretation'.[41] The rules of general international law that govern the construction of treaties are codified in Articles 31 and 32 of the Vienna Convention on the Law of Treaties (VCLT)[42] ('the Vienna rules'), which are generally taken to reflect 'approximations of the applicable rules' of customary international law[43] which in turn are 'essentially … a projection of the (valid) consent [of States]'.[44] The relevance of these general rules in the human rights context has been repeatedly confirmed by human rights bodies that are expressly mandated with the interpretation of human rights treaties;[45] a view that has been echoed in human rights scholarship.[46] A significant advantage of applying these general rules in the human rights context – apart from their doctrinal foundation – is that the rules provide objective criteria for interpretation: the often-cited statement that treaty interpretation is 'to some extent an art,

[40] See also Margaretha Wewerinke, 'The Role of the UN Human Rights Council in Addressing Climate Change' (2014) 7(1) *Human Rights and International Legal Discourse* 10.

[41] Shabtai Rosenne, 'Some Reflections Erga Omnes' in Antony Anghie and Garry Sturgess (eds), *Legal Visions of the 21st Century: Essays in Honour of Judge Christopher Weeramantry* (The Hague, Kluwer Law International, 1998) 515.

[42] VCLT.

[43] Martin Scheinin, 'Impact on the Law of Treaties' in Menno T Kamminga and Martin Scheinin (eds), *The Impact of Human Rights Law on General International Law* (Oxford; New York, Oxford University Press, 2009) 36. For a discussion of the customary law status of the rules of interpretation contained in the VCLT, see further Jan Klabbers, *The Concept of Treaty in International Law* (The Hague, Martinus Nijhoff, 1996).

[44] Crawford (n 2) 311.

[45] It is worth noting the argument of some human rights scholars that the practice of human rights treaty bodies may reflect the agreement of the parties regarding the treaties' interpretation. See Scheinin (n 42); Meron (n 21).

[46] See, eg, Manfred Nowak, *Introduction to the International Human Rights Regime* (Leiden, Martinus Nijhoff, 2003) 64 (suggesting that the general rules reflected in the VCLT apply to the ICCPR); Salomon (n 16) 304 (suggesting that the general rules of interpretation apply to the ICESCR) and Christine Chinkin, Marsha A Freeman and Beate Rudolf (eds), *The UN Convention on the Elimination of All Forms of Discrimination Against Women: A Commentary* (New York, Oxford University Press, 2012) 13 (suggesting that CEDAW should be interpreted in accordance with the rules of interpretation encapsulated in the VCLT because the treaty itself does not include provisions on interpretation).

not an exact science'[47] illustrates the need for 'meta-rules' of interpretation that would promote consistency between interpretative processes and safeguard their integrity.

At the same time, however, there are reasons to believe that the Vienna rules may need to be slightly modified in order to accommodate the normative content of provisions of human rights treaties. After all, the VCLT was drafted as a framework to be applied primarily to treaties without a compliance mechanism that contained reciprocal obligations and did not directly affect third parties.[48] Crawford considers that 'it is not too much to say that [the VCLT] looks at multilateral treaties from the perspective of bilateral treaties' or that it has a 'bifocal approach', dealing with the 'public order' aspects of multilateral treaties 'only peripherally … and then usually indirectly'.[49] Human rights treaties are perhaps the clearest example of treaties that deviate from the traditional type of treaties: they usually establish their own monitoring and enforcement mechanisms, contain objective rather than reciprocal obligations and have third party beneficiaries.[50] The implications of the objective nature of treaty obligations for their interpretation were recognised by the ICJ in *Reservations to the Convention on the Prevention and Punishment of the Crime of Genocide*, where the Court stated:

> The Convention was manifestly adopted for a purely humanitarian and civilizing purpose … [I]ts object on the one hand is to safeguard the very existence of certain human groups and on the other to confirm and endorse the most elementary principles of morality. In such a convention the contracting States do not have any interest of their own; they merely have, one and all, a common interest, namely, the accomplishment of those high purposes which are the raison d'être of the convention. Consequently, in a convention of this type one cannot speak of individual advantages or disadvantages to States, or of the maintenance of a perfect contractual balance between rights and duties.[51]

As Craven suggests, treaties of a humanitarian character 'cannot therefore simply be regarded as the accidental data of an otherwise disinterested legal system. … [T]o say that they are "only treaties" is merely to place them within a highly contingent set of understandings as to the nature of international legal relations'.[52]

Turning to the general rules themselves, we find a paradox: it is precisely the rules of treaty interpretation that minimise the relevance of the intention of the

[47] Martti Koskenniemi, *From Apology to Utopia: The Structure of International Legal Argument*, 2nd edn (Cambridge, Cambridge University Press, 2005) 396.

[48] Scheinin (n 43) 32.

[49] James R Crawford, 'Responsibility to the International Community as a Whole' (2001) 8 *Indiana Journal of Global Legal Studies* 303, 311.

[50] Scheinin (n 43) 28.

[51] *Reservations to the Convention on the Prevention and Punishment of the Crime of Genocide* [1951] ICJ Reports 15 23.

[52] Matthew Craven, 'Legal Differentiation and the Concept of the Human Rights Treaty in International Law' (2000) 11 *European Journal of International Law* 489, 519.

drafters of a treaty in the interpretative process. The VCLT lists preparatory works as 'supplementary means of interpretation' that may only be relied upon to determine the meaning of a treaty provision when its interpretation in accordance with the general rules 'leaves the meaning ambiguous or obscure', or leads to a result which is 'manifestly absurd or unreasonable'.[53] The Inter-American Court of Human Rights (IACtHR) emphasised the subsidiary nature of this rule in its Advisory Opinion on the death penalty, while stressing that devoting minimal attention to the intention of the drafters of human rights treaties is compatible with the special nature of those treaties. More specifically, it stated that objective criteria of interpretation that examine the texts themselves are more appropriate in interpreting human rights treaties than subjective criteria that only ascertain the intent of the parties involved.[54] Although there is an imperative rule, stated in Article 31(4), that 'A special meaning shall be given to a term if it is established that the parties so intended', this rule is unlikely to have much bearing on the interpretation of human rights treaties in the context of climate change given that the drafters of such treaties probably did not have an ascertainable and uniform intention, and quite possibly no intention at all, as to the meaning of treaty terms in relation to climate change. The rule is also unlikely to apply to the interpretation of the principles contained in the UNFCCC, given that the intention of the parties about the most crucial treaty terms was far from uniform.[55]

The most relevant rules for the treaty provisions analysed in this book are thus the general rules of treaty interpretation contained in Article 31 of the VCLT, which reflect customary international law.[56] Article 31(3) expresses the general rule that an international treaty 'shall be interpreted in good faith in accordance with the ordinary meaning to be given to the terms of the treaty in their context and in light

[53] VCLT, Art 32. See also Chinkin, Freeman and Rudolf (n 45) 13 (confirming its applicability to CEDAW) and Nowak (n 27) 14 (highlighting its relevance to the interpretation of the ICCPR).

[54] For a similar line of reasoning, see *Inter-American Court of Human Rights Restrictions to Death Penalty (Advisory Opinion)* 70 ILR (1986), 466 IACtHR 466. In particular, the ECHR has sought to reconcile the two perspectives by finding that 'the purpose of the High Contracting Parties in concluding the [ECHR] was not to concede to each other reciprocal rights and obligations in pursuance of their individual national interests but to realise the aims and ideals of the Council of Europe … and to establish a common public order of the free democracies of Europe with the object of safeguarding their common heritage of political traditions, ideals, freedom and the rule of law'. See *Austria v Italy* App no 788/60 (ECtHR, 11 January 1961) (*Austria v Italy*) 138–40, 116 *et seq*., endorsed in later cases including *Ireland v United Kingdom* Series A no 25 (1978) 2 EHRR 25 (*Ireland v United Kingdom*); *East African Asians v United Kingdom* (1973) 3 EHRR 76. Vierdag argues that this reasoning is 'essentially valid for human rights treaties generally, and … to be regarded as an accurate characterization of such instruments': EW Vierdag, 'Some Remarks About Special Features of Human Rights Treaties' (1994) 25 *Netherlands Yearbook of International Law* 119, 124.

[55] See also Daniel Bodansky, 'The United Nations Framework Convention on Climate Change: A Commentary' (1993) 18 *Yale Journal of International Law* 451, 465.

[56] See, eg, *Case Concerning Application of the Convention on the Prevention and Punishment of the Crime of Genocide (Bosnia and Herzegovina v Serbia and Montenegro)* [2007] ICJ Reports 43 *(Bosnia and Herzegovina v Serbia and Montenegro)* 109–10. For a discussion about the applicability of these rules to human rights treaties see Nowak (n 46) 64ff. See also Chinkin, Freeman and Rudolf (n 46) 13 (suggesting that human rights treaties should be interpreted in accordance with the rules of interpretation encapsulated in the VCLT if the treaty itself does not include provisions on interpretation).

of its object and purpose'.[57] The term 'context' refers to the text of the treaty including, when applicable, its preamble, annexes and agreements between the parties that relate to the treaty's conclusion.[58] The interpretative technique of 'systematic interpretation'[59] prevents the interpretation of treaty provisions in isolation. The book will demonstrate the importance of this technique when interpreting the UNFCCC provisions, which acquire a more specific meaning when interpreted in the light of Article 3 of the Convention. Another example is the significance of reading Article 1(2) of the ICCPR and ICESCR in conjunction with Article 47 of the ICCPR and Article 35 of the ICESCR respectively,[60] as the latter provisions prohibit an interpretation of individual rights that conflict with the right of self-determination. Furthermore, there is the principle that account must be taken of 'any subsequent practice in the application of the treaty which establishes the agreement of the parties regarding its interpretation'[61] which, according to scholars, may include the interpretative practice of human rights bodies.[62] This rule thus appears to consolidate the authoritative weight of human rights jurisprudence and instruments such as General Comments and advisory opinions.

The most significant feature of the general rule from the perspective of international human rights law is, however, that it calls for purposive interpretation. It is widely recognised that due to the special nature of human rights treaties the emphasis in their interpretation is, in Nowak's words, 'Essentially ... on interpreting treaties ... in the light of their object and purpose'.[63] And for human rights treaties 'naturally the main object is for states parties to protect the rights set out in the treaties'.[64] The IACtHR has emphasised 'the purpose of guaranteeing the enjoyment of individual human beings of those rights and freedoms rather than to establish reciprocal relations between States'.[65] Furthermore, in its Advisory Opinion on the Effect of Reservations on the Entry into Force of the ACHR, the Court emphasised:

> Modern human rights treaties in general ... are not multilateral treaties of the traditional type concluded to accomplish the reciprocal exchange of rights for the mutual

[57] VCLT, Art 31.

[58] Ibid Art 31(2). See also Jayawickrama (n 21) 160.

[59] Nowak (n 46) 65 (emphasis omitted).

[60] For a discussion, see Nowak (n 27) XXIII.

[61] VCLT, Art 31(3)(b).

[62] Scheinin, 'Characteristics of Human Rights Norms' in Krause and Scheinin (eds), *International Protection of Human Rights: a Textbook* (Turku, Åbo Akademi University Institute for Human Rights, 2009) 21 (citing as an example: 'Final Report on the Impact of Findings of the United Nations Human Rights Treaty Bodies' (International Law Association, Committee on Human Rights Law and Practice, 2004). Cf Nowak (n 27) XXIV (stating that subsequent practice may be derived from relevant reservations, declarations of interpretation and comments submitted by States).

[63] Nowak (n 27) XXIV. See also Alexander Orakhelashvili, 'Restrictive Interpretation of Human Rights Treaties in the Recent Jurisprudence of the European Court of Human Rights' (2003) 14 *European Journal of International Law* 529, 535.

[64] Nowak (n 46) 65.

[65] *Other Treaties Subject to the Advisory Jurisdiction of the Court (Advisory Opinion)* (1982) (1982) 3 *Hunam Rights Law Journal* 140, 1 IACtHR (ser A).

> benefit of the contracting States. Their object and purpose is the protection of basic rights of individual human beings, irrespective of their nationality, both against the State of their nationality and all other contracting States. In concluding these human rights treaties, the States can be deemed to submit themselves to a legal order within which they, for the common good, assume various obligations.[66]

Taking this object and purpose into account allows a 'dynamic reading' of human rights instruments, so that human rights law retains its relevance in a changing world.[67] Often cited is the ECtHR's characterisation of the ECHR as 'a living instrument which … must be interpreted in the light of the present-day conditions'. The IACtHR has similarly relied on the notion of 'evolving American law',[68] and scholars continue to emphasise that rights protected in international human rights treaties 'are not to be interpreted statically but rather in the light of relevant societal developments',[69] and that States' obligations to protect those rights are affected by 'changing social and moral assumptions'.[70]

For the purpose of this study, it is important to emphasise that the technique of purposive interpretation has led to a central role for the principle of effectiveness in human rights jurisprudence. In other words, the principle that provisions of human rights treaties should be interpreted and applied in a way that makes its safeguards practical and effective[71] (referred to by the ECtHR as '*effet utile*').[72] In *Soering v UK*,[73] the principle (first stated in *Ireland v UK*)[74] that 'In interpreting the Convention regard must be had to its special character as a treaty for the collective enforcement of human rights and fundamental freedoms'[75] led the

[66] *The Effect of Reservations on the Entry into Force of the American Convention of Human Rights* (*Advisory Opinion*) (1982) IHRL 3398, 2 IACtHR (Ser A).

[67] Although reliance on this technique of interpretation by human rights bodies has sometimes been criticised for overstepping their mandates, we can also argue, as Shelton does, that reliance on this technique is an inevitable consequence of the generic way in which human rights treaty texts are formulated. See Dinah L Shelton, 'An Introduction to the History of International Human Rights Law' (GWU Legal Studies Research Paper No 346, 2007) 24.

[68] Ibid.

[69] Nowak (n 27) XXIV.

[70] David Feldman, *Civil Liberties and Human Rights in England and Wales*, 2nd edn (Oxford, Oxford University Press, 2002) 53.

[71] Jayawickrama (n 21). See also D Nguyen, P Daillier and A Pellet, *Droit International Public*, 7th edn (Paris, Librairie Générale de Droit et de Jurisprudence, 2002) 264; Daniel Rietiker, 'The Principle of "Effectiveness" in the Recent Jurisprudence of the European Court of Human Rights: Its Different Dimensions and Its Consistency with Public International Law – No Need for the Concept of Treaty Sui Generis' (2010) 79 *Nordic Journal of International Law* 245.

[72] The ECtHR jurisprudence on the principle of effectiveness started with its judgment in *Airey v Republic of Ireland* Series A no 32 (1979) 2 EHRR, 305. The case concerned the scope of a State's obligations in relation to the right to a fair trial, and the Court held that these obligations included a positive obligation to ensure physical access to a courtroom. The principle has subsequently been applied in relation to most rights protected in the Convention, including the rights to life, to freedom of association and of public participation. See, eg, *Ireland v United Kingdom*, [239]; *Artico v Italy* Series A no 37 (1980) 3 EHRR 1, para 33.

[73] *Soering v UK* (1989) Series A no 161, 11 EHRR 439.

[74] *Ireland v United Kingdom*, para 239.

[75] *Soering v UK*, para 87.

Court to reason that although it agreed with the UK Government that the beneficial purpose of extradition in preventing offenders from evading justice cannot be ignored in determining the scope of application of the Convention;[76] 'These considerations cannot, however, absolve the Contracting Parties from responsibility under Article 3 for all and any foreseeable consequences of extradition suffered outside their jurisdiction'.[77]

As noted by commentators, the principle of effectiveness is 'nothing very exotic in international law'[78] and indeed exists as a cross-cutting principle: in general international law it is known as the principle *ut res magus valet quam pereat*, which means that law should be interpreted in a way that makes it effective.[79] In international human rights law, however, the principle acquires a specific meaning. Its effect on treaty interpretation is generally that in cases of doubt as to the meaning of a treaty provision, its interpretation should favour the protection of the substantive rights protected in the treaty *(in dubio pro libertate et dignitate)*.[80] The principle is also closely related to the maxim *Ubi jus ibi remedium:* where there is a right, there is a remedy[81] – a maxim that appears in Roman and Dutch law and that has long been recognised in common law systems.[82] Illustrations of how this principle operates in international human rights law are particularly plentiful in cases involving individuals who suffered harm whilst in custody. In *Dermit Barbato v Uruguay*, for example, the HRC could not reach a definite conclusion as to how the victim had died: he could have committed suicide, or he could have been killed by others. The HRC dealt with this uncertainty by finding that 'in all the circumstances the Uruguayan authorities *either by act or by omission* were responsible for not taking adequate measures to protect his life, as required by Article 6(1) of the Covenant'.[83] The significance of this decision is that it shows that human rights violations can be established when there is reason to assume that the State could have acted to prevent the violation, and that it triggers additional obligations on the part of the State to provide a remedy.[84] In another case

[76] Ibid para 86.

[77] Ibid.

[78] Rietiker (n 71) 276.

[79] John P Grant and Craig J Barker (eds), *Encyclopaedic Dictionary of International Law*, 3rd edn (New York, Oxford University Press, 2009). See also *Interpretation of the Peace Treaties with Bulgaria, Hungary, and Romania, Advisory Opinion (Second Phase)* [1950] ICJ Reports 65, 229; and *Corfu Channel Case (United Kingdom v Albania) (Merits)* [1949] ICJ Reports 4, 24–26.

[80] Nowak (n 46) 65–66. See also Orakhelashvili (n 63) 535.

[81] Henry Black, *Black's Law Dictionary*, 6th edn (Saint Paul, Springer, 1990) 1294. The entry adds that 'it is said that the rule of primitive law was the reverse: Where there is a remedy, there is a right.' For a discussion on its relation to the principle of effectiveness see Alistair R Mowbray, *The Development of Positive Obligations under the European Convention on Human Rights by the European Court of Human Rights* (Oxford, Hart Publishing, 2004) 3, 170, 221.

[82] Black (n 81) 1120.

[83] *General Comment No. 6: The right to life (Article 6)* (30 April 1982), UN Doc HRI/GEN/1/Rev 6, HRC, para 9.2 (emphasis added).

[84] With regard to: Hugo Dermit, the Committee found the State party under an obligation to establish the facts of his death, to bring to justice any persons found responsible for his death and to pay appropriate compensation to his family, ibid, para 11.

concerning death in custody, the ECtHR case of *Velikova v Bulgaria*,[85] it is even clearer that uncertainty can work in favour of the individual. The applicant, who was arrested for alleged cattle theft, had complained that he was not feeling well shortly after his arrest. The ECtHR considered the absence of medical evidence about the applicant's condition prior to his death not as a weakness of the applicant's case, but as an indication of the State's failure to safeguard his health.[86] The legal analysis of substantive obligations in chapter three (focusing on the rights to life, to the highest attainable standard of health, to enjoy a distinct culture and to self-determination) is largely concerned with the question what States are required to do to prevent a violation. The significance of purposive construction of human rights treaties is dealt with in more detail below, in relation to the territorial and personal scope of human rights treaties.

Territorial and Personal Scope of International Human Rights Treaties

This section examines the territorial and personal scope of States' obligations under international human rights treaties, taking the ICCPR and the ICESCR as a starting point. A first point to note is that the personal scope of human rights treaties – with the exception of those that protect the rights of specific groups – appears to be unrestricted. Indeed, the texts of human rights treaties suggest that the beneficiaries of human rights obligations include, as per the UDHR, 'all human beings', save for certain rights of political participation that are confined to 'citizens' or rights that specifically protect 'peoples' or 'minorities'. The presumption that States' obligations under these treaties may be territorially confined comes from the inclusion of jurisdiction clauses in some, but not all, human rights treaties. The need to examine this question also results from the prevalence of the presumption that most or all human rights treaties have a 'territorial scope' in human rights scholarship and (albeit to a lesser extent) in international jurisprudence.

Turning to the ICESCR first, we note that this treaty does not include a jurisdictional clause.[87] Article 2(1) of the Covenant provides that States Parties to the

[85] *Velikova v Bulgaria* App no 41488/98 (ECtHR, 18 May 2000).

[86] Ibid para 75.

[87] Opposite conclusions have been drawn from this omission. See, eg, Rolf Kunnemann, 'Extraterritorial Application of the International Covenant on Economic, Social and Cultural Rights' in Fons Coomans and Menno T Kamminga (eds), *Extraterritorial Application of Human Rights Treaties* (Antwerp, Intersentia, 2004) 201; and John H Knox, 'Climate Change and Human Rights Law' (2009) 50 *Virginia Journal of International Law* 198, 206 (finding that the obligations are not confined by territorial considerations). See also *Legal Consequences of the Construction of a Wall in the Occupied Palestinian Territory* (Advisory Opinion) [2004] ICJ Reports 9 (finding that the absence of a jurisdiction clause was due to 'the fact that this Covenant guarantees rights which are essentially territorial'). Cf *Bosnia and Herzegovina v Serbia and Montenegro* (finding that State responsibility could arise for acts committed by one State on the territory of another because the obligation of States to prevent and to punish the crime of genocide was 'not territorially limited by the [Genocide] Convention' in light of the absence of a jurisdiction clause).

ICESCR shall 'take steps, individually and through international assistance and cooperation, especially economic and technical, to the maximum of its available resources, with a view to achieving progressively the full realisation of the rights' protected in the present Covenant by all appropriate means, particularly the adoption of legislative measures.[88] A textual reading of this provision leads to the conclusion that 'the undertaking in Article 2(1) "to take steps" in itself, is not qualified or limited by other considerations'.[89] This is also clear from Article 23 of the Covenant, which provides that:

> The States Parties to the present Covenant agree that international action for the achievement of the rights recognised in the present Covenant includes such methods as the conclusion of conventions, the adoption of recommendations, the furnishing of technical assistance and the holding of regional meetings and technical meetings for the purpose of consultation and study organised in conjunction with the Governments concerned.[90]

Further references to international cooperation in the ICESCR are contained in Articles 11,[91] 15[92] and 22.[93] In accordance with these provisions, the Committee on Economic, Social and Cultural Rights (CESCR) has consistently interpreted the Covenant as imposing international cooperation obligations on States.[94] In General Comment No. 3 it states that 'the phrase "to the maximum of its available resources" was intended by the drafters of the Covenant to refer to both the resources existing within a State and those available from the international community international community through international cooperation and assistance'.[95] It goes on to state that it:

> wishes to emphasise that in accordance with Articles 55 and 56 of the Charter of the United Nations, with well-established principles of international law, and with the provisions of the Covenant itself, international cooperation for development and thus

[88] ICESCR, Art 2(1).

[89] *General Comment No. 3: The Nature of States Parties Obligations (Art 2, para 1)* (14 December 1990) E/1991/23, CESCR (*General Comment No. 3*), para 2.

[90] ICESCR, Art 23.

[91] Ibid Art 11 (providing an international cooperation obligation with regard to the rights to an adequate standard of living and the right to be free from hunger).

[92] Ibid Art 15 (providing that 'State Parties to the present Covenant recognize the benefits to be derived from the encouragement and development of international contacts and co-operation in the scientific and cultural fields').

[93] Ibid Art 22, mandating ECOSOC to 'bring to the attention of other organs of the United Nations, their subsidiary organs and specialized agencies concerned with furnishing technical assistance any matters arising out of [State reports] which may assist such bodies in deciding, each within its field of competence, on the advisability of international measures likely to contribute to the effective progressive implementation of the present Covenant'. These monitoring functions are now carried out by the CESCR in accordance with ECOSOC Resolution 185/17.

[94] See below for examples on the right to food, adequate housing, water and the highest attainable standard of health. Sigrun Skogly, *Beyond National Borders: States' Human Rights Obligations in International Cooperation* (Antwerp, Intersentia, 2006) 152.

[95] *General Comment No. 3*, para 13.

> for the realization of economic, social and cultural rights is an obligation of all States. It is particularly incumbent upon those States which are in a position to assist others in this regard.[96]

General Comment No 14 of the Committee on the right to the highest attainable standard of health contains an interpretation of Article 12 of the Covenant as providing an entire range of 'international obligations'.[97] The Committee also mentions a 'collective responsibility' on the part of the international community to address the problem of transmittable diseases and the 'special responsibility and interest' of economically developed States to assist poorer developing States in this regard.[98] In General Comment No 12 the Committee sets out similar international obligations in relation to the right to food.[99] In passing, we should note that the right of self-determination provided for in Article 1, which is common to the two Covenants, imposes transnational obligations per se, as 'peoples' may comprise the entire population of a State – in which case its protection necessarily depends on the conduct of other States.[100] The HRC highlighted in its General Comment No 12, stating that States' obligations under Article 1 exist 'not only in relation to their own peoples but *vis-à-vis* all peoples which have not been able to exercise or have been deprived of the possibility of exercising their right of self-determination'.[101]

Article 2(1) of the ICCPR provides that States must respect and ensure the rights of individuals 'within its territory and subject to its jurisdiction'.[102]

[96] Ibid para 14.

[97] The listed obligations are: first, to respect the enjoyment of the right to health in other countries; second, to prevent third parties from violating the right in other countries 'if they are able to influence these third parties by way of legal or political means'; third, 'depending on the availability of resources' to facilitate access to essential health facilities, goods and services in other countries, wherever possible and to provide the necessary aid when required; fourth, to ensure that the right to health is given due attention in international agreements and that other international agreements do not adversely impact upon the right to health; fifth, to ensure that their actions as members of international organisations take due account of the right to health; and sixth, to cooperate in providing disaster relief and humanitarian assistance in times of emergency with contributions 'to the maximum of [a State's] capacity'. See *General Comment No. 14: The Right to the Highest Attainable Standard of Health (Art 12)* (11 August 2000), UN Doc E/C12/2000/4, CESCR (General Comment No 14), paras 39–40. See also Craven (n 31) 253.

[98] General Comment No 14, paras 40 and 45.

[99] *General Comment No. 12: Substantive Issues Arising in the Implementation of the International Covenant on Economic, Social and Cultural Rights: The Right to Adequate Food (Art 11)* (12 May 1999), UN Doc E/C12/1999/5, CESCR paras 36–37.

[100] Knox (n 87) 205. See also Sarah Joseph, Jenny Schultz and Melissa Castan, *The International Covenant on Civil and Political Rights: Cases, Materials, and Commentary*, 2nd edn (Oxford, Oxford University Press, 2004) (pointing out that 'Article 1(3) is unusual as it imposes duties on States with regard to persons outside their jurisdiction, indeed even if those people are within the jurisdiction of another State Party').

[101] *General Comment No. 12: The Right to Self-Determination of Peoples (Art 1)* (13 March 1984), HRC, para 6.

[102] For further discussion, see Olivier de Schutter, *International Human Rights Law: Cases, Materials, Commentary* (Cambridge, Cambridge University Press, 2010) 123 (pointing out that the central question addressed in the literature is 'whether the notion of "jurisdiction" (taken separately or in combination with that of "territory") designates a condition for a finding of State responsibility which is distinct from that of attribution, or whether instead the two notion – "jurisdiction" and "attribution" – are

The HRC has insisted that this provision must be read in conjunction with Article 5(1) which states that 'Nothing in the present Covenant may be interpreted as implying for any State, group or person any right to engage in any activity or perform any act aimed at the destruction of any of the rights and freedoms recognised herein or at their limitation to a greater extent than is provided for in the present Covenant'.[103] It also emphasises the need to take account of the object and purpose of the treaty and the principle of *pacta sunt servanda* when considering the scope and nature of States' obligations,[104] and accordingly found that the word 'and' in Article 2(1) must be interpreted disjunctively. Its General Comment 31 spells out that 'States Parties are required by Article 2, paragraph 1, to respect and to ensure the Covenant rights to all persons who may be within their territory and to all persons subject to their jurisdiction'.[105] This disjunctive reading of the word 'and' has been endorsed by the International Court of Justice in its *Wall* opinion[106] and in the literature.[107]

In its General Comment No 31 the Committee interprets the word 'jurisdiction' as implying that 'a State party must respect and ensure the right laid down in the Covenant to anyone within the power or effective control of that State Party, even if not situated within the territory of the State Party'.[108] The Committee has not provided a clear indication of what would amount to 'power' or 'effective control'.[109] In the view of this author, the term 'power' is most relevant to climate

in fact synonymous and thus interchangeable'). See also Marko Milanovic, 'From Compromise to Principle: Clarifying the Concept of State Jurisdiction in Human Rights Treaties' (2008) 8 *Human Rights Law Review* 411, 7, 26 (arguing, at 7, that 'the word "jurisdiction" is meant to denote solely a sort of factual power that a State exercises over persons or territory'); and Cedric Ryngaert, 'Jurisdiction: Towards a Reasonableness Test' in Malcolm Langford et al (eds), *Global Justice, State Duties: The Extraterritorial Scope of Economic, Social and Cultural Rights in International Law* (Cambridge, Cambridge University Press, 2013) 218 (suggesting that a reasonableness test could be applied to interpret the term 'jurisdiction').

[103] *Sergio Euben Lopez Burgos v Uruguay* (Communication No R12/52) (*Sergio Euben Lopez Burgos v Uruguay*), para 12.3.

[104] *General Comment No. 31 (paras 3 and 5)*. See also Barbara Frey, 'Obligations to Protect the Right to Life: Constructing a Rule of Transfer Regarding Small Arms and Light Weapons' in Mark Gibney and Sigrid Skogly (eds), *Universal Human Rights and Extraterritorial Obligations* (Philadelphia, University of Pennsylvania Press, 2010) 50.

[105] Ibid para 10.

[106] *Legal Consequences of the Construction of a Wall in the Occupied Palestinian Territory*, (*Advisory Opinion*) [2004] ICJ Reports 136, 111.

[107] Theodor Meron, 'Extraterritoriality of Human Rights Treaties' (1995) 89 *Americal Journal of International Law* 78, 79.

[108] *General Comment No. 31 (para 10)*.

[109] In General Comment 31 the HRC only states, at para 10, that the principle that the enjoyment of rights is not limited to citizens of States Parties 'also applies to those within the power or effective control of the *forces of* a State Party acting outside its territory, regardless of the circumstances in which such power or effective control was obtained'. The notion of 'effective control' is derived from *Military and Paramilitary Activities in and against Nicaragua (Nicaragua v United States of America)* [1986] ICJ Reports 14 where the ICJ referred to control over military or paramilitary operations in foreign territory (paras 105–15). The test was subsequently adopted by the ECtHR, which initially used it to refer to effective control over territory, rather than over private actors acting abroad whose conduct was directly attributable to the State based on specific circumstances (eg *Loizidou v Turkey (Preliminary Objections and Merits)* App no 15318/89 (ECtHR 22 July 1989) para 52; *Bankovic et al v Belgium and*

change-related human rights violations, as it indicates that we must consider a State's capacity to prevent a violation within the limits set by international law. The concept of 'effective control' may help to address the more specific question of whether a State has 'effective control' over a private actor outside its territory (and thus cases covered by the rule of attribution articulated in Article 8 of the International Law Commission's Articles on Responsibility of States for Internationally Wrongful Acts (ARS), discussed below).[110] In either case, the principle that 'facticity creates normativity' could be relied upon to determine whether a State has violated its obligations under international human rights law.[111] This principle is derived from the HRC's practice of perusing a 'contextual assessment of the State's factual control in respect of facts and events that allegedly constitute a violation of a human right'.[112] The best known example is the HRC's decision in *Lopez v Uruguay*, where it found that a State should not be allowed 'to perpetrate violations of the Covenant on the territory of another state, which violations it could not perpetrate on its own territory'.[113] The approach pursued by the Committee essentially considers whether a State has control over a situation or instrumentality that interferes with Covenant rights, rather than over individuals whose rights are affected. Accordingly, Scheinin has considered that jurisdiction merely 'serves as a shorthand expression for the required factual link between a State and an individual (human rights accountability), or between a State's conduct and certain grievances (State responsibility)'.[114] This approach helps give effect to the object and

16 Other Contracting States App no 52207/99 (ECtHR, 19 December 2001), paras 54–81). This interpretation seems to have changed in recent cases (see ch 1). The ICJ's decision in the *Genocide* case keeps with the original meaning of the concept and emphasised that the rule is embodied in Art 8 of the ILC. See *Bosnia and Herzegovina v Serbia and Montenegro*, paras 398–99. For a critical assessment of the ICJ's application of the test see Antonio Cassese, 'The Nicaragua and Tadic Tests Revisited in Light of the ICJ Judgment on Genocide in Bosnia' (2007) 18 *European Journal of International Law* 649, 651.

[110] The question whether domestic conduct affecting individuals extraterritorially falls within Art 8 of the ARS has been discussed in the literature. Lawson and Den Heijer point out that there is overwhelming authority in European jurisprudence for a position that jurisdiction is not an issue in this type of case. See Maarten Den Heijer and Rick Lawson, 'Extraterritorial Human Rights and the Concept of "Jurisdiction"' in Malcolm Langford et al (eds), *Global Justice, State Duties: The Extraterritorial Scope of Economic, Social and Cultural Rights in International Law* (Cambridge, Cambridge University Press, 2013) 203 (with citations). This practice reflects an understanding that the obligations of States, both positive and negative, are not dependent on the geographical location or nationality of beneficiaries. Accordingly, it is safe to assume that attribution is established by considering the obligation rather than focusing on a State's control over a private actor. The situation is different in cases of private actors acting extraterritorially, because this may fall outside the scope of the obligation. In other words, there is a genuine question of attribution in such cases, which could possibly be resolved through the 'effective control' test that was used in *Military and Paramilitary Activities in and against Nicaragua (Nicaragua v United States of America) (Judgement)* [1986] ICJ Reports 14.

[111] Martin Scheinin, 'Extraterritorial Effect of the International Covenant on Civil and Political Rights' in Fons Coomans and Menno T Kamminga (eds), *Extraterritorial Application of Human Rights Treaties* (Antwerp, Intersentia, 2004) 76. See also Den Heijer and Lawson (n 110).

[112] Scheinin (n 111) 76 (emphasis in the original).

[113] *Sergio Euben Lopez Burgos v Uruguay*, para 12.3.

[114] Martin Scheinin, 'Just Another Word? Jurisdiction in the Roadmaps of State Responsibility and Human Rights' in Malcolm Langford et al (eds), *Global Justice, State Duties: The Extraterritorial Scope of Economic, Social and Cultural Rights in International Law* (Cambridge, Cambridge University Press, 2013) 229.

purpose of human rights treaties, as seen by the ECtHR's finding that the objective character of human rights obligations gives rise to an obligation for States to secure these rights and freedoms 'not only to its own nationals and those of the other … Parties but also to nationals of States not parties to the Convention and to stateless persons', as human rights obligations are 'designed rather to protect the fundamental rights of individual human beings from infringement by any of the … Parties than to create subjective and reciprocal rights for the … Parties themselves'.[115] At the same time, it fully recognises that the scope of States' human rights obligations is affected by the limits of their sovereign power.[116] The IACtHR recently developed the jurisprudence on extraterritorial State obligations, ruling that States could have obligations to people abroad who suffer human rights violations as a result of the State's conduct performed in its own territory.[117] However, though this is an important development, the IACtHR did not set out the limits of this new jurisdictional link.[118]

The analysis in the following chapters will build on the premise that the existence of a human rights violation allegedly caused by a State's acts and omissions and that affects people outside the State's territory must be assessed through a contextual analysis.[119] This premise is not only compatible with the practice of the HRC, but also with the CESCR's approach of assessing compliance with States' obligations by considering whether all appropriate means have been used to prevent a violation.[120] In accordance with this premise, normative consequences can be drawn from the factual reality that the consequences of climate change affect human beings everywhere,[121] while climate change mitigation is achieved primarily through national regulation and policies in countries other than the countries that are mostly affected by climate change, as well as through international decision-making, cooperation and the enforcement of existing legal

[115] *Austria v Italy*, 116 *et seq.*

[116] See also Dinah Shelton, 'Remedies and Reparation' in Malcolm Langford et al (eds), *Global Justice, State Duties: The Extraterritorial Scope of Economic, Social, and Cultural Rights in International Law* (Cambridge, Cambridge University Press, 2013) 413 (observing that the terms 'jurisdiction and control' contained in some human rights treaties '[reflect] the fact that in most instances States do not and cannot legally assert power over the exercise of civil and political rights in another State's territory'). See further *Austria v Italy*, 116 *et seq.*

[117] Inter-American Court of Human Rights, 'Advisory Opinion on the Environment and Human Rights', 15 November 2017, [95], [101]–[102].

[118] See Antal Berkes, 'A New Extraterritorial Jurisdictional Link Recognised by the IACtHR' (2018) available at www.ejiltalk.org/a-new-extraterritorial-jurisdictional-link-recognised-by-the-iacthr/.

[119] Cf Wouter Vandenhole, 'Is There a Legal Obligation to Cooperate Internationally for Development?' (2009) 23 *International Journal of Children's Rights* 23, 23 (implying that no contextual analysis would be needed where a State allegedly breaches obligations to 'fulfil' economic, social and cultural rights extraterritorially, as the existence of such obligations may be excluded a priori).

[120] *General Comment No. 3: The Nature of States' Parties' Obligations* (Adopted 14 December 1990) UN Doc E/1991/23, CESCR, para 3.

[121] This point is noted in virtually every academic commentary on human rights and climate change, but usually sets the stage for a discussion on 'extraterritorial' obligations. See, eg, Daniel Bodansky, 'Climate Change and Human Rights: Unpacking the Issues' (2010) 38 *Georgia Journal of Internaitonal and Comparative Law* 511, 521.

obligations that require climate change mitigation. Conceptually, this approach builds on the understanding that the cumulative norms derived from the various sources of human rights law create a web of legal relationships that involves all peoples and all nations. In this web of relationships the role of sovereign States is to ensure the protection of the human rights of those who are actually or potentially affected by the ways in which it exercises its sovereign power. It is worth noting that applying this approach in the context of climate change does *not* mean that State responsibility occurs 'whenever a chain of causation exists between a State's actions and extraterritorial harm'.[122] This will become clear in chapter six, which discusses the attribution of conduct to States, and chapter seven, which discusses the content of States' obligations.

Finally, it is worth highlighting the CESCR's position that the requirement of international cooperation to realise human rights derived from the UN Charter is relevant to the interpretation of the CESCR. This reflects the doctrinal position that norms derived from sources other than a specific treaty potentially affect the interpretation of that treaty as 'relevant rules of international law applicable between the Parties'. This interpretative technique of 'systemic integration' is discussed further in chapter five, which will also explain the significance of the no-harm rule and the UNFCCC for States' obligations under international human rights law.

[122] JH Knox, 'Diagonal Environmental Rights' in Mark Gibney and Sigrid Skogly (eds), *Universal Human Rights and Extraterritorial Obligations* (Philadelphia, University of Pennsylvania Press, 2010) 202, fn 187.

3

International Climate Change Law

Introduction

This chapter provides an overview of the international legal response to climate change, setting the stage for a comprehensive analysis of the role of international climate change law in rights-based climate action. The focus is on treaty-based law adopted under the auspices of the UNFCCC, including the Kyoto Protocol and the Paris Agreement.[1] In addition, the chapter discusses the no-harm rule and its potential to underpin State responsibility claims for human rights violations associated with climate change. As will be discussed in detail below, synergies between international climate change law on the one hand and human rights law on the other are increasingly being articulated in international legal instruments. The Conference of the Parties (COP) to the UNFCCC has now recognised the importance of human rights standards in the context of climate change, starting with the acknowledgment in a COP decision that 'Parties should, in all climate change related actions, fully respect human rights'.[2] Human rights advocacy at the climate negotiations intensified in the run-up to the 21st COP held in Paris, France in 2015,[3] and the Paris Agreement has become the first multilateral climate agreement to recognise States' human rights obligations, stating in its preamble that Parties 'should, when taking action to address climate change, respect, promote and consider their respective obligations on human rights, the right to health, the rights of indigenous peoples, local communities, migrants, children, persons with disabilities and people in vulnerable situations and the right to development'.[4] At the same time, however, international climate change law is a distinct legal

[1] See also Margaretha Wewerinke-Singh and Curtis Doebbler, 'The Paris Agreement: Some Critical Reflections on Process and Substance' (2016) 39(4) *University of New South Wales Law Journal* 1486, on which parts of this chapter draw.

[2] United Nations Framework Convention on Climate Change (UNFCCC), The Cancun Agreements: Outcome of the Work of the Ad Hoc Working Group on Long-Term Cooperative Action under the Convention, UN Doc FCCC/CP/2010/7/Add.1, Decision 1/CP.16 (10 December 2010) (The Cancun Agreements), para 8.

[3] For details see John Knox, Report of the Special Rapporteur on the Issue of Human Rights Obligations Relating to the Enjoyment of a Safe, Clean, Healthy and Sustainable Environment, UN Doc A/HRC/31/52 (1 February 2016) paras 7–22.

[4] UNFCCC, 'Paris Agreement' (adopted 12 December 2015, entered into force 4 November 2016) UN Doc FCCC/CP/2015/L.9/Rev.1 (Paris Agreement), preambular para 11.

framework, and understanding its features will enable us to identify a range of opportunities for addressing human rights violations associated with climate change under existing international law.

The UN Framework Convention on Climate Change

The UNFCCC is one of several multilateral environmental agreements concluded since the early 1970s, most of which have similar institutional arrangements. It establishes 'a conference or meeting of the parties (COP, MOP) with decision-making powers, a secretariat, and one or more specialist subsidiary bodies'.[5] There are currently 197 Parties to the UNFCCC (194 States plus the European Union),[6] which include all 193 UN Member States.[7] In order to understand the origins of the Convention, we need to bear in mind that climate change was placed on the agenda of the UN General Assembly in September 1988 under the agenda item – submitted by Malta – 'Declaration proclaiming climate as part of the common heritage of mankind'.[8] The item led to discussions and the adoption of a consensus resolution entitled 'Protection of Global Climate for Present and Future Generations of Mankind',[9] in which States expressed concern 'that certain human activities could change global climate patterns, threatening present and future generations with potentially severe economic and social consequences' and noted with concern 'that the emerging evidence indicates that continued growth in atmospheric concentrations of "greenhouse gases" could produce global warming with an eventual rise in sea levels, the effects of which could be disastrous for mankind if timely steps are not taken at all levels'.[10] The resolution called on 'Governments and intergovernmental organizations to collaborate in making every effort to prevent the detrimental effects on climate and activities which affect the ecological balance, and also calls upon non-governmental organizations, industry and other productive sectors to play their due role'.[11] In the last instance the concept of 'common

[5] Robin R Churchill and Geir Ulfstein, 'Autonomous Institutional Arrangements in Multilateral Environmental Agreements: A Little-Noticed Phenomenon in International Law' (2000) 94 *American Journal of International Law* 623.

[6] See 'Status of Ratification of the Convention' available at unfccc.int/essential_background/convention/status_of_ratification/items/2631.php. Niue and the Cook Islands are self-governing States in free association with New Zealand that are Parties to the UNFCCC and UN non-member States. Palestine is a Party to the UNFCCC and a UN General Assembly observer State.

[7] See 'Status of Treaties: Charter of the United Nations and Statute of the International Court of Justice' available at treaties.un.org/Pages/ViewDetails.aspx?src=TREATY&mtdsg_no=I-2&chapter=1&lang=en.

[8] Daniel Bodansky, 'The United Nations Framework Convention on Climate Change: A Commentary' (1993) 18 *Yale Journal of International Law* 451, 465.

[9] *Protection of Global Climate for Present and Future Generations of Mankind*, GA A/Res. 43/53 (6 December 1988) (*Protection of Global Climate for Present and Future Generations of Mankind 1988*).

[10] Ibid Preamble.

[11] Ibid para 9.

heritage of mankind' was not mentioned in the resolution: agreement had been reached to refer to a new concept, 'common *concern* of mankind'.[12] According to commentators, this concept 'is generally seen as being oriented to the fight specifically against ecological dangers threatening human survival'.[13] Through the resolution, the General Assembly also endorsed the establishment of the IPCC by the World Meteorological Organisation and the UN Environment Programme,[14] and urged governments, and intergovernmental and non-governmental organisations to implement programmes and research to enhance the understanding of climate change and its causes.[15]

It took another year for States to agree to adopt a legal framework specifically designed to address climate change, through another resolution again entitled 'Protection of Global Climate for Present and Future Generations of Mankind'.[16] The resolution urged governments, intergovernmental and non-governmental organisations and scientific institutions to 'collaborate in efforts to prepare, as a matter of urgency, a framework convention on climate and associated protocols containing concrete commitments in the light of priorities that may be authoritatively identified on the basis of sound scientific knowledge, and taking into account the specific development of developing countries'.[17]

When the UNFCCC was adopted three years after the 1989 Resolution, the Preamble stated that 'Acknowledging that change in the Earth's climate and its adverse effects are a common concern of humankind'.[18] The UNFCCC establishes both general principles that States must respect in their actions to address climate change,[19] as well as specific commitments that States must undertake in relation to mitigation, public information, education, financial resources and technology transfer.[20] The relevance of the UNFCCC for the protection of human beings is perhaps most evident from its ultimate objective enshrined in Article 2, which is 'to achieve, in accordance with the relevant provisions of the Convention,

[12] Ibid para 1. Daniel Bodansky notes that most Member States were reluctant to invoke the 'common heritage' concept in the context of climate change. Bodansky (n 8) 465.

[13] Kemal Baslar, *The Concept of the Common Heritage of Mankind in International Law* (The Hague, Martinus Nijhoff, 1998) 295 (comparing the concept with 'common heritage' which is concerned with 'allocating rights of use to state-free areas, or traditional global commons'). See also Malcolm N Shaw, *International Law*, 6th edn (New York, Cambridge University Press, 2008) 533; and SR Chowdhury, 'Intergenerational Equity: Substratum of the Right to Sustainable Development' in SR Chowdhury, Erik MG Denters and Paul JM de Waart (eds), *The Right to Development in International Law* (The Hague, Martinus Nijhoff, 1992) 240.

[14] *Protection of Global Climate for Present and Future Generations of Mankind 1988*, para 5.

[15] Ibid para 6.

[16] *Protection of Global Climate for Present and Future Generations of Mankind*, GA Res A/Res/44/207 (22 December 1989).

[17] Ibid paras 6–9, 12.

[18] UNFCCC, Preamble. This was the first time that a 'common concern' concept was incorporated into a legally binding instrument, and in an evolved version: apart from being framed in gender-neutral language, the concept now includes not just climate change, but also its 'adverse effects' as part of our common concern.

[19] Ibid Art 3.

[20] Ibid esp Art 4.

stabilization of greenhouse gas concentrations in the atmosphere at a level that would prevent dangerous anthropogenic interference with the climate system … within a time frame sufficient to allow ecosystems to adapt naturally to climate change … and to enable economic development to proceed in a sustainable manner'.[21] This objective must be read in the light of the Preamble, where the first paragraph reads 'Acknowledging that change in the Earth's climate and its adverse effects are a common concern of humankind'.[22] Adverse effects are defined in Article 1 as 'changes in the physical environment or biota resulting from climate change which have significant deleterious effects on the composition, resilience or productivity of natural and managed ecosystems or on the operation of socio-economic systems or on human health and welfare'.[23] All States commit to take precautionary measures 'to anticipate, prevent or minimize the causes of climate change and mitigate its adverse effects' to achieve the ultimate objective,[24] in accordance with the principle of 'common but differentiated responsibilities and respective capabilities' (CBDRRC).[25]

Article 3(3) specifies that 'Where there are threats of serious or irreversible damage, lack of full scientific certainty should not be used as a reason for postponing such measures',[26] reflecting (again) the precautionary principle. The precautionary principle is generally interpreted as pressing for precautionary regulation or action when there is no conclusive evidence of a particular risk scenario, when the risk is uncertain, or until the risk is disproved.[27] This principle is widely considered to be part of customary international law in the environmental field based on 'the importance of preventive action in environmental governance'.[28] This customary law status of the precautionary principle has since been confirmed by numerous findings of international courts and tribunals which unequivocally found the principle to be part of international law, despite some differences as to its exact meaning.[29] A recent interpretation of the principle was by the International

[21] Ibid Art 2.

[22] Ibid Preamble.

[23] Ibid Art 1(1).

[24] Ibid Art 3(3).

[25] Ibid Art 3(1).

[26] Ibid Art 3(3).

[27] Patricia Birnlie, Alan Boyle and Catherine Redgwell (eds), *International Law and the Environment* (Oxford, Oxford University Press, 2009) 604–07.

[28] Anja Lindroos and Michael Mehling, 'From Autonomy to Integration? International Law, Free Trade and the Environment' (2008) 77 *Nordic Journal of International Law* 253, 265 (with further references). It is worth noting that already a decade ago, scholars argued that the precaution principle 'has evolved into a general principle of environmental protection at the international level'. See J Cameron, 'The Status of the Precautionary Principle in International Law' in T O'Riordan and J Cameron (eds), *Interpreting the Precautionary Principle* (London, Earthscan Publications, 1994) 262 (with further references).

[29] *Gabčíkovo-Nagymaros Project (Hungary v Slovakia)* (Judgement) [1997] ICJ Reports 7 (*Gabčíkovo-Nagymaros Project*) and *Southern Bluefin Tuna Cases (New Zealand v Japan and Australia v Japan)* International Tribunal of the Law of the Sea, Order (27 August 1999). See also Philippe Sands, *Principles of International Environmental Law*, 2nd edn (New York, Cambridge University Press, 2003) 212 (noting that there is 'no uniform understanding of the meaning of the precautionary principle among States and other members of the international community').

Tribunal for the Law of the Sea (ITLOS) in its first Advisory Opinion, which cited it as a principle of customary international law.[30] The precautionary principle is also gradually gaining acceptance in social and economic fields, especially in international health law,[31] and attempts have been made in human rights scholarship to demonstrate that human rights treaty bodies could invoke the precautionary principle to achieve environmental protection.[32] As Birnlie, Boyle and Redgwell note, the consequences of applying the precautionary principle largely depend on the specific normative context.[33]

As regards the specific context of the UNFCCC, it is important to recall that Article 3(1) expressly states that the precautionary principle must be interpreted in accordance with the principle of CBDRRC. This principle is an extended version of the principle of 'common but differentiated responsibilities' (CBDR), which appears in the 1992 Rio Declaration on Environment and Development[34] and was subsequently incorporated into a large number of international treaties dealing with natural resources, many of which refer explicitly to States' common responsibilities and the need to take account of differentiated circumstances.[35] The principle of CBDR or CBDRRC is best understood as an application of the general principle of equity in international law. This acquires a specific meaning through the notion of 'common heritage of mankind'[36] or, in case of the UNFCCC, the notion of 'common concern of humankind'. As Sands explains, the CBDR principle 'entitles, or may require, all concerned States to participate in international response measures .... Second, it leads to environmental standards which impose

[30] See *Responsibilities and Obligations of States Sponsoring Persons and Entities with Respect to Activities in the Area (Advisory Opinion)*, Seabed Disputes Chamber of the International Tribunal for the Law of the Sea (1 February 2011) Case No 17, 125–30. For a discussion of the case, see D Anton, A Makgill and C Payne, 'Advisory Opinion on Responsibility and Liability for International Seabed Mining (ITLOS Case No. 17): International Environmental Law in the Seabed Disputes Chamber' (ANU College of Law Research Paper No 11–06, Australian National University, 2011).

[31] Marie-Claire Cordonier Segger et al, 'Prospects for Principles of International Sustainable Development Law after the WSSD: Common but Differentiated Responsibilities, Precaution and Participation' (2003) 12 *Review of European Community and International Environmental Law* 54, 62 and 567.

[32] Séverine Fiorletta Leroy, 'Can the Human Rights Bodies be Used to Produce Interim Measures to Protect Environment-Related Human Rights?' (2006) 15 *Review of European Community and International Environmental Law* 66, 58. See also Olivier de Schutter et al, 'Commentary to the Maastricht Principles on Extraterritorial Obligations of States in the Area of Economic, Social and Cultural Rights' (2012) 34 *Human Rights Quarterly* 1084, 1084ff.

[33] Birnlie, Boyle and Redgwell (n 27) 161.

[34] Rio Declaration on Environment and Development, United Nations Conference on Environment and Development, UN Doc A/CONF.151/1 (3–14 June 1992) (Rio Declaration), Principle 7 ('In view of the different contributions to global environmental degradation, States have common but differentiated responsibilities'). The principle followed in turn from the 'need', recognised in the 1972 Stockholm Declaration on the Human Environment, to consider 'the applicability of standards which are valid for the most advanced countries but which may be inappropriate and of unwarranted social cost for the developing countries'. Stockholm Declaration of the United Nations Conference on the Human Environment, UN Doc A/CONF.48/14/Rev.1 (16 June 1972), printed in International Legal Materials (1972), 1416 (Stockholm Declaration), Principle 23.

[35] Cordonier Segger et al (n 31) 56.

[36] Ibid.

differing obligations on States'.[37] This produces higher standards of achievement for 'developed' countries than for developing countries.[38]

In the UNFCCC, the inclusion of 'respective capabilities' as a marker of differentiation indicates that 'common but differentiated responsibilities' are distinct from 'capabilities' and thus principally based on States' individual responsibility for contributions to accumulated greenhouse gases in the global atmosphere.[39] The Preamble clarifies that States' obligations are differentiated based on the understanding that 'the largest share of historical and current global emissions of greenhouse gases has originated in developed countries, that *per capita* emissions in developing countries are still relatively low and that the share of global emissions originating in developing countries will grow to meet their social and development needs'.[40] The principle of CBDRRC expressed in the UNFCCC thus embodies the understanding that 'developing' (non-Annex I) countries have reaped fewer benefits from historic emissions than 'developed' (Annex I) countries, and have a lower capacity for addressing climate change.[41] As a matter of factual background, we should note that it continues to be the case that the States contained in Annex I, which represent only around 20 per cent of the global population, are those that have contributed the most to greenhouse gases that have accumulated in the global atmosphere. This is true despite the fact that it excludes some of the wealthiest States in the world (namely Brunei, Kuwait, Qatar, Singapore and the United Arab Emirates).[42]

CBDRRC acts as a cornerstone of the international climate change regime. It is reiterated throughout the Convention and reflected in its substantive provisions. States' common obligations proceed from the Convention's ultimate objective, which requires all State Parties to cooperate and to participate in response measures, including through reporting to the Conference of the Parties about their emission levels and, when applicable, measures taken to mitigate climate change and to adapt to the adverse effects.[43] The UNFCCC operationalises CBDRRC

[37] Philippe Sands, *Principles of International Environmental Law*, vol. 3 (Cambridge, Cambridge University Press, 2012) 217.

[38] Cordonier Segger et al (n 31) 60.

[39] Joanne Scott and Lavanya Rajamani, 'EU Climate Change Unilateralism' (2012) 23 *European Journal of International Law* 469, 494.

[40] UNFCCC, Preamble.

[41] Duncan French, 'Developing States and International Environmental Law: The Importance of Differentiated Responsibilities' (2000) 49 *International and Comparative Law Quarterly* 35, 47.

[42] See also Tim Crosland, Aubrey Meyer and Margaretha Wewerinke-Singh, 'The Paris Agreement Implementation Blueprint: a Practical Guide to Bridging the Ambition Gap (Part 1) (2017) 25(1) *Environmental Liability* 114.

[43] Art 4(1) specifically obliges State Parties to develop, update and publish national inventories of anthropogenic emissions by sources and removals by sinks of all greenhouse gases not covered by the Montreal Protocol; to formulate, implement and update national and, where appropriate, regional programmes continuing mitigation measures; to promote and co-operate in the development, application and transfer of technologies and processes to control, reduce or prevent such anthropogenic emissions; to promote sustainable management and conservation of sinks and reservoirs of all greenhouse gases not controlled by the Montreal Protocol; to take climate change considerations into account

by imposing different obligations on Annex I and non-Annex I Parties,[44] based on the explicitly stated principle that 'developed country parties should take the lead in combating climate change'[45] while 'the specific needs and circumstances of developing country parties, especially those that are particularly vulnerable to the adverse effects of climate change, and of those Parties, especially developing country Parties, that would have to bear a disproportionate or abnormal burden under the Convention, should be given full consideration'.[46] Article 4 contains specific commitments for developed country Parties, and obliges them to take action, including the adoption of national policies to help cut their emissions and to protect and enhance greenhouse gas sinks and reservoirs in a way that 'will demonstrate that developed countries are taking the lead in modifying longer-term trends in anthropogenic emissions'.[47] This entails an obligation for these Parties to periodically submit detailed information on such matters with a view to lowering their anthropogenic emissions to 1990 levels. This information must be reviewed periodically by the Conference of the Parties (COP).[48]

Developed country Parties and other developed Parties listed in Annex II are also obliged to provide 'new and additional financial resources' to offset developing country Parties' implementation costs,[49] and to assist any developing country Parties that are particularly vulnerable to the adverse effects of climate change in terms of meeting the costs of adaptation to those effects,[50] 'taking into account the need for adequacy and predictability in the flow of funds'.[51] The same States are obliged to 'take all practicable steps to promote, facilitate and finance, as appropriate, the transfer of, or access to, environmentally sound technologies and know-how to other Parties, particularly developing country Parties, to enable them to implement the provisions of the Convention' whereby developed country Parties must 'support the development and enhancement of endogenous capacities and technologies of developing country Parties'.[52] The commitments of developing country Parties under the Convention are conditional on the provision of financing by developed country Parties: Article 4(7) states that the extent to which developing country Parties implement their commitments under the

to the extent feasible in their relevant social, economic and environmental policies; and to promote and co-operate in research, exchange of information and education in the field of climate change. Sinks are defined in Art 1(8) as 'any process, activity or mechanism which removes a greenhouse gas, an aerosol or a precursor of a greenhouse gas from the atmosphere'.

44 UNFCCC, Preamble. See also Scott and Rajamani (n 39) 477 (these preambular recitals show that the CBDRRC principle 'takes into account both current and historic contributions to the stock of global greenhouse gases').

45 UNFCCC, Art 3(1).

46 Ibid Art 3(2).

47 Ibid Art 4(2)(a).

48 Ibid Art 4(2)(b).

49 Ibid Art 4(4).

50 Ibid Art 4(3).

51 Ibid Art 4(4).

52 Ibid Art 4(5).

Convention will depend on the effective implementation of developed country Parties' obligations in terms of financial resources and technology transfer, and repeats the provision in the Preamble that this 'will take fully into account that economic and social development and poverty eradication are the first and overriding priorities of developing country Parties'.[53]

The Conference of the Parties (COP) to the UNFCCC is, as 'the supreme body of' the UNFCCC,[54] responsible for the Convention's implementation. The COP resembles institutional arrangements established under the other multilateral environmental agreements (MEAs) that have been made since the early 1970s. Like most MEAs, it establishes not only 'a conference or meeting of the parties (COP, MOP) with decision-making powers' but also a secretariat and several subsidiary bodies.[55] The purpose of these institutional arrangements is 'to develop the normative content of the regulatory regime established by [the agreement] and to supervise the States parties' implementation of and compliance with that regime'.[56] As regards the legal status of the COP and MOP, Churchill and Ulfstein explain that these bodies are 'not intergovernmental organisations (IGOs) in the traditional sense' because of their *ad hoc* nature.[57] At the same time, the COP and MOP are created by treaties, possess law-making powers and compliance mechanisms, and are therefore 'more than just diplomatic conferences'.[58] It is also clear that the COP is, like any body created by a treaty, bound by the terms of its constituting treaty as well as by obligations conferred on States under international law.[59] Indeed, the State Parties to the UNFCCC have not agreed to exempt the COP from the general rules of international law, and Article 7 makes it expressly subject to the international law created in the UNFCCC.[60]

Article 7 authorises the COP 'to make, within its mandate, the decisions necessary to promote the effective implementation of the Convention'. In addition, COP decisions are one of the ways in which it exercises its power to 'exercise such other functions as are required for the achievement of the objective of the Convention

[53] Ibid Art 4(7).
[54] Ibid Art 7(3).
[55] Churchill and Ulfstein (n 5) 623.
[56] Ibid (note omitted).
[57] Ibid.
[58] Ibid.
[59] As noted above, this is the consequence of the non-derogable, and more broadly the objective nature of human rights norms.
[60] This is important for the assessment of the consequences of COP decision for the enjoyment of human rights. See, eg, Naomi Roht-Arriaza, 'Human Rights in the Climate Change Regime' (2010) 1 *Journal of Human Rights and the Environment* 211 (discussing projects under the Clean Development Mechanism (including large hydropower and biomass projects), biofuels, choices on energy and adaptation, and avoided deforestation (REDD and REDD+) as 'problematic areas where the climate change regime may cause human rights violations'); and Margaux J Hall and David C Weiss, 'Avoiding Adaptation Apartheid: Climate Change Adaptation and Human Rights Law' (2012) 37 *Yale Journal of International Law* 309 (discussing human rights violations that might occur in the context of adaptation).

as well as all other functions assigned to it under the Convention'.[61] COP decisions are thus not legally binding *per se* and cannot themselves give rise to new substantive obligations that are not already contained in the Convention.[62] Technically, COP decisions constitute 'subsequent agreement between the Parties regarding the interpretation of the treaty or the application of its provisions',[63] and this makes them relevant for interpreting the treaty.[64] Rajamani has pointed out that the COP nonetheless has 'indirect law-making powers', on the basis that 'it is authorized to negotiate amendments and Protocols to agreements' which 'require ratification by Parties'.[65] In addition, Rajamani explains that the COP has 'direct' or 'genuine' law-making powers because 'it is authorized in some cases to develop rules, as for instance for emissions trading, and these rules, although not legally binding, have mandatory force'.[66]

The Kyoto Protocol

The Kyoto Protocol[67] has been ratified by 191 States plus the European Union.[68] It was negotiated pursuant to an agreement reached between the Parties to the Convention at the first COP held in Berlin in 1994. At COP1 in Berlin, parties agreed that existing pledges by developed country Parties to stabilise emission levels to 1990 levels by 2000 would fall short of achieving the ultimate objective of the UNFCCC. It was also agreed that developing country Parties would not undertake new commitments but would instead focus on the implementation of their existing commitments under the UNFCCC with assistance from developed country Parties.[69] The Protocol is thus an operationalisation of the provisions of the UNFCCC and based on the principle of CBDRRC. Its stated objective is to pursue the 'ultimate objective of the Convention'.[70]

[61] UNFCCC, Art 7(2)(m).

[62] Lavanya Rajamani, 'Addressing the "Post-Kyoto" Stress Disorder: Reflections on the Emerging Legal Architecture of the Climate Regime' (2009) 58 *International and Comparative Law Quarterly* 803, 824 (pointing at the lack of explicit authorisation for binding law-making, which is provided for in other multilateral environmental agreements).

[63] Vienna Convention on the Law of Treaties (adopted 23 May 1969, entered into force 27 January 1980) 1155 UNTS 331, Art 31(3)(a).

[64] See also Rajamani (n 62) 824.

[65] Ibid 825 (footnotes omitted; references to Arts 15 and 17 of the UNFCCC, Art 17 of the Kyoto Protocol).

[66] Ibid.

[67] Kyoto Protocol to the United Nations Framework Convention on Climate Change (adopted 11 December 1997, entered into force 16 February 2005) 1771 UNTS 107 (Kyoto Protocol).

[68] Website of the UNFCCC Secretariat, 'Kyoto Protocol: Status of Ratification' available at unfccc.int.

[69] Berlin Mandate, UNFCCC Conference of the Parties: Decisions Adopted by the 1st Session, UN Doc FCCC/CP/1995/7/Add.1 (7 April 1995); (1995) 34 International Legal Materials 1671.

[70] Kyoto Protocol, Preamble.

In order to achieve its objective, the Protocol sets legally binding quantified emission limitation and reduction commitments for developed country parties based on an aggregate reduction target.[71] It also establishes a more rigorous reporting system and a Compliance Committee with the power to sanction non-compliance, thus representing what Bodansky and Rajamani refer to as a 'progressively harder approach' to mitigation than the UNFCCC.[72] However, the collective commitment of developed country Parties to cut their emissions by 5 per cent from 1990 levels during the first commitment period of 2008 to 2012 was highly inadequate.[73] Developing country Parties are expressly required to meet existing commitments under Article 4(1) of the Convention in order to achieve sustainable development, taking into account developed country obligations to provide assistance in the form of finance, technology transfer and capacity building.[74] The Protocol also sets up a range of market-based mechanisms to facilitate developed country Parties' compliance with their mitigation obligations under the Protocol.[75]

The concept of emission trading as a mitigation strategy remains controversial for a number of reasons, including: the apparent inadequacy of existing legally binding targets; uncertainty as to future targets; and the lack of effective national and international mechanisms for monitoring, verifying and compelling compliance with procedural rules designed to safeguard the environmental integrity of the system (ie the existence of 'loopholes').[76] Moreover, human rights scholarship has shed light on the negative impact of sponsored projects on local communities in some cases and suggested ways of using procedural rights to improve the functioning of these mechanisms.[77] The multiple controversies surrounding the market mechanisms indicate areas of tension between these mechanisms on the one hand and the protection of human rights on the other. However, other key features of the Protocol – most notably its legally binding emission reduction targets and provisions related to compliance – may still be evaluated positively

[71] Ibid Arts 2–3. The quantified emission limitation or reduction commitments are contained in Annex B.

[72] Daniel Bodansky and Lavanya Rajamani, 'The Evolution and Governance Architecture of the Climate Change Regime' in Detlef Sprinz and Urs Luterbacher (eds), *International Relations and Global Climate Change*, 2nd edn (Cambridge, MIT Press, 2013) 2. See also generally David Freestone and Charlotte Streck, *Legal Aspects of Implementing the Kyoto Protocol Mechanisms: Making Kyoto Work* (Oxford, Oxford University Press 2005).

[73] Kyoto Protocol, Art 3(1).

[74] Ibid Art 10.

[75] These include 'joint implementation' (JI) (allowing States to receive carbon credits for supporting emission reduction projects in other developed States), the 'clean development mechanism' (similar to joint implementation, but for supporting projects in developing States) and 'emissions trading' (for purchasing unused emission quotas from other States with binding commitments).

[76] See Farhana Yamin and Joanna Depledge, *The International Climate Change Regime: A Guide to Rules, Institutions and Procedures* (Cambridge, Cambridge University Press, 2004) 156; and Thomas H Tietenberg, *Emissions Trading: Principles and Practice* (Washington D.C., Resources for the Future Press, 2006) 170.

[77] See, eg, Naomi Roht-Arriaza and Svitlana Kravchenko, 'Procedural Rights as a Crucial Tool to Combat Climate Change' (2010) 38 *Georgia Journal of International and Comparative Law* 613.

from an international human rights law perspective insofar as they contribute to accountability for environmental harm that affects the enjoyment of human rights.

In accordance with the Protocol's provision that 'commitments for subsequent commitment periods shall be established',[78] negotiations on new commitments started in 2005 under the Ad Hoc Working Group on Further Commitments for Annex I Parties under the Kyoto Protocol (AWG-KP).[79] This culminated in a decision of the Conference of the Parties acting as the Meeting of the Parties to the Kyoto Protocol (CMP) to set an aggregate target of reducing developed country Parties' overall emissions by at least 18 per cent below 1990 levels in the period 2013–20 (the Doha Amendment).[80] However, Japan,[81] New Zealand[82] and the Russian Federation[83] refused to undertake new commitments and Canada became the first Party to withdraw from the Protocol in December 2012. Moreover, the Doha Amendment never gained formal legal effect: at present, only 83 Parties to the Protocol have ratified the Doha Amendment, while 144 ratifications are required for its entry into force.[84] The formal significance of the Protocol has therefore severely diminished, and the future of the Protocol remains uncertain. Amongst issues to be resolved are the future of the Kyoto market mechanisms, and whether the Protocol will eventually be formally terminated. What is clear, however, is that the Paris Agreement adopted in December 2015 is set to take over from the Protocol as the main vehicle for international accountability for emission reductions. The relationship between the Protocol and this new legal instrument remains to be resolved by the CMP and by the COP serving as the Meeting of the Parties to the Paris Agreement (CMA).

The Paris Agreement

At COP21 in Paris, 195 states and the European Union adopted the Paris Agreement.[85] The Agreement, which was attached as an annex to a COP decision,

[78] Kyoto Protocol, Art 3(9).

[79] In accordance with Art 3(9) of the Protocol, negotiations had started in December 2005 when the COP, serving as a Meeting of the Parties to the Kyoto Protocol (CMP), established the Ad Hoc Working Group on Further Commitments for Annex I Parties under the Kyoto Protocol (AWG-KP). See 'Consideration of commitments for subsequent periods for Parties included in Annex I to the Convention under Art 3, para 9, of the Kyoto Protocol', UN Doc FCCC/KP/CMP/2005/8/Add.1, p. 3, Dec. 1/CMP.1 (30 March 2006), 3. In 2012, the CMP, at its 8th session, adopted decision 1/CMP.8 (the Doha Amendment).

[80] Decision 1/CMP.8, C, Amendment to Art 3(1) of the Kyoto Protocol.

[81] Ibid fn 14.

[82] Ibid fn 15.

[83] Ibid fn 16.

[84] See 'The Doha Amendment' available at unfccc.int/kyoto_protocol/doha_amendment/items/7362.php.

[85] Report of the Conference of the Parties on Its Twenty-First Session, Held in Paris from 30 November to 13 December 2015 – Addendum – Part Two: Action Taken by the Conference of the Parties at Its Twenty-First Session, Dec 1/CP.21, UN Doc FCCC/CP/2015/10/Add.1 (29 January 2015) (Adoption of the Paris Agreement). The Agreement is included as an annex to this document (Paris Agreement).

opened for signature on 22 April 2016[86] and entered into force on 4 November 2016.[87] The Agreement was adopted following decades of politically complex negotiations under the UNFCCC and the Kyoto Protocol, and has been widely hailed as a breakthrough in multilateral climate governance.[88] The new treaty marks a radical departure from the Kyoto Protocol's system of targets and timetables, replacing it with a pledge-and-review system under which each Party chooses its own commitment. Like the Kyoto Protocol, the Agreement references the ultimate objective in its Article 2, which reads: 'This Agreement, in enhancing the implementation of the Convention, including its objective, aims to strengthen the global response to the threat of climate change, in the context of sustainable development and efforts to eradicate poverty'. Although the formulation is somewhat confusing, it does make it clear that the Agreement is subsidiary to the Convention. Articles 22–24 of the Agreement reinforce this understanding by referring to the provisions on amendments and dispute settlements in the Convention as applying mutatis mutandis to the Agreement. Further, Article 17 notes that the UNFCCC Secretariat that serves the Convention shall also serve the Agreement.

Article 2 also sets out a so-called 'long-term goal' of 'Holding the increase in the global average temperature to well below 2°C above pre-industrial levels and pursuing efforts to limit the temperature increase to 1.5°C above pre-industrial levels, recognizing that this would significantly reduce the risks and impacts of climate change'. The incorporation of a 1.5°C limit is the result of strong advocacy by small island developing States and other climate vulnerable developing States, notably supported by UN human rights experts who have highlighted that any increase in temperature rise will also increase the risks of large-scale and irreversible impacts that would infringe on a range of human rights.[89] The Agreement further aims to '[increase] the ability to adapt to the adverse impacts of climate change[90] and to '[make] finance flows consistent with a pathway towards low greenhouse gas emissions and climate resilient development'.[91] The second clause of Article 2 places these goals in the context of equity and the principle of common but differentiated responsibilities and respective capabilities, 'in the light of different national circumstances'. The latter formulation first emerged in

[86] Ibid annex Art 20(1).

[87] At the time of writing the Paris Agreement has been ratified by 166 States. See 'Paris Agreement – Status of Ratification' available at unfccc.int/paris_agreement/items/9444.php.

[88] See, eg, Peter Christoff, 'The Promissory Note: COP 21 and the Paris Climate Agreement' (2016) 25 *Environmental Politics* 765, 782.

[89] See 'The Effects of Climate Change on the Full Enjoyment of Human Rights' (Special Procedures of the Human Rights Council, 2015) available at www.thecvf.org/wp-content/uploads/2015/05/humanrightsSRHRE.pdf, 3ff.

[90] Paris Agreement, Art 2(1)(b).

[91] Paris Agreement, Art 2(1)(c).

the US–China bilateral agreement on climate change[92] and found its way into the climate change regime through a COP decision adopted at COP20 in Lima, Peru.[93] Although the language appears to be intended to dilute the principle of CBDRRC by shifting the emphasis from historical responsibility to climate change to a more amorphous concept of national variation, the fact that the Agreement remains anchored in the Convention and its principles means that the additional seven words are unlikely to have much legal impact.[94]

Unlike the Kyoto Protocol, the Paris Agreement does not contain legally binding emission reduction commitments. Instead, in a lengthy Article 4, the Paris Agreement establishes a system of emission reduction reporting that is based on 'nationally determined', rather than internationally negotiated, 'contributions'. Although nationally determined contributions (NDCs) are to be prepared, communicated and maintained 'with the aim of achieving the objectives of such contributions'[95] the language of Article 4 falls short of requiring that parties actually achieve or implement their NDCs. There is no sanction or corrective action foreseen for a State that does not undertake the action it reports it will take. Clause 3 of Article 4 stipulates that each party's successive NDC 'will represent a progression beyond the Party's then current [NDC] and reflect its highest possible ambition, reflecting its common but differentiated responsibilities and respective capabilities, in the light of different national circumstances'. However, it must be emphasised that there is no sanction or corrective action foreseen for a State that reports that it will only undertake *de minimis* action. Because this framework is based almost exclusively on procedural obligations, it will in practice be difficult to hold States accountable for emission reduction action or inaction under international law.[96]

Article 7 of the Agreement establishes a qualitative global goal for adaptation, namely of 'enhancing adaptive capacity, strengthening resilience and reducing vulnerability … with a view to contributing to sustainable development and ensuring an adequate adaptation response in the context of the temperature goal'.[97] The link between adaptation and the long-term temperature goal is reaffirmed by

[92] Office of the Press Secretary, The White House, 'US–China Joint Announcement on Climate Change' (Press Release, 12 November 2014) para 2, available at www.whitehouse.gov/the-press-office/2014/11/11/us-china-joint-announcement-climate-change: 'committed to reaching an ambitious 2015 agreement that reflects the principle of common but differentiated responsibilities and respective capabilities, in light of different national circumstances'.

[93] *Lima Call for Climate Action* (2 February 2015) UN Doc FCCC/CP/2014/10/Add.1, para 3.

[94] Cf Lavanya Rajamani, 'Ambition and Differentiation in the 2015 Paris Agreement: Interpretative Possibilities and Underlying Politics' (2016) 65 *International and Comparative Law Quarterly* 493, 508.

[95] Paris Agreement, Art 4(2).

[96] See however ch 9 on climate litigation before domestic courts.

[97] Ibid Art 7(1).

paragraph 4 of Article 7 in which parties recognise 'that greater levels of mitigation can reduce the need for additional adaptation efforts'. Article 7 further provides that:

> adaptation action should follow a country-driven, gender-responsive, participatory and fully transparent approach, taking into consideration vulnerable groups, communities and ecosystems … based on and guided by the best available science and, as appropriate, traditional knowledge, knowledge of indigenous peoples and local knowledge systems.[98]

The Agreement stipulates that international support provided should enable developing countries to cooperate on enhancing adaptation action,[99] plan and implement adaptation actions,[100] and submit and update adaptation communications.[101] From a doctrinal perspective, however, the mitigation and adaptation sections of the Agreement remain as aspirational text with procedures, but little substance. Articles 9, 10 and 11, on finance, access to technology, and capacity building, respectively, offer the same procedural enticements, but little other action.

A significant development in international climate change law is the inclusion of a provision on loss and damage resulting from climate change in the Paris Agreement. The first time loss and damage was expressly mentioned in a formal decision was in the Cancun Agreements, which initiated consideration on 'approaches to address loss and damage associated with climate change impacts' in particularly vulnerable developing countries,[102] and in 2013 the Warsaw International Mechanism on Loss and Damage (WIM) was established. The WIM was to be the main vehicle under the Convention to 'promot[e] the implementation of approaches to address loss and damage associated with the adverse effects of climate change … in a comprehensive, integrated and coherent manner'.[103] Article 8 of the Paris Agreement anchors the WIM into the Agreement, thus giving it a durable legal basis while making it subject to the authority and guidance of the CMA. The WIM will be able to work in crucial areas including, amongst other areas: early warning systems, emergency preparedness, slow onset events, irreversible and permanent loss and damage, risk insurance facilities, and climate risk pooling. Furthermore, the COP decision accompanying the Agreement requests the Executive Committee of the WIM 'to establish, according to its procedure and mandate, a task force to complement, draw upon the work of and involve, as appropriate, existing bodies and expert groups under the Convention … to develop recommendations for

[98] Ibid Art 7(5).
[99] Ibid Art 7(7).
[100] Ibid Art 7(9).
[101] Ibid Art 7(10)–(11).
[102] The Cancun Agreements, UN Doc FCCC/CP/2010/7/Add.1, para 26.
[103] Report of the Conference of the Parties on Its Nineteenth Session, held in Warsaw from 11 to 23 November 2013 – Addendum – Part Two: Action Taken by the Conference of the Parties at Its Nineteenth Session, Dec 2/CP.19, UN Doc FCCC/CP/2013/10/Add.1 (31 January 2014) para 5.

integrated approaches to avert, minimize and address displacement related to the adverse impacts of climate change'.[104] This builds on the workplan of the WIM, which aims to 'enhance the understanding of and expertise on how the impacts of climate change are affecting patters of migration, displacement and human mobility; and the application of such understanding and expertise'.[105] However, the loss and damage package came with a trade-off: in the decision accompanying the Agreement the Parties 'agree[d] that Article 8 of the Agreement does not involve or provide a basis for any liability or compensation'.[106] This statement reflects a significant compromise from small island States and other vulnerable countries, which had wanted to see liability and compensation addressed as part of the loss and damage package.[107] Nonetheless, Article 8 of the Paris Agreement reflects international consensus on the notion that some impacts of climate change extend beyond mitigation and adaptation. This recognition could support legal arguments that States have human rights obligations to address the impact of climate change, and additional obligations to ensure victims' right to a remedy for human rights violations associated with climate change. The relationship between Article 8, human rights law and the general law of State responsibility is addressed further in chapters four and five.

The No-Harm Rule

It is widely believed, and supported by authority, that under general international law all States are under an obligation to prevent transboundary environmental damage (the 'no-harm rule').[108] This obligation was first articulated in the *Trail Smelter* (1907), where the arbitral tribunal stated that:

> Under the principles of international law … no state has the right to use or permit the use of territory in such a manner as to cause injury by fumes in or to the territory of another of the properties or persons therein, when the case is of serious consequence and the injury is established by clear and convincing evidence.[109]

[104] COP Decision 1/CP.21, UN Doc FCCC/CP/2015/L.9/Rev.1 (12 December 2015) para 50.

[105] Report of the Executive Committee of the Warsaw International Mechanism for Loss and Damage Associated with Climate Impacts, UN Doc FCCC/SB/2014/4, Annex II (24 October 2014) 11.

[106] Adoption of the Paris Agreement, UN Doc FCCC/CP/2015/10/Add.1, para 52.

[107] See further Meinhard Doelle, 'Loss and Damage in the UN Climate Regime' in Daniel A Farber and Marjan Peeters (eds), *Elgar Encyclopedia of Environmental Law vol 1: Climate Change Law* (Cheltenham, Edward Elgar 2016) 617.

[108] Sands (n 37) 236 (mentioning the views of writers, the apparent approval of Judge de Castro in his dissent in the *Nuclear Tests* case and an examination of State practice by the Rapporteur to the International Law Association's Committee on Legal Aspects of the Environment). For a more critical view see John H Knox, 'The Myth and Reality of Transboundary Environmental Impact Assessment' (2002) 96 *American Journal of International Law* 291, 294.

[109] *Trail Smelter Case (United States v Canada)* [1941] 3 Reports of International Arbitral Awards 1905, 1965.

Although the arbitral tribunal in *Trail Smelter* specifically referred to injury caused by fumes, the principle expressed in this case has a more general application to all sorts of environmental damage. It is also thought to apply to the world's common spaces, in addition to damage that is inflicted by one State on the environment of another.[110] The scope of the principle has been extended to include cases where damage is inflicted on parts of the environment in which all States have an interest. This development is specifically stated in the Stockholm Declaration, which provides that:

> States have, in accordance with the Charter of the United Nations and the principles of international law ... the responsibility to ensure that activities within their jurisdiction or control do not cause damage to the environment of other States or of areas beyond the limits of national jurisdiction.[111]

The rule was expressed in almost identical wording in Principle 2 of the Rio Declaration on Environment and Development[112] and is restated in the Preamble to the UNFCCC.[113] The International Court relied on the principle in its Advisory Opinion *Legality of the Threat or Use of Nuclear Weapons* that 'States have, in accordance with the Charter of the United Nations and the principles of international law, the sovereign right to exploit their own resources pursuant to their own environmental policies, and the responsibility to ensure that activities within their jurisdiction or control do not cause damage to the environment of other States or of areas beyond the limits of national jurisdiction'.[114] The Court restated this formulation, in almost identical terms, in *Gabcikovo-Nagymaros Project*.[115] And in *Pulp Mills*, the Court found that customary international law requires a State 'to use all the means at its disposal in order to avoid activities which take place in its territory, or in any area under its jurisdiction, causing significant damage to the environment of another State'.[116] It is clear from these formulations that the no-harm rule limits the sovereign rights of a State to perform, or to authorise third parties to perform, damaging activities within its own territory.[117] The key element here is to balance States' sovereignty and their territorial integrity in '[protecting] within the territory the rights of other states, in particular their right to integrity and inviolability in peace and war'.[118]

State responsibility for a violation of the no-harm rule will only be established when a threshold of damage is crossed. The arbitrators in the *Lac Lanoux*

[110] Jonathan I Charney, 'Third State Remedies for Environmental Damage to the World's Common Spaces' in Francesco Francioni and Tullio Scovazzi (eds), *International Responsibility for Environmental Harm* (London, Graham & Trotman, 1991) 149.

[111] Stockholm Declaration (n 34) Principle 21.

[112] Rio Declaration on Environment and Development, United Nations Conference on Environment and Development, UN Doc A/ CONF.151/1 (3–14 June 1992).

[113] UNFCCC, Preamble.

[114] *Legality of the Threat or Use of Nuclear Weapons (Advisory Opinion)* [1996] ICJ Reports 241 para 29.

[115] *Gabčíkovo-Nagymaros Project*, para 41.

[116] *Case concerning Pulp Mills on the River Uruguay (Argentina v Uruguay)* [2010] ICJ Reports 14 (*Pulp Mills Case*), para 101.

[117] Sands (n 37) 236.

[118] *Island of Palmas Case (Netherlands, USA)* [1928] 2 Reports of International Arbitral Awards 829, 839.

suggested that the threshold is one of 'serious injury',[119] while the ILC in its Articles on Prevention of Transboundary Harm from Hazardous Activities (ILC Articles on Prevention of Harm) refers to a threshold of 'significant damage'.[120] It defines 'significant' as 'something more than detectable but … not at the level of "serious" or "substantial"'.[121] It adds that 'The harm must lead to a real detrimental effect on matters such as, for example, human health, industry, property, environment or agriculture in other States'.[122] Most climate change damage – including damage resulting from extreme weather events, sea level rise, droughts, flooding and heatwaves linked to climate change – would seem to be more than *de minimis* or insignificant, and would therefore meet this threshold.[123] And when 'damage' involves interferences with human rights, we can assume that the damage is 'significant' based on the legal and moral importance attached to human rights.

An important point to note here is that despite the emphasis on damage, State responsibility arises as a result of wrongful conduct.[124] The Commentaries to the International Law Commission's Articles on the Responsibility of States for Internationally Wrongful Acts (ARS) provide implicit support for the proposition that the no-harm rule is actually a preventive obligation. *Trail Smelter* is taken as the single authority for the rule, understood as a rule of customary international law, that 'The breach of an international obligation requiring a State to prevent a given event occurs when the event occurs and extends over the entire period during which the event continues and remains not in conformity with that obligation',[125] based on the understanding that the obligation in *Trail Smelter* 'was breached for as long as the pollution continued to be emitted'.[126] This suggests that the term 'harm' must be understood in the context of risk prevention. The existing authorities suggest that the relevant standard of care that States must uphold to comply with the rule is one of 'due diligence' or 'best efforts'.[127] It is worth noting that the principle of 'due diligence', as a principle of international law, has a common origin

[119] *Lac Lanoux Case* [1959] XII Reports of International Arbitral Awards 281, reprinted in (1959) 53 *American Journal of International Law* 50 (*Lac Lanoux Case*), 306.

[120] International Law Commission, 'Articles on Prevention of Transboundary Harm from Hazardous Activities and Commentaries thereto', 53rd sess, UN Doc A/56/10 (2001) (ILC Articles on Prevention of Harm).

[121] Ibid Commentary to Art 2, para 4.

[122] Ibid.

[123] Roda Verheyen, *Climate Change Damage and International Law: Prevention Duties and State Responsibility* (Leiden, Martinus Nijhoff, 2005) 52.

[124] *Pulp Mills Case*, para 101. See also Sands (n 37) 246 fn 62 and accompanying text. This interpretation suggests that a State that permits or carries out potentially hazardous activities may incur international responsibility if it fails to ensure that these activities do not cause damage to the environment of other States or to the world's common spaces.

[125] James Crawford, *The International Law Commission's Articles on State Responsibility: Introduction, Text, Commentaries* (New York, Cambridge University Press, 2002) Art 14(3).

[126] Ibid Commentary to Art 14(3), para 14.

[127] See also Verheyen (n 122) 170 (with references, all rejecting the alternative standard of fault or intent as a prerequisite for breach of the no-harm rule). See also Ian Brownlie, *State Responsibility* (New York, Clarendon Press, 1983) 161 (recognising that State responsibility automatically arises from an established 'breach of duty to exercise due diligence in control of private persons').

with the general law of State responsibility and international human rights law: it is derived from the laws on diplomatic protection, requiring States to protect the rights of non-nationals in their territory.[128] The notion is generally considered to originate from the 1872 *Alabama* case,[129] in which the arbitral tribunal relied on the notion of due diligence as an international and objective standard that imposed obligations on the State to prevent causing damage to another State.[130] In *Neer* (1926)[131] and *Lac Lanoux* (1957)[132] this interpretation is confirmed in almost identical wording. The understanding of due diligence obligations as embodying a precautionary approach is also reflected in various multilateral environmental agreements (MEAs) that have included the standard.[133] In its 2011 *Advisory Opinion on the Responsibilities and Obligations of States* the Seabed Disputes Chamber of ITLOS confirmed that the precautionary approach is 'an integral part of the due diligence obligation of sponsoring States, which is applicable even outside the scope of the [Nodules and Sulphides] Regulations'.[134]

The ILC has elaborated on the due diligence standard in its Articles on Prevention of Harm and the related Commentaries, which draw extensively on the notion of due diligence as a means of risk prevention.[135] The Commentaries set out that:

> The duty of due diligence ... is not intended to guarantee that significant harm be totally prevented, if it is not possible to do so. In that eventuality, the State of origin is required, as noted above, to exert its best possible efforts to minimize the risk.[136]

The International Court's interpretation of the no-harm rule in *Pulp Mills* confirms that States' due diligence obligations must be understood as 'best effort' obligations, and that it 'entails not only the adoption of appropriate rules and measures but also a certain level of vigilance in their enforcement and the exercise of administrative control applicable to public and private operators, such as the monitoring of activities undertaken by such operators'.[137] The ILC has similarly suggested

[128] Brownlie (n 127) 161.

[129] Blomeryer-Bartenstein, 'Due Diligence' in R Berhardt (ed), *Encyclopedia of Public International Law*, vol. I (New York, Elsevier, 1992), 1110.

[130] *Alabamaî Arbitration* (1872), in Moore, *International Arbitrations* vol. IV, 4144 *(Alabamai Arbitration)* 4156–57, para 10 (concerning a damage claim by the United States against Great Britain for assistance provided to the Confederate cause during the American Civil War).

[131] *Neer Case* Mexico–United States General Claims Commission, Award of 1926 [1951] IV Reports of International Arbitral Awards 60, 61.

[132] *Lac Lanoux Case*, 50.

[133] See, eg, Art 194(1) of the United Nations Convention on the Law of the Sea (adopted 10 December 1982, entered into force 16 November 1994) 1833 UNTS 397, Art 194(1); Convention on the Prevention of Marine Pollution by Dumping of Wastes and Other Matter (adopted 29 December 1972, entered into force 30 August 1975) 1046 UNTS 120, Arts I and II and Art VII(2); and Convention on Environmental Impact Assessment in a Transboundary Context (adopted 25 February 1991, entered into force 10 September 1997) 1989 UNTS 309, Art 2(1).

[134] *Responsibilities and Obligations of States Sponsoring Persons and Entities with Respect to Activities in the Area (Advisory Opinion)*, International Tribunal of the Law of the Sea (1 February 2011) para 131.

[135] ILC Articles on Prevention of Harm, Art 3.

[136] Ibid Commentary to Art 3, para 7.

[137] *Pulp Mills Case*, para 197.

that the rule obliges States to take certain monitoring and enforcement measures, including consideration of relevant scientific evidence of the risks resulting from potentially harmful activities. Further, States must '[formulate] policies designed to prevent significant transboundary harm or to minimise the risk thereof and [implement] those policies'.[138] The precise standard of care for each State should be assessed on the basis of appropriateness and proportionality to the degree of risk in the particular situation,[139] whereby consideration must be given to the economic level of States.[140] The ILC stipulates in its commentaries, however, that a State's economic level 'cannot be used to dispense the State from its obligations [to prevent transboundary harm]'.[141] This interpretation reflects the principle of CBDRRC reflected in the international climate change regime: whereas all States have a positive obligation to take measures to prevent dangerous climate change, the content of those obligations is affected by a State's level of economic development.

Conclusion

International climate change law consists of a complex system of norms, procedures and institutions that has developed significantly over time. The treaty-based system developed under the UNFCCC in particular provides a carefully balanced framework for international cooperation on climate change, which has involved to include not only mitigation but also adaptation, capacity building and loss and damage. The no-harm rule continues to underpin this system and has gained legal strength through the elaboration of its prevention and due diligence requirements. However, the precise meaning and scope of the no-harm rule in the context of climate change remains unclear, in part because there is limited case law to elucidate what the rule means in practice. The rules and principles contained in the UNFCCC are open-textured and unclear by design, and because the regime lacks a dedicated enforcement mechanism there is a similar lack of jurisprudence to shed light on the substantive norms contained in the Kyoto Protocol, the Paris Agreement and the UNFCCC itself. The following chapters will explore to what extent and how synergies between international climate change law, international human rights law and the general law of State responsibility could make the international legal response to climate change more effective.

[138] ILC Articles on Prevention of Harm, para 10.
[139] Ibid para 11.
[140] Ibid. See also *Alabamaî Arbitration*, para 13 (finding that due diligence must be exercised 'by neutral governments in exact proportion to the risks to which either of the belligerents may be exposed, from a failure to fulfil the obligations of neutrality on their part').
[141] ILC Articles on Prevention of Harm. See also, *Alabamaî Arbitration*, para 13 (finding that due diligence must be exercised 'by neutral governments in exact proportion to the risks to which either of the belligerents may be exposed, from a failure to fulfil the obligations of neutrality on their part').

4

The Law of State Responsibility

Introduction

This chapter discusses the potential of the law of State responsibility as an overarching framework for climate change-related human rights claims, focusing on its role in the international legal system. The chapter also unpacks the interrelationships between State responsibility and human rights, and between State responsibility and the international climate change regime. The analysis shows that neither international human rights law nor international climate change law precludes the application of the law of State responsibility to the substantive obligations contained in these two frameworks. This conclusion opens the door to an integrative approach to the three different legal frameworks – human rights law, climate change law and State responsibility – in the context of fragmentation.

The Law of State Responsibility

The law of State responsibility may be called 'the general secondary law of international obligations, in the same way that the Vienna Convention [on the Law of Treaties] provides the general secondary law of treaties'.[1] Today it is codified in the International Law Commission (ILC)'s Articles on the Responsibility of States for Internationally Wrongful Acts (ILC ARS). In brief, the law of State responsibility contains 'the general conditions under international law for the State to be considered responsible for wrongful actions or omissions, and the legal consequences which flow therefrom'.[2] It is thus important for answering legal questions related to the human rights implications of climate change in two respects: First, its rules on attribution determine the types of State conduct that could potentially breach a State's obligations relating to the human rights implications of climate change. Second, the law of State responsibility stipulates the legal consequences of established breaches of obligations, including obligations owed to victims of human rights violations associated with climate change.

[1] James R Crawford, 'Responsibility to the International Community as a Whole' (2001) 8 *Indiana Journal of Global Legal Studies* 303, 310.

[2] James R Crawford, *The International Law Commission's Articles on State Responsibility: Introduction, Text, Commentaries* (Cambridge, Cambridge University Press, 2002) 31.

The constituent elements of an internationally wrongful act of a State are listed in Article 2 of the ILC ARS, which states that a State has committed an internationally wrongful act when an action or omission:

(a) is attributable to the State under international law; and
(b) constitutes a breach of an international obligation of the State.[3]

Shelton points out that the two elements of an internationally wrongful act encompass a range of complex questions that are specific to the international legal system, including 'the nature and range of attributable acts giving rise to responsibility, the standard of care owed and the nature and scope of reparations'.[4] The premise of this book is that the simplicity, generality and flexibility embedded in these two elements of wrongful conduct make it possible to establish State responsibility for acts and omissions of States that contribute to the human rights implications of climate change.

Two conceptual breakthroughs in the development of the law of State responsibility ensured that this body of law would be amenable to application in connection with the human rights implications of climate change: its generality, and its capacity to address *erga omnes* obligations, or obligations that are owed 'towards all' rather than to a particular State or States. The law of State responsibility was traditionally conceived as a framework that applied primarily in bilateral relations between States. Moreover, the ILC and the League of Nations' Committee of Experts initially focused on a specific issue, namely responsibility of States for injuries to aliens.[5] The first conceptual breakthrough that underpins the law of State responsibility as it is understood today came with the second ILC Special Rapporteur on State responsibility, Roberto Ago, who started dealing with State responsibility as a generic concept confined to 'secondary' rules related to the breach of any international obligation, that is, a breach of a substantive or 'primary' rule.[6] Ago's rationale is captured in his statement (now cited in the Commentaries to the ILC ARS) that 'It is one thing to define a rule and the content of the obligation it imposes, and another to determine whether that obligation has been violated and what should

[3] International Law Commission's Articles on the Responsibility of States for Internationally Wrongful Acts (ILC ARS), Art 2.

[4] Crawford (n 2) 50.

[5] To be precise, the area it had identified as in need of regulation was the responsibility of States for 'injury caused in their territory to the person or property of foreigners'. For a discussion see Roberto Ago, 'First Report on State Responsibility – Review of Previous Work on Codification of the Topic of the International Responsibility of States, UN Doc A/CN.4/SERA/1969/Add.1' (Yearbook of the International Law Commission, 1969) 131; and Daniel Bodansky and John R Crook, 'Symposium: The ILC's State Responsibility Articles – Introduction and Overview' (2002) 96 *American Journal of International Law* 773, 776. See also Patrick Daillier, 'The Development of the Law of Responsibility Through The Case Law' in James Crawford, Alain Pellet and Simon Olleson (eds), *The Law of International Responsibility* (Oxford, Oxford University Press, 2010) 39.

[6] The first ILC Special Rapporteur on State responsibility, FV García-Amador, submitted six reports to the ILC which were all focused on responsibility for injury to aliens. Roberto Ado produced eight reports, which according to the ILC Commentaries to the ASR established 'the basic structure and orientation of the project'. See Crawford (n 2) 31, para 2.

be the consequences of the violation'. This newly introduced generality enabled by the distinction between 'primary' and 'secondary' obligations, allowed the law of State responsibility to evolve into a field of law that 'covers the field of the responsibility of States for internationally wrongful conduct'.[7]

Today the law of State responsibility is still largely, if not entirely, premised on the distinction between primary and secondary rules.[8] The ILC ARS are understood to contain 'secondary' rules which determine the legal consequences of a breach of a primary (substantive) rule.[9] The distinction between primary and secondary rules translates into two types of obligations: as Crawford puts it, 'a breach of a *primary* obligation gives rise, immediately by the operation of the law of State responsibility, to a *secondary* obligation or a series of such obligations (cessation, reparation …)'.[10] It is thus clear that although the concept of State responsibility has 'a particular substantive content of its own',[11] and is as such a 'legal category',[12] it is only an intermediary category in the analytical sense. Indeed, an internationally wrongful act is still understood in accordance with the principles of State responsibility reflected in *Phosphates in Morocco*, namely as a 'violation of international law' and a 'definitive act which would, by itself, directly involve international responsibility'.[13] Moreover, it remains the case that when the act is 'attributable to the State and … contrary to the treaty right of another State, international responsibility would be established *as immediately as* between the two States'.[14] This follows from the basic principle that 'Every internationally wrongful act of a State entails the international responsibility of that State'.[15] These basic principles are important, because they suggest that internationally wrongful conduct relating to the human rights implications of climate change has immediate legal consequences, even if these consequences do not immediately materialise because of a lack of enforcement.

Another important conceptual breakthrough in connection with climate change is the capacity of the law of State responsibility to address *erga omnes* obligations. While the original conception of State responsibility reflected a bilateral view of inter-State relations, the diversity (and volume) of substantive norms of international law increased significantly during the protracted drafting of the

[7] James Crawford, Alain Pellet and Simon Olleson (eds), *The Law of International Responsibility* (Oxford, Oxford University Press, 2010) 20.

[8] See, however, Bodansky and Crook (n 5) (arguing that some parts of the Articles, including the part on reparations, actually codify primary rules).

[9] See generally James R Crawford, 'The ILC's Articles on Responsibility of States for Internationally Wrongful Acts: a Retrospect' (2002) 96 *American Journal of International Law* 874.

[10] Ibid 876 (emphasis added).

[11] Philip Allott, 'State Responsibility and the Unmaking of International Law' (1988) 29 *Harvard Environmental Law Review* 1, 12.

[12] Ibid 14.

[13] *Phosphates in Morocco (Italy v France)* [1938] PCIJ Ser A/B No 74 10, para 48.

[14] Ibid (emphasis added).

[15] ILC ARS, Art 1.

ILC ARS. In particular, there was a proliferation of obligations with third-party beneficiaries and obligations concerning common areas, including outer space, the high seas and the Earth's climate system.[16] The ILC ARS reflect these developments and accommodate for obligations that are owed to the 'international community as a whole' into the general law of obligations, marking a departure from the 'classical bilateralism of the duty/right paradigm'.[17] And although much of the relevance of the law of State responsibility still consists of the doctrine expressed by the Permanent Court in the *Factory at Chorzów* case, that 'it is a principle of international law, and even a general conception of law, that any breach of an engagement involves an obligation to make reparation',[18] the law of State responsibility is not a liability system with the primary or exclusive goal of providing injured persons with compensation. Indeed, the ILC ARS make it clear that wrongful conduct can be established even when no-one has been injured as a result of the wrongful act. This means that (in contrast to what some scholars have suggested) it is evidently not necessary to 'disentangle the cobweb of individual acts by States and societal forces'[19] in order to establish the wrongful nature of certain climate change-related conduct. In other words, even in the context of a complex global problem involving both public and private actors, establishing State responsibility still turns on the simple question of whether or not a particular State has acted in accordance with its international obligations. The simplicity of this question is no coincidence: it was specifically designed to address classic bilateral issues as well as issues of concern to humanity as a whole.

Against this backdrop, the law of State responsibility seems prima facie relevant to addressing the human rights implications of climate change. However, its relevance to the international human rights regime – a regime with its own quasi-judicial enforcement mechanisms based on non-reciprocal obligations – merits critical analysis.[20] Similarly, we must consider whether and if so, to what extent and how the general law of State responsibility applies in cases of breaches of norms derived from international climate change law. In this regard, an important point to consider is that the ILC ARS are based on a 'presumption against

[16] Dinah Shelton, 'Righting Wrongs: Reparations in the Articles on State Responsibility' (2002) 96 *American Journal of International Law* 833, 834.

[17] International Law Commission, 'Third Report on State Responsibility by Mr. James Crawford, Special Rapporteur on State Responsibility' (UN Doc A/CN.4/507, International Law Commission Report, 2000) 43, para 96. See also Malgosia Fitzmaurice, 'International Responsibility and Liability' in Daniel Bodansky, Jutta Brunnée and Ellen Hey (eds), *The Oxford Handbook of International Environmental Law* (New York, Oxford University Press, 2007) 1020 (pointing out that one of the problems with the law of State responsibility has been how to overcome this paradigm, and 'how to reflect the features of the many environmental obligations that have as a goal the protection of the common interest').

[18] *Case Concerning the Factory at Chorzów (Germany v Poland)* [1927] PCIJ Rep Series A no 17, 29.

[19] Christian Tomuschat, 'Global Warming and State Responsibility' in Holger Hestermeyer et al (eds), *Law of the Sea in Dialogue* (Heidelberg, Springer, 2011) 9.

[20] Dinah Shelton, *Remedies in International Human Rights Law*, 2nd edn (Oxford, Oxford University Press, 2005) 98.

the creation of wholly self-contained regimes in the field of reparation',[21] thus reflecting what Simma and Pulkowski have called 'a universalistic concept of international law'.[22] Nonetheless, the ILC Articles open the door to the exclusion of the general rules of State responsibility in Article 55, entitled *lex specialis*. This article stipulates that the articles do not apply 'where and to the extent that the conditions for the existence of an internationally wrongful act or the content or implementation of the international responsibility of a State are governed by special rules of international law'.[23] The Commentaries specify that Article 55 is intended to cover 'strong' forms of *lex specialis*, including what are often referred to as self-contained regimes, as well as 'weaker' forms such as specific treaty provisions on a single point.[24] According to Crawford, this provision was created to mitigate the difficulties arising from the creation of 'general legal categories in relation to particular regimes', mentioning trade law as the clearest example of a particular regime with its own 'internal economy'.[25] Simma and Pulkowski argue that Article 55 accordingly accommodates for the notion of self-contained regimes; that is, regimes which exist in normative isolation.[26] The effect of Article 55 is that the law of State responsibility is presumed to be subordinate to such regimes. However, Article 55 also reflects and accommodates a much more nuanced view of how general and specific secondary norms interact with each other.[27] This is best understood in the light of Crawford's observation that the ILC ARS allow for special regimes and 'at the same time [influence] those regimes'.[28] This is particularly clear in relation to international human rights law, as discussed in the following section.

[21] International Law Commission, 'Third Report on State Responsibility by Mr. James Crawford, Special Rapporteur on State Responsibility' (UN Doc A/CN.4/507, International Law Commission Report, 2000) 43, para 147.

[22] Bruno Simma and Dirk Pulkowski, 'Leges Speciales and Self-Contained Regimes' in James Crawford, Alain Pellet and Simon Olleson (eds), *The Law of International Responsibility* (Oxford, Oxford University Press, 2010) 146.

[23] For a discussion see Bruno Simma, 'Self-Contained Regimes' (1985) 16 *Netherlands Yearbook of International Law* 111, 115.

[24] ILC ARS, Commentary to Art 55, para 5. The notion of self-contained regime stems from the ICJ's ruling in *United States Diplomatic and Consular Staff in Tehran (United States of America v Iran) (Judgement)* [1980] ICJ Reports 3, 40, para 86, where the Court held that 'The rules of diplomatic law … constitute a self-contained regime which, on the one hand, lays down the receiving State's obligations regarding the facilities, privileges and immunities to be accorded to diplomatic missions and, on the other, foresees their possible abuse by members of the mission and specifies the means at the disposal of the receiving State to counter any such abuse'.

[25] Crawford (n 1) 305.

[26] Simma and Pulkowski (n 22) 139.

[27] Anja Lindroos and Michael Mehling, 'From Autonomy to Integration? International Law, Free Trade and the Environment' (2008) 77 *Nordic Journal of International Law* 253, 253 (arguing that the notion of self-contained regimes reflects an 'overly simplistic appreciation of how … regimes interact with each other and with the larger body of international law'). See also Martti Koskenniemi, 'Doctrines of State Responsilbility' in James Crawford, Alain Pellet and Simon Olleson (eds), *The Law of International Responsibility* (Oxford, Oxford University Press, 2010) 47 (stating that 'The fact that human rights protection has been confined under specific treaty regimes does not mean that State responsibility is inapplicable to human rights treaties').

[28] Crawford (n 1) 305. It is worth noting the results of a study on 'Diversity in Secondary Rules and Unity of International Law' carried out by the Netherlands Yearbook of International Law. These

State Responsibility and International Human Rights Law

The influence of international human rights law on the ILC ARS is made explicit in its Commentaries, which make extensive reference to the jurisprudence of international human rights bodies. This influence is particularly apparent from the rules expressed in Articles 33 and 42(b) of the ILC ARS. According to these articles the beneficiaries of human rights obligations are the ultimate beneficiaries of rights accrued as a result of State responsibility incurred by a rights-violating State. Indeed, the Commentaries to Article 33(1) specifically point out that 'a State's responsibility for the breach of an obligation under a treaty concerning the protection of human rights may exist towards all the other parties to the treaty, but the individuals concerned should be regarded as the ultimate beneficiaries and in that sense as the holders of the relevant rights'.[29] Conversely, the relevance of the general rules of State responsibility to human rights obligations has been expressly and widely recognised by international human rights bodies;[30] examples of cases where human rights bodies relied on these rules for the interpretation of human rights treaties are increasingly numerous.[31] The idea that human rights treaties with inter-State procedures constitute self-contained regimes must also be rejected: McGoldrick points out that the ICCPR must be understood as providing 'a modern text, and the HRC a modern institutional forum, in which the principles of State responsibility are applied in an empirical fashion'.[32] He emphasises that

demonstrated ways in which various branches of international law (including international human rights law) have developed secondary rules which are applied in their respective fields. The study concluded that the effect of these synergies can be evaluated as positive, as 'special rules' were used 'in a way which, at the same time, promoted and guaranteed the growing effectiveness of their own particular set of primary rules, without putting in jeopardy the unity and coherency of the international legal order'. See KC Wellens, 'Diversity in Secondary Rules and the Unity of International Law' (1994) 25 *Netherlands Yearbook of International Law* 28, 3–333. This issue was subsequently published as a book: LANM Barnhoorn and KC Wellens (eds), *Diversity in Secondary Rules and the Unity of International Law* (The Hague, Martinus Nijhoff, 1995).

[29] Crawford (n 2) 95, para 3.

[30] *Patrick Coleman v Australia* (Communication No 1157/2003), para 6.2; *S Jegatheeswara Sarma v Sri Lanka* (Communication No 950/2000), para 9.2; *Humberto Menanteau Aceituno and Mr. José Carrasco Vasquez (represented by counsel Mr. Nelson Caucoto Pereira of the Fundación de Ayuda Social de las Iglesias Cristianas) v Chile* (Communication No 746/1997), para 5.4. See also the Individual concurring opinion of Kurt Herndl and Waleed Sadi in *Cox v Canada* (Communication No 539/1993).

[31] For a clear example see *The Mayagna (Sumo) Awas Tingni Community v Nicaragua* (2003) 10 IHRR 758; (2001) IACtHR Series C No 789, para 154; and *Marino López et al. v Colombia* (2007) Inter-American Commission on Human Rights Report No 86/06, para 42. See also Dominic McGoldrick, *The Human Rights Committee* (New York, Oxford University Press, 1991) 169. It is also worth noting that the mandates of some human rights bodies (such as the mandate of the ACHPR) explicitly allow them to draw on any instruments of international law relevant to the treaty that enlighten their understanding of the human rights in the instruments that they are expressly mandated to apply.

[32] Dominic McGoldrick, 'State Responsibility and the International Covenant on Civil and Political Rights' in Malgosia Fitzmaurice and Dan Sarooshi (eds), *Issues of State Responsibility Before International Judicial Institutions* (Oxford, Bloomsbury Publishing, 2004) 199.

State practice, UN practice and the history of the regime indicate that the ICCPR 'was not intended to be a self-contained regime'.[33] And Vierdag notes that 'Almost all the provisions in [the ICCPR and the ECHR] contain elements that have corresponding rules in the law of State responsibility'.[34]

It seems justified to conclude that international human rights law can be interpreted in accordance with the general law of State responsibility, while at the same time (as recognised in Article 55) adding its own substantive and procedural caveats. The single most important caveat is that under international human rights law, a victim's right to a remedy is a substantive right, which is protected under customary international law,[35] and expressed in human rights treaties in various forms. Most treaties guarantee both the right of access to procedures through which claims of human rights violations are heard, and a substantive right to redress.[36] The ICCPR in particular contains comprehensive provisions on remedies in three separate articles. The broadest of these is Article 2(3) which spells out the obligations of State Parties to the Covenant to ensure that any person whose rights are violated shall have an 'accessible, effective and enforceable' remedy.[37] The right to a remedy exists not only *ex post facto* but also when there is a threat of a violation,[38] and is intertwined with the principle of effectiveness. An example of this is the ACHPR's understanding that 'The rights and freedoms of individuals enshrined in the [African] Charter can only be fully realized if governments provide structures which enable them to seek redress if they are violated'.[39] Accordingly, from a human rights perspective the law of State responsibility is best understood as providing a structure through which redress for human rights violations can be obtained by States on behalf of the victims of the violation. This understanding is in line with the principle of effectiveness; a principle that must be relied upon to give effect to the right of a remedy in the light of threats that adverse effects

[33] Ibid. See also: McGoldrick (n 31) 169 (noting that the HRC has generally interpreted the ICCPR in accordance with the general law on State responsibility).

[34] EW Vierdag, 'Some Remarks about Special Features of Human Rights Treaties' (1994) 25 *Netherlands Yearbook of International Law* 119, 135.

[35] See *Basic Principles and Guidelines on the Right to a Remedy and Reparation for Victims of Gross Violations of International Human Rights Law and Serious Violations of International Humanitarian Law*, UNGA Res 60/147 (16 December 2005) Annex, Principles 1(b), 2, 3 and (pertaining to gross violations of international human rights law and international crimes) 11. See also Shelton (n 20) 103 (noting that '[t]he decision to afford a domestic remedy formerly was left to the discretion of the wrongdoing State, subject to the vague and uncertain doctrine of denial of justice. Today, human rights law requires States to afford an effective remedy for any violation of rights').

[36] For an overview of global and regional human rights treaties that incorporate the right to a remedy see Shelton (n 20) 113–20. See also Crawford (n 2) 95, paras 3–4.

[37] For a discussion of the evolution of the Human Rights Committee's position on the right to a remedy see generally Martin Scheinin, 'The Human Rights Committee's Pronouncements on the Right to an Effective Remedy: An Illustration of the Legal Nature of the Committee's Work under the Optional Protocol' in Nisuke Ando (ed), *Towards Implementing Universal Human Rights* (Leiden, Martinus Nijhoff, 2004) (esp 101–03). See also Shelton (n 20) 50.

[38] Shelton (n 20) 104ff.

[39] *Jawara v The Gambia* (Communications 147/95, 149/96 74).

of climate change pose to the enjoyment of human rights. Part II of this book explains the practical implications of this premise for victims of climate change. A preliminary question to address is the relationship between the general law of State responsibility on the one hand and the international climate change regime on the other. This question is addressed in the following section.

State Responsibility and the Climate Change Regime

The conclusion that the law of State responsibility is amenable to application in conjunction with international human rights law can also be drawn with regard to the UNFCCC, the Kyoto Protocol and the Paris Agreement. Drawing this conclusion is straightforward in the case of the UNFCCC, because it does not contain 'special rules' regarding conditions for the existence of a wrongful act, nor does it refer to the consequences of breaches of obligations under the treaty.[40] Moreover, the UNFCCC's one article that spells out options for enforcing treaty provisions is fully compatible with the assumption that the full body of 'secondary rules' contained in the general law of State responsibility is applicable to the treaty regime.[41] It is worth nothing that, during their respective ratifications of the UNFCCC, several States including Fiji, Kiribati, Nauru and Papua New Guinea, added the reservation that the provisions of this treaty 'shall in no way constitute a renunciation of any rights under international law concerning State responsibility for the adverse effects of climate change and that no provisions in the Convention

[40] The framework for addressing loss and damage concluded at COP 19 at Warsaw, Poland, was established under the adaptation provisions of the UNFCCC, and did not use terms related to breaches of obligations. This means, in my view, that it cannot be plausibly argued that this framework constitutes *lex specialis* which excludes the applicability of the general law of State responsibility. See Warsaw International Mechanism for Loss and Damage Associated with Climate Change Impacts (22 November 2013) UN Doc FCCC/CP/2013/L.15. For a discussion on the (then proposed) loss and damage mechanism under the UNFCCC, see Ilona Millar, Catherine Gascoigne and Elizabeth Caldwell, 'Making Good the Loss' in Michael B Gerrard and Gregory E Wannier (eds), *Threatened Island Nations: Legal Implications of Rising Seas and a Changing Climate* (Cambridge, Cambridge University Press, 2013). See also Roda Verheyen, *Tackling Loss & Damage: A New Role for the Climate Regime?* (Loss and Damage in Vulnerable Countries Initiative, 2012) and Roda Verheyen, *Climate Change Damage and International Law: Prevention Duties and State Responsibility* (Leiden, Martinus Nijhoff, 2005).

[41] Art 14(1) of the UNFCCC provides that parties can jointly seek settlement of their dispute 'through negotiation or any other peaceful means of their own choice'; Art 14(2) entitles parties to unilaterally refer a dispute involving the UNFCCC to the ICJ or to a binding arbitration, subject to each of the parties having made a declaration accepting the jurisdiction of the relevant forum over such disputes; and Art 14(6) provides that where resort to the procedures provided for under paras 1–2 has failed, any party to the dispute can submit the dispute to a conciliation commission that would be created upon the request of that party. No State has so far made a declaration under Art 14. Andrew Strauss rightly observes that the lack of such a declaration would not affect the jurisdiction of the ICJ under Art 36(1) and (2) of the Statute of the ICJ as there is no need for States to consent to the jurisdiction of the Court more than once. See Andrew Strauss, 'Climate Change Litigation: Opening the Door to the International Court of Justice' in William CG Burns and Hari M Osofsky (eds), *Adjudicating Climate Change: State, National and International Approaches* (Cambridge, Cambridge University Press, 2009) 343.

can be interpreted as derogating from the principles of general international law'.[42] These reservations can be seen as a formal confirmation of an existing legal situation.

A slightly more complex situation exists under the Kyoto Protocol as a result of the Compliance Committee established under the treaty. As noted, this body may instigate sanctions on State Parties that fail to comply with their treaty obligations, usually consisting of restrictions on parties' eligibility to participate in carbon trading mechanisms.[43] This function could be interpreted as creating *lex specialis* pertaining to the legal consequences of violations of the Kyoto Protocol that could, as per Article 15 of the ILC ARS, exclude the applicability of (relevant parts of) the general law of State responsibility. However, it is suggested here that this interpretation is not correct. Instead, it the correct approach is to consider the situation as analogous to that of human rights treaties with enforcement mechanisms. First, as a result of the principle of effectiveness, we can assume that these treaty bodies are established to enhance the effectiveness of the treaty regime, and not to weaken it by annulling rights and legal consequences that would normally arise from a breach in accordance with the law of State responsibility. Second, the Kyoto Protocol and the UNFCCC are expressly concerned with a 'common concern of mankind' and thus, like international human rights treaties, protect the legitimate interests of the international community as a whole rather than merely the interests of State Parties.[44] For the Kyoto Protocol, this means that it can be safely assumed that neither the existence of the Compliance Committee nor its actual practice replaces the rights of State Parties to invoke the responsibility of other State Parties that violate its substantive provisions in accordance with the general law of State responsibility to seek an end to the wrongful conduct and reparations for its effects. This conclusion makes it clear that breaches of the Kyoto Protocol may be taken into account as part of State conduct that is wrongful in the aggregate under international human rights law.

The situation is no different for the Paris Agreement. As mentioned above, the COP decision that accompanied the Paris Agreement contained a clause stating that Article 8 of the Agreement 'does not involve or provide a basis for any liability or compensation'.[45] This language seeks to exclude compensation for damage caused by the actions of States that contribute the most to climate change from the mandate of the Warsaw International Mechanism on Loss and Damage. Although some observers were concerned about the potential broader implications of this

[42] Declarations made by Fiji, Kiribati, Nauru and Papua New Guinea. See 'Status of Ratification of the UNFCCC and the Kyoto Protocol', available at www.unfccc.int.

[43] For a detailed discussion see René Lefeber, 'Holding Countries to Account: the Kyoto Protocol's Compliance System Revisted After Four Years of Experience' (2010) 1 *Climate Law* 133, 134.

[44] As argued by Verheyen (n 40) 266 and Fitzmaurice (n 17) 1020. Cf Tomuschat (n 19) 14.

[45] Report of the Conference of the Parties on Its Twenty-First Session, 'Addendum – Part Two: Action Taken by the Conference of the Parties at Its Twenty-First Session', Dec 1/CP.21, UN Doc FCCC/CP/2015/10/Add.1, para 52.

language for States' existing rights to compensation under general international law,[46] a COP decision – which is not in itself binding – cannot override the general rules of State responsibility under international law that require full reparation for internationally wrongful conduct.[47] In fact, the exclusion of liability clause could even be taken as a confirmation that the Paris Agreement does not create new *lex specialis* that would preclude the application of the law of State responsibility to internationally wrongful acts relating to climate change. To be on the safe side, however, several States that are particularly vulnerable to the adverse effects of climate change have made declarations upon ratification of the Agreement to preserve their rights to compensation for climate damages under general international law.[48] These declarations confirm – perhaps superfluously – that no new *lex specialis* that could set aside the law of State responsibility was created in Paris.

Conclusion

The general law of State responsibility offers a broad and highly flexible framework to hold States accountable for internationally wrongful conduct. Neither international human rights law nor international climate change law can be considered a self-contained regime, which would render the general law of State responsibility inapplicable to the norms contained in those regimes. International climate change law does not have its own secondary rules or enforcement mechanisms, and the law of State responsibility can therefore be invoked to deal with breaches of obligations derived from the international climate change regime. However, international human rights law has its own 'secondary rules' that need to be taken into account when considering issues of State responsibility for human rights violations. Perhaps the most important of those special rules is the right to a remedy. The following chapters will consider the special features of international human rights law and their implications for State responsibility for human rights violations associated with climate change.

[46] See, eg, Laurie Goering, 'Climate Deal Could Bar Poor from Seeking Compensation for Losses' (Reuters, 2015) available at uk.reuters.com/article/uk-climatechange-summit-damage-idUKKBN-0TU23R20151211; Alex Pashley, 'Did the Paris Deal Rule Out Climate Compensation?' (Climate Home, 2015) available at www.climatechangenews.com/2015/12/18/did-the-paris-deal-rule-out-climate-compensation.

[47] See further ch 4.

[48] See, eg, *Declaration by the Marshall Islands* (United Nations Treaty Collection, 2016), available at treaties.un.org/pages/ViewDetails.aspx?src=TREATY&mtdsg_no=XXVII-7-d&chapter=27&clang=_en: 'the Republic of the Marshall Islands declares its understanding that ratification of the Paris Agreement shall in no way constitute a renunciation of any rights under any other laws, including international law'. The Cook Islands, the Federated States of Micronesia, Nauru, the Solomon Islands, Tuvalu and Vanuatu made similar declarations.

5

Integrating Legal Frameworks in a Context of Fragmentation

Introduction

The increasing number of specialised branches of international law has led to concerns that fragmentation is undermining the coherence and effectiveness of the international legal system. In relation to climate change specifically, it has been said that the plural, fragmented character of the international legal system undermines rather than enhances the collective action that is needed to address the problem. However, great strides have been made in recent years in promoting synergies between different branches of international law in connection with climate change. This book is part of a growing movement in legal scholarship that studies the linkages between the international climate change regime and other branches of international law, with a view to identify ways to create and enhance productive synergies.[1]

Perhaps the greatest promise of enhanced linkages between climate change, human rights and State responsibility is improved access to remedies for the victims of climate change. The doctrinal question at stake here is the role of human rights law in the international legal system where *lex specialis* is already in place and appears to create parallel obligations and fora for discussion and cooperation. However, principles of general international law such as *lex specialis derogate legi generali* (ie special law prevails over general law),[2] or the understanding that *lex specialis* may be used 'to apply, clarify, update or modify as well as set aside' general law,[3] appear of limited guidance for answering this question. After all, international human rights law itself is considered to be a special regime, with norms that reflect the unified purpose of protecting universal human rights as entitlements of all human beings by virtue of their humanity. This unified purpose

[1] See, eg, Rosemary Rayfuse and Shirley V Scott (eds), *International Law in the Era of Climate Change* (Cheltenham, Edward Elgar, 2012); Harro van Asselt, Francesco Sindico and Michael A Mehling, 'Global Climate Change and the Fragmentation of International Law' (2008) 30(4) *Law and Policy* 423.

[2] Fragmentation of International Law: Difficulties Arising from the Diversification and Expansion of International Law, Report of the Study Group of the International Law Commission, A/CN/4/L.702, 13 July 2006, paras 5, 14.

[3] Ibid para 8.

must be reflected in the interpretation of human rights norms, even when these norms are interpreted in connection with other norms such as those derived from international climate change law.

This chapter discusses how legal norms derived from climate change law and human rights law, respectively, can be interpreted in a way that enhances coherence and effectiveness while doing justice to the special characteristics of human rights law. It explores the institutional disconnect related to climate change and human rights in terms of the debate on the fragmentation of international law, and asks whether and if so, how apparent fragmentation can be overcome at the normative level through an evolutive interpretation of relevant norms. The analysis demonstrates that overcoming fragmentation is possible, but it requires that the special characteristics of both international human rights law and international climate change law are taken into account. The chapter concludes by setting out a number of ways in which normative synergies can be created between substantive norms derived from the two different regimes, in a manner that allows the law of State responsibility to serve as an overarching framework that comes into effect when there is an actual or alleged breach of international norms relating to the human rights implications of climate change.

The Work of the International Law Commission on Fragmentation

From a doctrinal perspective, the natural starting point for examining the relationship between the international climate change regime on the one hand and international human rights law on the other is the general rule for treaty interpretation where in determining the meaning of treaty provisions, account may be taken of 'any relevant rules of international law applicable in the relations between the parties'.[4] This rule is generally considered to fall within the scope of customary international law, requiring consideration of 'the wider normative environment' of a given norm. It was considered to be the single most important interpretative device for dealing with relationships between different branches of international law in the groundbreaking ILC study 'Fragmentation of International Law', by Special Rapporteur Martti Koskenniemi, conducted in response to the perceived problem that 'specialized law-making and institution-building tends to take place with relative ignorance of legislative and institutional activities in the adjoining fields and of the general principles and practices of international law'.[5] The study

[4] See also Margaretha Wewerinke, 'The Role of the UN Human Rights Council in Addressing Climate Change' (2014) 8 *Human Rights and International Legal Discourse* 10, on which part of this chapter draws.

[5] Fragmentation of International Law: Difficulties Arising from the Diversification and Expansion of International Law, Report of the Study Group of the International Law Commission, A/CN/4/L.702, 13 July 2006, 11.

provides a valuable outline of the key principles that allow for interpretative relationships and synergies between branches of international law, and was received by the General Assembly with appreciation.[6] The study concludes that international law must, in principle, be considered as a harmonious system;[7] a conclusion that has generally been met with approval. Yet the study has also been criticised for its formalistic approach to addressing relationships between norms and rule-systems almost exclusively in terms of potential conflicts,[8] and for its over-reliance on the VCLT. Indeed it did not provide a satisfactory answer to the problem of 'the loss of an overall perspective on the law'.[9] The underlying difficulty is that the ILC did not recognise differences in normativity, except for recognising existing provisions in the VCLT when stating that 'the *lex specialis* maxim cannot be used to set aside types of international law that are non-derogable, such as (but not only) peremptory norms which are expressly recognised as such'.[10] The ILC considered human rights law as a 'special regime', whose importance lies in 'the way its norms express a unified object and purpose' which must be reflected in the interpretation of its norms.[11] According to this perspective, the *lex specialis* of human rights law may technically limit States' discretion in the interpretation of norms that are contained in the climate change regime or otherwise aid in the interpretation of the provisions of the UNFCCC, especially where these provisions are vague.[12]

The Special Characteristics of Human Rights Law as a Central Part of a Holistic Legal Framework

The limits to an excessively technical approach to dealing with various regimes become evident when considering that the 'principle of harmonisation' recognised

[6] Resolution 61/34 of 4 December 2006.

[7] Ibid para 4 ('It is a generally accepted principle that when several norms bear on a single issue they should, to the extent possible, be interpreted so as to give rise to a single set of compatible obligations'). See also para 9 (proposing reconciliation between general and specific norms) and para 11 (allowing for self-contained regimes).

[8] Sahib Singh, 'The Potential of International Law: Fragmentation and Ethics' (2011) 24 *Leiden Journal of International Law* 23 (arguing that 'the Report's rule-centric approach to a polarized discourse results only in the propagation of ethical deficiencies').

[9] Fragmentation of International Law: Difficulties Arising from the Diversification and Expansion of International Law, Report of the Study Group of the International Law Commission, A/CN/4/L.702, 13 July 2006. See also Mario Prost, *The Concept of Unity in Public International Law* (Oxford, Hart Publishing, 2012) 210.

[10] Fragmentation of International Law: Difficulties Arising from the Diversification and Expansion of International Law, Report of the Study Group of the International Law Commission, A/CN/4/L.702, 13 July 2006, para 9.

[11] Ibid paras 12–13.

[12] Siobhán McInerney-Lankford, 'Human Rights and Climate Change' in Michael B Gerrard and Gregory E Wannier (eds), *Threatened Island Nations: Legal Implications of Rising Seas and a Changing Climate* (Cambridge, Cambridge University Press, 2012) 232, 234.

by the ILC falls short of a rule that prescribes systemic integration.[13] It has already been noted with regard to Article 31(3)(c) that it is unclear when or how the provision should be applied.[14] I argue that the ambiguity is best resolved in accordance with the ILC's broader observation that 'whatever their subject matter, treaties are a creation of the international legal system and their operation is predicated upon that fact'.[15] This understanding can explain the relevance of international human rights law as embodying norms that constitute intransgressible principles of customary law,[16] not all of which are recognised as peremptory norms.[17] This understanding of the international legal system finds doctrinal support in the law of treaties itself: in its Preamble the VCLT emphasises (mirroring Article 1 of the UN Charter) the rule of customary international law that international treaties must be interpreted and disputes settled 'in conformity with principles of justice', including specifically 'human rights and fundamental freedoms for all'.[18] It thus stands to reason that the general rules of treaty interpretation require that effect be given to the different branches of international law, not just in a coherent way, but also in accordance with 'principles of justice' that include human rights. Accordingly, human rights norms can also be applied as 'horizontal' norms that influence the interpretation of other treaties.[19] Article 103 of the UN Charter helps consolidate the doctrinal basis for this understanding, as it clarifies that the human rights obligations derived from the Charter prevail over obligations under any other international agreement in the event of a conflict between those obligations.

[13] See also *Case Concerning Oil Platforms (Islamic Republic of Iran v United States of America)* [2003] ICJ Reports 161 (Separate Opinion of Judge Simma) para 9 (noting that when general principles of international law with a *jus cogens* character are concerned, the principle of systemic integration 'turns into a legally insurmountable limit to the permissible treaty'). However, observers have noted that 'It is hard to see how any treaty could be interpreted in a way that violates such a rule, and why reference to Article 31(3)(c) is necessary in the first place'. See Anja Lindroos and Michael Mehling, 'From Autonomy to Integration? International Law, Free Trade and the Environment' (2008) 77 *Nordic Journal of International Law* 253, 269.

[14] Lindroos and Mehling (n 13) 268. See also *Case Concerning Oil Platforms (Islamic Republic of Iran v United States of America)* [2003] ICJ Reports 225 (Separate Opinion of Judge Higgins) para 46 (stating that resort to Art 31(3)(c) would have required 'more explanation than the Court provides').

[15] Fragmentation of International Law: Difficulties Arising from the Diversification and Expansion of International Law, Report of the Study Group of the International Law Commission, A/CN/4/L.702, 13 July 2006, 13.

[16] *Legality of the Threat or Use of Nuclear Weapons (Advisory Opinion)* [1996] ICJ Reports 241, para 79. See also Shabtai Rosenne, 'Some Reflections Erga Omnes' in Antony Anghie and Garry Sturgess (eds), *Legal Visions of the 21st Century: Essays in Honour of Judge Christopher Weeramantry* (The Hague, Kluwer Law International, 1998) 515.

[17] For a discussion, see Martin Scheinin, 'Impact on the Law of Treaties' in Menno T Kamminga and Martin Scheinin (eds), *The Impact of Human Rights Law on General International Law* (Oxford, Oxford University Press, 2009) 30 (arguing that in the case of human rights law, its normative weight 'may manifest itself in softer forms [than *jus cogens*] that afford a special status to human rights law in respect of "merely" contractual treaties between states').

[18] Vienna Convention on the Law of Treaties (adopted 23 May 1969, entered into force 27 January 1980) 1155 UNTS 331, Preamble and UN Charter, Art 1.

[19] See also Scheinin (n 17) 30.

One perspective that pushes 'systemic integration' of human rights norms to its limits is what Mario Prost calls an 'axio-logical perspective' on international law, which emphasises the role of values in upholding the principle of harmonisation through contextual interpretation. As Prost puts it, 'Value-driven unity rests on the idea of a common denominator of fundamental values that transcend individual rules and provide the legal order with a general sense of direction'.[20] From this perspective, fragmentation is not understood as a conflict of norms: 'It occurs where a regime, a government, or a tribunal undermines the axio-logical core of international law, whether this core is already well established or simply in the making'.[21] Human rights obligations may accordingly be seen as creating thresholds of minimum acceptability, or as 'levels of protection for individual rights which can be regarded as the minimum acceptable outcome under given scenarios'.[22] In interpreting the rules and principles of the UNFCCC, the protection of the Earth's climate as a prerequisite to human life and well-being could become a central consideration.[23] Conversely, specific value-based norms such as equity and common but differentiated responsibilities and respective capabilities (CBDRRC) could strengthen the objective of substantive equality that is inherent in human rights law.[24] However, this approach is open to criticism if the interpreter fails to demonstrate how 'values' or 'axioms' are embodied in substantive norms, or how the existing secondary rules of international law support or require their application.

The answer proposed here is that substantive norms themselves offer relatively clear guidance on the relationship between human rights law and climate change law, as long as the object and purpose of the respective substantive norms is taken into consideration. In this context, it is significant that the practice of international human rights bodies increasingly builds on the conceptual understanding of international law as one legal system, while at the same time emphasising the special nature of human rights law,[25] and that provisions of international instruments other than human rights instruments may be invoked based on the understanding that these provisions enlighten their understanding of the human rights in the instruments that they are expressly mandated to apply.[26] Furthermore, the

[20] Mario Prost, *The Concept of Unity in Public International Law* (Oxford, Hart Publishing, 2012) 200.
[21] Ibid.
[22] Ibid.
[23] See also John Dernbach, *Acting as if Tomorrow Matters: Accelerating the Transition to Sustainability* (Washington DC, Environmental Law Institute, 2012) (pointing out that 'the texts and beliefs of each of the world's major religions teach responsibility toward other humans as well as the environment' and 'Because unsustainable actions adversely affect others, more-sustainable actions are not simply better for us; they reflect our ethical and religious values').
[24] Report of the Office of the United Nations High Commissioner for Human Rights on the Relationship between Climate Change and Human Rights, UN Doc A/HRC/10/61 (15 January 2009) 28.
[25] See, eg, *The Effect of Reservations on the Entry into Force of the ACHR (Articles 74 and 75)* (1982) 3 *HRLJ* 153, 2 IACtHR (Ser A); *Austria v Italy* App no 788/60 (ECtHR, 11 Jan 1961) (*Austria v Italy*) 138-40; and *Ireland v United Kingdom* Series A no 25 (1978) 2 EHRR 25 (*Ireland v United Kingdom*).
[26] *Marino López et al. v Colombia* (2007) Inter-American Commission on Human Rights Report No 86/06 (*Marino López et al. v Colombia*).

principle of systemic integration may be considered as intrinsically linked with the principle of effectiveness, both in the context of human rights law (for considering when resort may or must be had to climate change law) and in the context of international law as a legal system which embodies universally applicable human rights norms.[27]

Exploiting Synergies between International Human Rights Law and International Climate Change Law

There are several norms of international climate change law that can be invoked to clarify States' obligations under international human rights law. First, the no-harm rule could clarify States' obligations under international human rights law vis-a-vis persons outside their own territories. The rationale here is that it would be illogical, and contrary to the object and purpose of human rights law, to interpret human rights obligations as allowing conduct that interferes with human rights if this conduct is unlawful under the no-harm rule. De Schutter supports this view, suggesting that the no-harm rule and prevention obligations under international human rights law could be mutually reinforcing.[28] Along similar lines, Ryngaert argues that States may 'have a duty to protect human rights outside their territory … if their rights are violated as a result of an act initiated in those States' territory, in line with the *Trial Smelter* principle'.[29] Others have argued that the obligation to prevent human rights violations from occurring elsewhere is 'the logical consequence of the duty under general international law not to harm foreign nationals and to make reparations for breaches'.[30] In accordance with this rationale, the no-harm rule could reinforce the argument that human rights obligations arise from a State's capacity to regulate anthropogenic greenhouse gases; a pollutant that causes transboundary harm and thereby affects the enjoyment of human rights. However, in the light of the *lex specialis derogate legi generali* doctrine it would seem to be more appropriate to rely on the *lex specialis* of the UNFCCC to highlight the content of States' obligations to prevent transboundary harm

[27] Daniel Rietiker, 'The Principle of "Effectiveness" in the Recent Jurisprudence of the European Court of Human Rights: Its Different Dimensions and Its Consistency with Public International Law – No Need for the Concept of Treaty Sui Generis' (2010) 79 *Nordic Journal of International Law* 245, 275. See also above, on the principle of effectiveness.

[28] Olivier de Schutter, *International Human Rights Law: Cases, Materials, Commentary* (Cambridge, Cambridge University Press, 2010) 165. See also Bruno Simma and Philip Alston, 'The Sources of Human Rights Law: Custom, Jus Cogens, and General Principles' (1988–89) 12 *Australian Yearbook of International Law* 104.

[29] Cedric Ryngaert, 'Jurisdiction: Towards a Reasonableness Test' in Malcolm Langford et al (eds), *Global Justice, State Duties The Extraterritorial Scope of Economic, Social and Cultural Rights in International Law* (Cambridge, Cambridge University Press, 2012) 222 (footnotes omitted, emphasis omitted).

[30] Siobhán McInerney-Lankford, Mac Darrow and Lavanya Rajamani, *Human Rights and Climate Change: a Review of the International Legal Dimensions* (World Bank Study no 61308, 2011) 46.

resulting from activities that cause climate change, or alternatively to consider the more specific obligations derived from the UNFCCC and its ultimate objective in conjunction with the no-harm rule as a co-existing norm of customary international law. The better view is that the provisions of the UNFCCC and its subsidiary instruments do embody the no-harm rule, but give it a more specific meaning through the ultimate objective of the UNFCCC and the agreed understanding that this objective must be achieved in accordance with the principles of equity and CBDRRC.

The precautionary principle is another example of a norm contained in international climate change law that may be relevant to human rights protection. If it is accepted that this principle has a bearing on States' obligations under international human rights law related to climate change, it could help interpret international human rights law as requiring States to take preventive action to reduce the risk that the adverse effects of climate change have on the enjoyment of internationally protected human rights. In the light of the high degree of scientific certainty concerning the causes and consequences of climate change, the precautionary principle creates a fairly high threshold that States must overcome to justify their actions when their compliance with international human rights obligations is assessed. The principle could accordingly ease the evidential burden on claimants in international human rights litigation, which is significant given the various evidential obstacles that may arise in claims of climate change-related State responsibility. However, the 'threshold' of risk that triggers the precautionary principle is to a great extent norm-specific and related to the seriousness of the consequences.[31] In the context of human rights, the principle must therefore be read in conjunction with specific human rights norms. The principle is examined in chapter three, which discusses rights-specific obligations.

It is also worth highlighting the significance of Article 3(4) of the UNFCCC, which provides for a right to sustainable development,[32] for the substance of States' obligations under the UNFCCC as well as under international human rights law. The right to sustainable development can be understood as a modification of the right to development, which has arguably become a norm of customary international law through its repeated reiteration by the overwhelming majority of States in the international community. The right evolved from a number of UN General Assembly resolutions, in particular, the Declaration on the Right to Development that was adopted by an overwhelming majority of States in 1986,[33] which were

[31] Marie-Claire Cordonier Segger and Markus W Gehring, 'Precaution, Health and the World Trade Organization: Moving toward Sustainable Development' (2004) 29 *Queen's Law Journal* 139.

[32] Art 3(4) provides that 'The Parties have a right to, and should, promote sustainable development. Policies and measures to protect the climate system against human-induced change should be appropriate for the specific conditions of each party and should be integrated into the national development programmes, taking into account that economic development is essential for adopting measures to address climate change'.

[33] *Declaration on the Right to Development*, GA Res 41/128, 97th mtg (4 December 1986) (*Declaration on the Right to Development*).

based on the ideas of equity, common interest, interdependence and international solidarity as the foundation for a nation's right to development. The UN and other international fora subsequently adopted a number of declarations linking development to human rights.[34] Further legal basis for the right to development is being provided by widely ratified human rights treaties containing a range of substantive rights that are the basis of development of the individual. Some human rights instruments, such as the CEDAW and the African Charter on Human and Peoples' Rights, even include express provisions on the right to development.[35]

In the context of climate change, the right to development has sometimes been understood as allowing developing countries to maintain or increase current emission levels.[36] However, this interpretation seems simplistic and possibly incorrect, as the right acquires a specific meaning in the context of the UNFCCC due to its codification as a right to *sustainable* development in Article 3(4) of this treaty. We should bear in mind that the term 'sustainable development' is a distinct legal concept which is commonly understood in accordance with the definition in the Brundtland Report as 'development that meets the needs of the present generation without compromising the ability of future generations to meet their own needs'.[37] It should also be noted that the text of Article 3(4) suggests – in line with the CBDRRC principle – that both developed and developing States are required to take policies and measures to protect the climate system against human-induced change, which should be 'appropriate for the specific conditions of each party and … integrated into the national development programmes'.[38] The phrase 'taking into account that economic development is essential for adopting measures to address climate change' makes it particularly clear that economic and social development and protection of the Earth's climate system should be considered as mutually reinforcing objectives within the framework of the Convention.[39] In light of recent evidence which suggests that the realisation of sustainable development in all developing countries requires scaled-up international cooperation to ensure access to electricity, clean cooking conditions and other forms of energy to meet

[34] These include: *Declaration on the Establishment of a New International Economic Order*, GA Res 3201 (S-VI), 2229th mtg (1 May 1974).

[35] Convention on the Elimination of All Forms of Discrimination against Women (adopted 18 December 1979, entered into force 3 September 1981) 1249 UNTS 13 (CEDAW), Art 3.

[36] For a discussion, see Paul Baer, et al, 'The Greenhouse Development Rights Framework: Drawing Attention to Inequality within Nations in the Global Climate Policy Debate' (2009) 40 *Development and Change* 1121.

[37] GH Brundtland and World Commission on the Environment and Development, *Our Common Future: Report of the World Commission on Environment and Development ('Brundtland Report')* (Oxford, Oxford University Press, 1987). See also James Crawford, *Brownlie's Principles of Public International Law*, 8th edn (Croydon, Oxford University Press, 2012) 358.

[38] United Nations Framework Convention on Climate Change (adopted 9 May 1992, entered into force 19 June 1993) 1771 UNTS 107 (UNFCCC), Art 3(4).

[39] Failure to integrate the sustainability element into the right to development would make the right self-contradictory, given that adverse effects of climate change have such significant impacts on the ability of individuals and nations to develop. For further discussion, see Flavio Comim, 'Climate Injustice and Development: A Capability Perspective' (2008) 51 *Development* 344.

basic human and development needs (which correlate with the enjoyment of a range of human rights),[40] the greatest added-value of the right to sustainable development from the perspective of international human rights law is that it requires States to cooperate with each other to enhance development for all nations, whilst simultaneously addressing the risks posed by climate change.[41]

To recapitulate: the general rules of interpretation allow for the 'systemic integration' of norms when interpreting provisions of international human rights law but preclude interpretations of other laws that are inconsistent with the object and purpose of protecting the rights of peoples and individuals.[42] Indeed, the principle of harmonisation works towards the consideration of human rights norms when other norms are interpreted and applied. At the same time, the principle of effectiveness works in favour of taking account of relevant obligations of States derived from the principles and commitments contained in the UNFCCC which could potentially strengthen the existing provisions of international human rights law when applied in the context of climate change. The precautionary principle, CBDRRC and the right to sustainable development are examples of provisions that are prima facie amenable to interpretation in conjunction with international human rights norms in a way that enhances the effectiveness of each regime. The next chapter will consider the normative synergies between international human rights law and the UNFCCC in order to determine when a State is responsible for a breach of international human rights law based on action or inaction connected with climate change. To set the stage for this analysis, the next section addresses some preliminary issues related to State responsibility.

Conclusion

This chapter considered the so-called fragmentation of international law, including the position of the ILC that international law must, in principle, be considered as a harmonious system. This position is consistent with the general rule of treaty interpretation that, in order to determine the meaning of treaty provisions, any relevant rules of international law applicable in the relations between the parties can be taken into account. From the perspective of international human rights law, it is significant that the practice of international human rights bodies increasingly

[40] Ibid 117.

[41] *Declaration on the Right to Development*, Arts 3-4. See also Report of the Independent Expert on Human Rights and International Solidarity, UN Doc A/HRC/12/27 (22 July 2009); and Margot E Salomon, *Global Responsibility for Human Rights: World Poverty and the Development of International Law* (Oxford, Oxford University Press, 2007).

[42] See also Siobhán McInerney-Lankford, 'Fragmentation of International Law Redux: The Case of Strasbourg' (2010) 32 *Oxford Journal of Legal Studies* 609 (emphasising the importance of distinguishing between harmonisation and teleological interpretation, and that fragmentation might be justified where it serves to defend a higher standard of human rights protection).

builds on the understanding of international law as one legal system, despite the emphasis placed on the special nature of human rights law.[43] Indeed, human rights bodies have made it clear that they may use any instruments that improve their understanding of human rights in the instruments that they are expressly mandated to apply.[44] However, a nuanced approach to systemic integration is needed: neither the rule contained in Article 31(3)(c) of the VCLT nor the ILC's 'principle of harmonisation' actually prescribe systemic integration. Moreover, international law does not necessarily assume the compatibility of its different branches or the norms contained therein; instead, it requires consideration of the wider normative environment when a particular norm is applied. The relationship between human rights, the UNFCCC and the law of State responsibility cannot be understood a priori or mechanically. Instead, it must be explained through an analysis of the substantive norms contained in the two legal regimes and in the light of their objects and purposes.

A brief examination of specific norms has provided examples of the implications of this approach. The no-harm rule is significant from an international human rights law perspective. This is because its incorporation into general international law means that the risk that climate change will interfere with the enjoyment of human rights in a third country (by definition a risk of 'significant' harm) triggers positive obligations for States that use or permit the use of their territory for activities that cause climate change. The *lex specialis* of the UNFCCC gives a more specific meaning to the no-harm rule by categorising States into 'developed' and 'developing' countries with differentiated obligations. This must be understood in terms of the provisions contained in Article 4. These oblige all State Parties to cooperate in areas relevant to climate change – including the development, application and spread of technologies; adaptation; research, and the exchange of information – while imposing specific obligations on developed countries in these areas to help prevent dangerous climate change without perpetuating existing inequalities. Accordingly, the no-harm rule is most appropriately seen as a more general expression of the principles and commitments contained in the UNFCCC. The analysis of the principles and commitments contained in the UNFCCC and its subsidiary instruments underlines the importance of this legal framework for international human rights protection.

The importance of the law of State responsibility for legal responses to climate change-related infringements with human rights follows from its generality and its potential to accommodate various forms of *lex specialis*. Exploring the interrelationships between legal frameworks leads to the conclusion that the law of State responsibility is applicable to the legal framework of the UNFCCC, even though the UNFCCC, the Kyoto Protocol and the Paris Agreement have created platforms for continuous international collaboration on climate change. It is important to

[43] See, eg, *The Effect of Reservations on the Entry into Force of the ACHR (Articles 74 and 75)* (1982) 3 *HRLJ* 153, 2 IACtHR (Ser A); *Austria v Italy* and *Ireland v United Kingdom.*

[44] *Marino López et al. v Colombia.*

highlight that this law applies not only to specific procedural obligations but also to broad substantive obligations that emanate from the principles and commitments of the UNFCCC. Indeed, the specificity of the provisions that give rise to the obligations is immaterial as long as it can be established through evidence that the State acted contrary to its obligations. If a breach of a State's obligations can indeed be established, then the responsibility of that State is automatically activated, imposing obligations of cessation and reparations on the responsible State that complement their already existing obligations.

One practical difference between the respective legal frameworks of the UNFCCC and international human rights law is that the framework of the latter entitles individuals and sometimes other non-State actors to invoke the responsibility of a State for violations of international law, whereas the former does not. Moreover, neither the UNFCCC nor its subsidiary treaties create a body of adjudication. The implication is that the formal change in the legal relationship between States caused by a breach of international climate change law will only have a practical effect when another State invokes this law through the traditional framework of State responsibility, 'as between the States'. In other words, the invoking State must give notice of a claim of State responsibility to the allegedly responsible State.[45] Yet the probability that a State would resort to this diplomatically crude 'mechanism' of State responsibility is low in cases where a breach of obligations is not immediately apparent. This creates a potential stalemate where ambiguity as to the exact meaning of obligations (normally resolved through judicial interpretation) makes it difficult for a State to identify a violation. However, the chances that States will resort to enforcement by invoking the responsibility of another State are bound to increase as the severity of climate change risks and damage are becoming more apparent.[46] The remainder of this book will demonstrate that the specific

[45] International Law Commission's Articles on the Responsibility of States for Internationally Wrongful Acts, Arts 43 and 48. Art 43(2) suggests that the invoking State may specify the allegedly wrongful conduct and request reparations but is not required to do so.

[46] In relation to climate change liability see generally Brunnée, Goldberg et al. talk about a 'risk quadrant' on which the future significance of change liability may depend: on the one axe of the quadrant is the future extent of climate change damage; on the other axe is the effectiveness of the regulatory response. See Jutta Brunnée et al, 'Policy Considerations' in Richard Lord et al (eds), *Climate Change Liability: Transnational Law and Practice* (Cambridge, Cambridge University Press, 2012) 63. See also Joyeeta Gupta, 'Legal Steps Outside the Climate Convention: Litigation as a Tool to Address Climate Change' (2007) 16 *Review of European Comparative and International Environmental Law* 76; David B Hunter, 'The Implications of Climate Change Litigation' in William CG Burns and Hari M Osofsky (eds), *Adjudicating Climate Change: State, National, and International Approaches* (Cambridge, Cambridge University Press, 2009); and Jacob David Werksman, 'Could a Small Island Successfully Sue a Big Emitter? Pursuing a Legal Theory and a Venue for Climate Justice' in Michael B Gerrard and Gregory E Wannier (eds), *Threatened Island Nations: Legal Implications of Rising Seas and a Changing Climate* (Cambridge, Cambridge Uuniversity Press, 2012). On human rights-based climate change litigation specifically see Eric A Posner, 'Climate Change and International Human Rights Litigation: A Critical Appraisal' (2007) 155 *University of Pennsylvania Law Review* 1925 (focusing on litigation under the Alien Tort Statute and arguing that for principled, jurisdictional and pragmatic reasons 'it is unlikely that American courts can provide remedies that are economically sound and politically acceptable' [to plaintiffs who argue that 'major emitters of greenhouse gases have violated rights to life and health by contributing to environmental and health injuries associated with global warming']).

standards of international human rights law, now consolidated through the interpretation of human rights treaties, can help to close the apparently widening accountability gap in international climate change law. It peruses States' obligations under specific provisions of international human rights law, after examining the general rules for attributing potentially wrongful conduct to States. Based on the rules of attribution and substantive human rights norms, conclusions can be drawn about the potential wrongfulness of action or inaction that contributes to negative effects of climate change on the enjoyment of human rights and the legal consequences thereof.

PART II

State Responsibility and Remedies for Violations

6

Attributing Climate Change-Related Conduct to States

Introduction

This chapter sets out how conduct relating to climate change is attributed to States under general international law and international human rights law. Specific attention is placed on the rules of causation and joint liability, given that virtually all States are involved in conduct leading to climate change while the resulting damage is remote and indivisible. The chapter shows that from an international law perspective, causation and joint liability are not the obstacles to establishing State responsibility that they may at first seem to be.

The Rules on Attribution

Although international human rights law may sometimes require a modified application of the principles of State responsibility, its rules on attribution are overwhelmingly compatible with, if not identical to, the rules of attribution contained in the general law of State responsibility.[1] The rules on attribution exist because States can rarely, if ever, guarantee the conduct of all private persons or entities on its territory.[2] Understanding how these rules apply to the substantive norms discussed in chapters 2 and 3 is essential for understanding questions of State responsibility for human rights violations associated with climate change. After all, a large proportion of the greenhouse gases that cause climate change are emitted

[1] One exceptional case is Art 1 of the Convention Against Torture, which specifies that torture is attributed to a State only 'when such pain or suffering is inflicted by or at the instigation of or with the consent or acquiescence of a public official or other person acting in an official capacity'. It may also be argued that the Committee on Economic, Social and Cultural Rights (CESCR) sought to create a special rule of attribution with its notion of 'minimum core obligations', the breach of which would be apparent from, eg, a lack of access to essential drugs (*General Comment No. 14: The Right to the Highest Attainable Standard of Health (Art 12)* (11 August 2000), UN Doc E/C12/2000/4, CESCR) or to water facilities and services (*General Comment No. 15: The Right to Water* (29 Nov 2002), UN Doc E/C12/2002/11, CESCR, para 37). However, in the view of the present author this concept reflects the CESCR's (then sole) focus on the examination of State reports and is not to be considered a special rule of attribution.

[2] James R Crawford, 'The ILC's Articles on Responsibility of States for Internationally Wrongful Acts: a Retrospect' (2002) 96 *American Journal of International Law* 874, 879.

by entities other than States: corporations that exploit fossil fuels, utility companies that produce electricity, enterprises that manufacture products, airlines and car companies that allow travel, and producers and consumers who supply and demand these products and services. An analysis of the rules of attribution will clarify in what circumstances conduct contributing to climate change is directly or indirectly attributable to States, thus paving the way for an in-depth analysis of substantive rules based on which State responsibility for human rights violations associated with climate change can be established.

The rules on attribution are expressed in Articles 4–11 of the International Law Commission's Articles on the Responsibility of States for Internationally Wrongful Acts (ILC ARS). None of these rules contain a causal requirement.[3] This is a deliberate omission, which was discussed by the ILC in relation to the question whether the occurrence of damage or injury should be a precondition for an internationally wrongful act. Special Rapporteur Ago put forward the argument that damage or injury should be a precondition for wrongful conduct, but only for obligations characterised by Ago as 'obligations of result'. Ago proposed making a distinction between those obligations from 'obligations of conduct', which could be breached irrespective of whether damage occurs.[4] Yet the distinction proved to be a simplistic and, for the purposes of the ILC ARS, superfluous categorisation of obligations. As Crawford later pointed out, some 'conduct-based obligations are breached through a combination of a failure to act and the occurrence of a prohibited consequence, whereas other conduct-based obligations might be breached without the occurrence of any damage ('as a matter of pure luck')'.[5] This led the ILC to conclude that the precise requirements for wrongfulness to occur must be determined through the examination of the primary rules,[6] and hence to the deletion of all references to damage and causation from the first part of the ILC ARS.

[3] Art 2 of the ILC ARS does not mention causation at all, and the Commentaries to Part I of the International Law Commission's Articles on the Responsibility of States for Internationally Wrongful Acts (ILC ARS) ('The Internationally Wrongful Act of a State') clarify that the establishment of State responsibility does not necessarily involve establishing causation. The Commentaries do mention causation in Part II ('Content of the International Responsibility of a State') in the context of reparations that must be made when an internationally wrongful act has already been established. See James Crawford, *The International Law Commission' s Articles on State Responsibility: Introduction, Text, Commentaries* (Cambridge, Cambridge University Press, 2002), 295. For this reason this author respectfully disagrees with Malgosia Fitzmaurice, 'International Responsibility and Liability' in Daniel Bodansky, Jutta Brunnée and Ellen Hey (eds), *The Oxford Handbook of International Environmental Law* (Oxford, Oxford University Press, 2007) 1018 stating that the Commentary to Art 31 of the ILC ARS 'describes the link that must exist between the wrongful act and the injury *in order for state responsibility to arise* as a sufficient causal link, which is not too remote' (emphasis added).

[4] Roberto Ago, First Report on State Responsibility – Review of Previous Work on Codification of the Topic of the International Responsibility of States, UN Doc A/CN.4/SERA/1969/Add.1 (Yearbook of the International Law Commission, 1969) 132.

[5] James R Crawford, 'Revising the Draft Articles on State Responsibility' (1999) 10 *European Journal of International Law* 435, 441.

[6] This point has been emphasised by other several other authors. See, eg, Léon Castellanos-Jankiewicz, *Causation and International State Responsibility* (Amsterdam Centre for International Law, SHARES Series 2012), and Richard SJ Tol and Roda Verheyen, 'State Responsibility and Compensation for Climate Change Damages: a Legal and Economic Assessment' (2009) 32 *Energy Policy* 1112.

The general rule of attribution is now contained in Article 4 (entitled 'Conduct of organs of a State'), which provides that 'The conduct of any organ shall be considered an act of that State under international law, whether the organ exercises legislative, executive, judicial or any other functions, whatever position it holds in the organisation of the State, and whatever its character as an organ of the central Government or of a territorial unit of the State'.[7] As suggested above, these rules operate similarly, if not identically, in international human rights law: the HRC, for example, has found violations of the Covenant that were attributable to central government and its legislature, federal governments, municipal authorities, judicial authorities, police and security forces and various types of State agents.[8] The Commentaries clarify that the reference to a State organ in Article 4 extends to organs of government 'of whatever kind or classification, exercising whatever functions, and at whatever level in the hierarchy…'.[9] The type of conduct that is generally attributable to a State as a consequence of these rules includes national legislation, decisions of the judiciary or administrative measures.[10] The conduct of a person or entity that is not a government agent or organ but nonetheless exercises governmental authority must also be attributed to the State (Article 5).[11] This is true even if the organ or agent exceeds its authority or contravenes instructions (Article 7).[12] The practice of human rights bodies also reflects these special rules; for example, the HRC has considered that the conduct of persons or entities empowered to exercise elements of governmental authority is attributable to the State.[13] Other special rules of attribution are contained in ILC ARS articles on the conduct of organs placed at the disposal of a State by another State (Article 6), the conduct of private actors directed or controlled by a State (Article 8), conduct carried out in the absence or default of the official authorities (Article 9), conduct of an insurrectional or similar type (Article 10), and conduct acknowledged and adopted by a State as its own (Article 11).

Some commentators have identified the rules contained in Articles 8 and 11 of the ILC ARS as particularly relevant for establishing State responsibility in the context of climate change. The rule in Article 8 provides that the conduct of

[7] ILC ARS, Art 4(2) clarifies that 'An organ includes any person or entity which has that status in accordance with the internal law of the State'. See also Richard B Lillich et al, 'Attribution Issues in State Responsibility' (1990) 84 *Proceedings of the Annual Meeting (American Society of International Law)* 51, 52 (pointing out that the principle that 'a state may act through its own independent failure of duty or inaction when an international obligation requires state action in relation to non-State conduct' is reflected in all codifications and restatements of the law on State responsibility).

[8] Dominic McGoldrick, 'State Responsibility and the International Covenant on Civil and Political Rights' in Malgosia Fitzmaurice and Dan Sarooshi (eds), *Issues of State Responsibility Before International Judicial Institutions* (Oxford, Bloomsbury Publishing, 2004) fnn 74–83 and accompanying text, containing citations.

[9] ILC ARS, Commentary to Art 4, para 5.

[10] Ibid.

[11] Ibid Art 5.

[12] Ibid Art 7.

[13] McGoldrick (n 8).

a person or group of persons acting either on the instruction of, or under the direction or control of, a State will be directly attributable to that State.[14] Article 11 allows for the attribution of conduct of private actors to a State if it 'acknowledges or adopts the conduct as its own'.[15] Verheyen argues that a State may exercise effective control over polluting activities carried out by private actors (Article 8) as well as adopting such conduct as its own by 'approving such private conduct through active (permitting) policies' (Article 11).[16] Although this argument appears to make sense, it is ultimately not convincing: interpreting the rules this broadly would make virtually all private conduct directly attributable to States. It also seems far-fetched to argue that polluting activities carried out by companies, individuals and other private actors are 'directed' or 'approved of' by States in the sense of Articles 8 and 11 where attribution might be established in accordance with the general rule reflected in Article 4.

However, it is not necessary to attribute the conduct of emission-producing private actors to States in order to establish State responsibility for climate change damage (or associated human rights violations). The crux here is that the general rule of attribution reflected in Article 4 of the ILC ARS allows omissions to be attributed to States (ie a failure on the part of the State's organs or agents to carry out an international obligation).[17] This rule is particularly important for establishing human rights violations associated with climate change, as international human rights law imposes a wide range of 'positive obligations' on States (discussed in more detail in chapter seven). The Commentaries to the ILC ARS stress that 'Cases in which the international responsibility of a State has been invoked on the basis of an omission are at least as numerous as those based on positive acts, and no difference in principle exists between the two'.[18] The Commentaries clarify that an 'act of a State' 'must involve some action or omission by a human being or group … What is crucial is that a given event is sufficiently connected to conduct (whether an act or omission)

[14] The Commentaries suggest that this rule embodies two rules of custom: the first relating to the conduct of persons acting under the instructions of States, such as 'auxiliaries' or 'volunteers' recruited or instigated by a State to carry out 'particular missions' abroad, the second relating to private persons acting under the direction or control of a State in situations where the State directed or approved of the allegedly wrongful activities. The second rule is based on *Military and Paramilitary Activities in and against Nicaragua (Nicaragua v United States of America)* [1986] ICJ Reports 14, para 86. See ILC ARS, Commentary to Art 8, paras 2–4.

[15] ILC ARS, Art 11, paras 3–4 of the Commentary clarifies that this rule has been applied only in exceptional cases, especially those related to State succession (where a successor State adopted conduct of the predecessor State) and in *United States Diplomatic and Consular Staff in Tehran (Judgement)* [1980] ICJ Reports 3, 35 (where Iran's subsequent unequivocal and unqualified 'approval' of the conduct of militants who attacked the US Embassy in Tehran gave the approval retroactive effect, thus making this private conduct directly attributable to Iran).

[16] Roda Verheyen, *Climate Change Damage and International Law: Prevention Duties and State Responsibility* (Leiden, Martinus Nijhoff, 2005) 239.

[17] This formulation was used in Art 1 of the Outcome Document of the Third Committee of the 1930 Hague Conference, reproduced in Yearbook of the United Nations 1956, vol II, Document A/CN.4/96, 225, Annex 3.

[18] Crawford (n 3) 35 and Commentary to Art 2, para 4.

which is attributable to the State.'[19] For example, in *Corfu Channel (UK v Albania)*,[20] Albania was held responsible for the consequences of mines that had been laid in its territorial waters, not for the act of laying mines (which was not attributable to it), but based on its failure to mitigate or eliminate the danger.[21] This case also illustrates an important practical consequence of the general rule of attribution, namely that where a wrongful act consists of an omission, the question of attribution may become evidentially indistinguishable from the question whether the State has complied with the substantive obligation. The ILC ARS Commentaries confirm that establishing the standards for determining whether or not a breach of obligation has occurred 'is a matter for the interpretation and application of the primary rules engaged in the given case'.[22]

Sir Ian Brownlie has pointed out that the wrongfulness of an omission that causes harm to another State can usually be established without specifying which organ or agent should have carried out the acts, based on the understanding that it is often 'impossible to specify which officials or organs were the source of the harm'.[23] This practice safeguards the effectiveness of the international legal system, and can be seen as an application of the principle of effectiveness.[24] Reflecting the importance of this principle in the human rights context, attribution is rarely considered separately when the allegedly wrongful conduct is a State's failure to prevent the violation of a human right or rights. At the practical level, this is because human rights norms exist, at least in part, to protect individuals against State abuse,[25] and the State (in the words of the Inter-American Court of Human Rights (IACtHR)) 'controls the means to verify acts occurring within its territory'.[26] At the normative level, it reflects the importance of the principle that a State will exercise its legislative, regulatory or other functions in a way that is consistent with its human rights obligations. An example is the European Court of Human Rights (ECtHR) case *Young, James and Webster v UK*.[27] This dealt with interference with the right to associate (Article 11 of the ECHR) resulting from British Rail policies. The applicants claimed that British Rail was controlled by the government and therefore its allegedly wrongful conduct was attributable to the State.[28] In deciding the case, the Court thought it unnecessary to establish whether or not the acts of British Rail were attributable to the State, based on its observation that 'it was the

[19] Ibid Commentary to Art 2, paras 5–6.

[20] *Corfu Channel Case (United Kingdom v Albania)* (Merits) [1949] ICJ Rep 4.

[21] Ibid 23 ('These grave … omissions involve the international responsibility of Albania [which] is responsible under international law for the explosions which occurred … and for the damage and loss of human life which resulted from them').

[22] ILC ARS, Commentary to Art 2, para 3.

[23] Ian Brownlie, *State Responsibility* (Oxford, Oxford University Press, 1983) 151.

[24] Crawford (n 3) Commentary to Art 8, para 1.

[25] Dinah Shelton, 'Protecting Human Rights in a Globalized World' (2002) 25 *Boston College International and Comparative Law Review* 273.

[26] *Velásquez Radríguez v Honduras* (1988) 95 ILR 232; IACtHR (Ser C) No 4, para 136.

[27] *Young, James and Webster v UK* Series A no 44 (1982), 4 EHRR 38.

[28] Ibid para 52.

domestic law in force at the relevant time that made lawful the treatment of which the applicants complained'.[29] The obligation to secure the rights contained in the ECHR (Article 1) involved an obligation to secure those rights in the enactment of national legislation, and thus the State was responsible for any breach of the Convention that resulted from the enactment of this national law.[30]

In relation to climate change, we must emphasise that even if it is difficult to differentiate between questions of attribution and breach, this does not affect the basic principle that attributable conduct is only wrongful if it breaches an international obligation. The distinction between attribution and breach remains important precisely because the generality of the rule of attribution reflected in Article 4 means that an extremely broad range of conduct linked with climate change may be attributable to States. First, and perhaps most importantly, a potential source of evidence for attributable conduct is the information reported by States themselves to the COP, the CMP and the CMA. As noted above, this information is submitted in accordance with a legal obligation imposed on all State Parties to the UNFCCC to 'Develop, periodically update, publish and make available to the Conference of the Parties … national inventories of anthropogenic emissions by sources and removals by sinks of all greenhouse gases not controlled by the Montreal Protocol, using comparable methodologies'.[31] Under the Kyoto Protocol, Annex I parties (listed in Annex B) are obliged to report supplementary information relating to their national greenhouse gas inventories and participation in market mechanisms.[32] Finally, the system of Nationally Determined Contributions (NDCs) established under the Paris Agreement, discussed in chapter three, requires State Parties not only to prepare, communicate and maintain NDCs, but also to report on progress towards their achievement.[33] Moreover, the Paris Agreement requires that States provide information about support provided and received in the context of mitigation, adaptation, technology development and transfer and capacity building.[34] In relation to mitigation obligations, it is worth emphasising that under the UNFCCC as well as its subsidiary treaties, State Parties account for emissions produced by public as well as private actors.[35]

[29] Ibid para 49.

[30] Ibid.

[31] United Nations Framework Convention on Climate Change (adopted 9 May 1992, entered into force 19 June 1993) 1771 UNTS 107 (UNFCCC), Art 1(a).

[32] Kyoto Protocol to the United Nations Framework Convention on Climate Change (adopted 11 December 1997, entered into force 16 February 2005) 1771 UNTS 107 (Kyoto Protocol), Art 7(1).

[33] UNFCCC, 'Paris Agreement' (adopted 12 December 2015, entered into force 4 November 2016) UN Doc FCCC/CP/2015/L.9/Rev.1 (Paris Agreement), Art 13(5).

[34] Ibid Art 13(6).

[35] Two possibly exceptional cases are aviation and marine bunker fuels, and 'emissions resulting from multilateral operations pursuant to the Charter of the United Nations'. It debateable whether aviation and marine bunker fuels are attributable to Annex I States: on the one hand, there is an obligation to report these emissions, but on the other hand, they are not included in national totals. 'Report of the Conference of the Parties on its third session', Dec 1/cp.2, UN Doc FCCC/CP/1997/7/Add.1 (25 March 1998) 31. We could argue that this construction signals the limited scope of obligations of the UNFCCC, rather than non-attributability of these emissions. This interpretation is supported by

This suggests that international climate change law contains a special rule of attribution for reported emission-producing activities of States. At a more general level, examples of potentially attributable acts include government interventions such as payment of subsidies and tax concessions for coal power plants, exploration and development of fossil fuels, and activities that facilitate such exploration and development.[36] The export of oil, gas and coal are other examples of acts that might be attributable to States, either directly or (more likely) through the act of issuing permits and licences.[37] Attributable conduct could also consist of a State's failure to enforce its own national law, including decisions of domestic courts,[38] or to uphold international standards related to environmental protection[39] or international cooperation and assistance.

The scope for attribution is extended even further through the rule that an internationally wrongful act may consist of several acts and omissions that cumulatively amount to a breach of obligations.[40] In the ILC ARS, this is expressed in Article 15 which states that State responsibility can arise from a 'breach consisting of a composite act'.[41] The breach has to extend over the entire period 'starting with the first of the actions or omissions of the series and lasts for as long as these actions or omissions are repeated and remain not in conformity with the international obligation'.[42] Verheyen has argued that in accordance with this rule,

Art 2(2) of the Kyoto Protocol, which provides that 'The Parties included in Annex I shall pursue limitation or reduction of emissions of greenhouse gases not controlled by the Montreal Protocol from aviation and marine bunker fuels, working through the International Civil Aviation Organization and the International Maritime Organization, respectively'. This provision shows that the exclusion of this category from national totals regards delegation to another treaty regime rather than an assumption against attribution. In other words, we could argue that all emissions reported to the Conference of the Parties are attributable to the State for the purpose of establishing State responsibility. This does not, of course, in itself trigger the international responsibility of the State unless a breach of obligation is established.

[36] Although OECD countries have gradually cut back these subsidies, OECD subsidies for fossil-fuel energy still averaged US$20–22 billion per year in 2008. For a comparative discussion see United Nations Development Programme, *Fighting Climate Change: Human Solidarity in a Divided World* (Human Development Report 2007/2008) 128.

[37] Christian Tomuschat, 'Global Warming and State Responsibility' in Holger Hestermeyer et al (eds), *Law of the Sea in Dialogue* (Berlin, Springer, 2011) 9.

[38] See eg *Okyay et al. v Turkey* App no 36220/97 (ECtHR, 12 July 2005) para 74.

[39] See eg *Oneryildiz v Turkey* App no 48939/99 (ECtHR GC, 30 Nov 2004) para 71.

[40] *Paul and Audrey Edwards v United Kingdom* (App 46477/99) Judgement of 14 March 2002; (2002) 35 EHRR 487 (on the cumulative failure of several public agencies including doctors, the police, the courts and the Crown Prosecution Service that amounted to a breach of obligations under Art 2 of the ECHR).

[41] ILC ARS, Art 15(1). This provides that 'The breach of an international obligation by a State through a series of actions or omission occurs which, taken with the other actions or omissions, is sufficient to constitute the wrongful act'.

[42] ILC ARS, Art 15(2). See also *Ireland v United Kingdom* Series A no 25 (1978) 2 EHRR 25, para 159, in which the ECtHR discussed the concept of a 'practice incompatible with the Convention'. It found that such a practice 'consists of an accumulation of identical or analogous breaches which are sufficiently numerous and inter-connected to amount not merely to isolated incidents or exceptions but to a pattern or system; a practice does not of itself constitute a violation separate from such breaches'. The significance of the concept here was its effect on the applicability of the rule of exhaustion of domestic

State responsibility could arise for climate change damage 'where the cumulative behaviour of a State does not conform to a standard of care for preventing damage or the risk thereof, in the context of the no harm rule'.[43] This argument seems convincing, with the caveat that the no-harm rule would need to be analysed in conjunction with the *lex specialis* of the UNFCCC when it is applied in the context of climate change. In the context of human rights, the rule supports the conclusion drawn in chapter two that a 'contextual analysis' of a State's conduct and the obligations by which it is bound is the most appropriate method for determining whether a human rights violation has occurred. Such an analysis could take account of a range of conduct as attributable to the State – from information reported to the COP, CMP or CMA to its national legislation and regulatory framework, energy subsidies, trade policies and the extent of assistance provided and received in accordance with technology transfer and financial obligations – to determine whether the totality of this conduct is in accordance with its international human rights obligations. The next section demonstrates that this approach is equally suitable for establishing violations of international law in cases of joint or collective conduct.

Responsibility and Involvement of Multiple States

Seeing that anthropogenic climate change is generated by human action and inaction attributable to multiple States, it is important to understand how the rules of attribution apply to States acting jointly or collectively. Article 47 of the ILC ARS codifies the rule that applies joint or collective conduct, stating that 'Where several States are responsible for the same internationally wrongful act, the responsibility of each State may be invoked in relation to that act'.[44] The Commentary to Article 47 emphasises that the responsibility of other States for the same act does not diminish or reduce the responsibility of individual States, reflecting the basic principle that States are individually and independently responsible for any breaches of their international obligations. Thus, although Article 47 is concerned with invoking responsibility rather than establishing it, it implies that conduct, including wrongful conduct, can be attributed to multiple States simultaneously.[45]

remedies embodied in Art 26 of the Convention. The Court found that the rule did not apply where 'an applicant State complains of a practice as such, with the aim of preventing its continuation or recurrence, but does not ask the Commission or Court to give a decision on each of the cases put forward as proof or illustration of that practice'.

[43] Verheyen (n 16) 236.

[44] ILC ARS, Art 47.

[45] It is worth noting that Art 48(1) of the ARIO suggests that this principle extends to wrongful acts committed by international organisations, or by international organisations and one or more States. See Articles on the Responsibility of International Organizations, *Report of the ILC on the Work of its 63rd session*, Official Records of the General Assembly, 55th session, Supplement No 10, UN Doc A/66/10 (2011) ('Where an international organization and one or more States or other international organizations are responsible for the same internationally wrongful act, the responsibility of each State or organization may be invoked in relation to that act').

This is an important rule of attribution, as it implies that State responsibility can arise, for example, from the actions of States acting collectively in negotiations and decision-making under the UNFCCC. Reference to the 'sameness' of the wrongful act indicates that the Article does not apply to joint conduct that amounts to a different wrongful act for each State (eg as a result of different obligations of respective States). The reason is probably simple, namely that the usual rules of attribution apply to these situations. Article 47 can be understood as a clarification to the effect that the usual rules also apply to joint wrongful conduct, which is accordingly no more and no less than internationally wrongful acts for which States are individually and independently responsible.[46]

The *Corfu Channel* case is a textbook example of conduct involving multiple States, which led to the establishment of a separate internationally wrongful act of one State based on its own obligations. As already noted, Albania was held to have committed an internationally wrongful act, based on its knowledge of the mines and its failure to warn foreign vessels so as to prevent the risk of death and injury.[47] The fact that another State appeared to have been responsible for laying the mines that caused the damage did not affect, let alone diminish, Albania's responsibility.[48] The *Soering* case illustrates that the principle of independent responsibility operates similarly in cases of alleged violations of international human rights law involving multiple States: the ECtHR held that the United Kingdom was responsible for a violation of Article 3 of the ECHR based on the Court's finding that exposure to the so-called 'death row phenomenon', a form of inhuman or degrading treatment or punishment, was a foreseeable consequence of the applicant's extradition to the United States.[49] The fact that the United States, and not the United Kingdom, would be responsible for directly inflicting the treatment did not affect the United Kingdom's responsibility for a violation of its own obligation under Article 3.[50]

A case where the rule expressed in Article 47 applies occurred in *Certain Phosphate Lands in Nauru*.[51] Here Australia had challenged the admissibility of the claim against it, based on the argument that its alleged international responsibility was inseparably linked with the responsibility of two other States, the

[46] Exceptions to this general rule are 'aid or assistance' (Art 16) and direction or control (Art 17), which can trigger the responsibility of a State for the wrongful conduct of another State.

[47] *Corfu Channel Case (UK v Albania)* 4.

[48] The United Kingdom alleged that the mines had been laid by Yugoslavia, but this was not proven. Ibid 16–17. See also James Crawford, *State Responsibility: The General Part* (Cambridge, Cambridge University Press, 2013) 335.

[49] *Soering v UK* Series A no 161 (1989) 11 EHRR 439. See also *Cruz Varas et al. v Sweden* App no 15576/89 (ECtHR 20 March 1991); *Vilvarajah and Others v United Kingdom* App nos 13163/87; 13164/87; 13165/87; 13447/87; 13448/87 (ECtHR, 30 October 1991) and the more recent cases *Al Nashiri v Poland* App no 28761/11 (ECtHR GC, 24 July 2014); and *Husayn (Abu Zubaydah) v Poland* App no 7511/13 (ECtHR GC, 24 July 2014).

[50] *Soering v UK*, para 86 (stating that the fact that the United Kingdom had no power over the practices and arrangements of the Virginia authorities could not absolve the United Kingdom from responsibility under Art 3 'for all and any foreseeable consequences of extradition suffered outside [its] jurisdiction').

[51] *Corfu Channel Case (UK v Albania).*

United Kingdom and New Zealand, over which the Court had no jurisdiction. The ICJ rejected Australia's argument but was willing to consider the case on its merits, emphasising the principle of independent responsibility.[52] Another example is *Mox Plant (Ireland v United Kingdom)*, where the International Tribunal for the Law of the Sea (ITLOS) order for provisional measures indicated that the parties' failure to cooperate to exchange information and to find measures to prevent harm being caused by the proposed project could constitute a violation of the duty to cooperate to ensure the protection of the marine environment.[53] This order not only implies that the violation of obligations to cooperate with other States may give rise to the 'parallel' responsibility of multiple States, but is also one of the clearest illustrations of enforceable rights derived from such obligations.

In passing, it is worth noting that some human rights scholars have advocated the introduction of a principle of joint and several liability to address cases of indivisible damage caused by joint State conduct, such as regional biofuel policies and agricultural subsidies.[54] The ICJ itself stated in *Certain Phosphate Lands in Nauru* that 'a rule of joint and several responsibility … should certainly exist as a matter of principle',[55] adding that it should 'be developed internationally rather than drawn from municipal analogies'. The wisdom of this statement is perhaps clear from the dissenting opinion of Judge Simma in *Islamic Republic of Iran v United States of America (Oil Platforms)*,[56] which stated that the generic counterclaim of the United States against Iran should have been upheld despite the fact that some of the allegedly wrongful acts may have been carried out by Iraq, and not by Iran. Judge Simma found that it would be 'more objectionable not to hold Iran liable than to hold Iran liable for the entire damage caused … even though it did not directly cause it all',[57] and found that it was possible to hold Iran responsible because 'the principle of joint-and-several responsibility … can properly be regarded as a "general principle of law" within the meaning of Article 38, paragraph 1 (c), of the Court's Statute'.[58]

[52] *Certain Phosphate Lands in Nauru (Nauru v Australia) (Preliminary Objections)* [1992] ICJ Reports 240, 258–59; *Corfu Channel Case (UK v Albania)*, 301.

[53] *Mox Plant Case (Ireland v United Kingdom) (Provisional measures)* International Tribunal of the Law of the Sea; [2001] 41 ILM 405.

[54] Discussed in Margot E Salomon, 'Deprivation, Causation, and the Law of International Cooperation' in Malcolm Langford et al (eds), *Global Justice, State Duties: The Extraterritorial Scope of Economic, Social and Cultural Rights in International Law* (Cambridge, Cambridge University Press, 2013) 311. See also reports and statements of the UN Special Rapporteur on the Right to Food; eg Contribution of the Special Rapporteur on the right to food to the 17th session of the UN Commission on Sustainable Development (4–15 May 2009) available at www.srfood.org.

[55] *Certain Phosphate Lands in Nauru (Nauru v Australia) (Preliminary Objections)* [1992] ICJ Rep 240, 554 (citing Ian Brownlie, *Principles of Public International Law*, 3rd edn (New York, Oxford University Press, 1979) 456).

[56] *Case Concerning Oil Platforms (Islamic Republic of Iran v United States of America) (Separate Opinion of Judge Simma)* [2003] ICJ Rep 161.

[57] Ibid para 73.

[58] Ibid para 74.

In relation to this, at the outset is that Judge Simma used a questionable methodology for ascertaining a general principle of law, namely a comparative analysis of relevant tort law in only five jurisdictions.[59] Secondly, and perhaps more importantly, we can observe that Judge Simma could have reached the conclusion that Iran was responsible for violating the relevant treaty provision without resorting to private law analogies. The crux of the matter lies in Judge Simma's observation that the treaty provision, which protected the parties' freedom of commerce, imposed a prohibition on the parties to prevent each other's use of existing capabilities to engage in commerce, also in the future.[60] Although Simma did not say so, it is clear from his opinion that he considered that this treaty provision could be breached through a pattern of conduct (ie what Article 15 of the ILC ARS calls a 'composite act'). This meant that 'the particular extent to which Iran was responsible for separate acts that were potentially wrongful [did not need] to be determined with precision'.[61] Instead, what needed to be established, according to the judge, was that 'Iran, because of the Iran–Iraq war, was responsible for a significant portion of those actions, and that such actions impaired the freedom of commerce between the United States and Iran guaranteed by the 1955 Treaty in ways not justifiable simply because of the existence of a state of war'.[62] The implicit point here seems to be that the 'significant portion of those actions' would amount to a composite act that violated the treaty provision that was binding on Iran. Simma's subsequent point that the lack of certainty as to the potential attribution of some specific activities to Iran (and not Iraq) constituted an obstacle to establishing responsibility seems to contradict his own finding that Iran had breached its obligation through the 'significant portion of the actions' in which both Iran and Iraq were engaged, and which impaired the freedom of commerce. The flip side of this analysis is that if the finding of State responsibility were not actually supported by evidence regarding Iran's responsibility, the finding would not have been justifiable under existing international law.

Overall, the analysis of the rules of international law relating to joint or collective conduct confirms that inconclusive evidence about attribution is not a bar to establishing State responsibility for human rights violations associated with climate change. The direct or indirect involvement of multiple States in the activities that cause climate change does not pose an obstacle to redress either, as under general international law each State is responsible for its own conduct. It is worth recalling here that State responsibility can be established not only based on specific wrongful acts, but also based on acts and omissions of a State that are wrongful in the aggregate. In addition, we should recall that some rules and principles relevant to climate change, such as the precautionary principle, could shift the burden of

[59] Ibid.
[60] Ibid para 26.
[61] Ibid para 60.
[62] Ibid.

proof to a State whose international responsibility is invoked by a beneficiary of the obligation or by another State based on a claim that the State has failed to comply with obligations to prevent harm. This means that even the *absence* of evidence could sometimes substantiate or consolidate a State responsibility claim connected with the human rights implications of climate change. In such cases, questions of attribution would only be dealt with implicitly, as part of the assessment of a State's compliance with its substantive obligations. This conclusion paves the way for an examination of the substantive content of States' obligations related to specific human rights in the light of the facts related to climate change.

7

Establishing Violations of Human Rights Affected by Climate Change

Chapter six has shown that a wide range of climate change-related conduct is attributable to States under international law. Attributable conduct includes a failure to take adequate action to respond to climate change, insofar as an obligation exists to take specific action. Whether or not a State can be held responsible for climate change-related human rights violations therefore depends on the content of the human rights obligations that are binding on the State in question. Nevertheless, States' human rights obligations to respond to climate change are not yet well understood. This chapter attempts to unpack these obligations through an analysis of substantive human rights norms as expressed in treaties and spelt out in human rights jurisprudence. The chapter also examines how the effectiveness of international human rights law can be enhanced by taking the framework of the United Nations Framework Convention on Climate Change (UNFCCC) into account when assessing compliance with human rights obligations.

Human rights obligations are to a large extent rights-specific and delimited by human rights law itself. Thus, this chapter considers obligations derived from four specific rights, each representing a different category of rights: the right of self-determination (a group right); the right to life (a civil and political right); the right to enjoy one's culture (a cultural right); and the right to the highest attainable standard of health (an economic and social right). All four of these rights are contained in the International Bill of Rights, and their content has been clarified through the jurisprudence of regional as well as international human rights bodies, including the UN Human Rights Committee (HRC), and the UN Committee on Economic, Social and Cultural Rights (CESCR). For each right, this chapter addresses five questions. First, how is the enjoyment of this right affected by climate change? Second, how is the right protected under international law? Third, who are the beneficiaries of the right? Fourth, what are States' obligations associated with the right? Fifth, what do these obligations mean in relation to the threats posed by climate change? The chapter then considers how human rights themselves can limit States' obligations to respond to climate change.

The analysis of specific rights demonstrates that international human rights law imposes standards of protection on States, and that these standards can be ascertained by analysing the evidence while taking account of the environmental standards that are already binding on the State.[1] This opens the door to considering States' existing obligations under the UNFCCC, the Kyoto Protocol and the Paris Agreement in order to clarify the content of human rights obligations of States with differing responsibilities for climate change and different capacities to address it. These parallel obligations are particularly important for resolving conflicts between rights, including conflicts between the rights of people within and outside the territory of a particular State. The resolution of such conflicts by reference to States' obligations under international climate change law paves the way for a workable allocation of legal responsibility for human rights violations associated with climate change.

The Right of Self-determination

When it comes to the threats posed by climate change to the enjoyment of human rights, Small Island Developing States (SIDS) are the proverbial canary in the coalmine. The threat is most severe for SIDS such as Kiribati, the Maldives, the Marshall Islands and Tuvalu, whose entire territory consists of one or more atoll islands that are highly vulnerable to rising sea levels, coral bleaching and other climate impacts. For these States, the threat posed by climate change is of an existential nature: scientists project that 'sea-level rise is likely to end the history of many of the low-lying islands, even at 2 degrees Celsius warming'.[2] The Maldives, for example, has informed the Office of the UN High Commissioner for Human Rights (OHCHR), in a submission on the relationship between climate change and human rights, that most of its territory will be under water by 2100 according to conservative scenarios of rising sea levels.[3] The legal implications of a situation where a State's territory can no longer sustain a human population or where it is submerged altogether remain unclear. An extreme implication is that the affected State would lose its statehood; a situation that would have severe implications for the legal rights and cultural identity of its citizens.[4] The prospect of States losing

[1] See also Margaretha Wewerinke-Singh, 'State Responsibility for Human Rights Violations Associated with Climate Change' in Sébastien Jodoin, Sébastien Duyck and Alyssa Johl (eds), *Routledge Handbook of Human Rights and Climate Governance* (Oxford, Routledge, 2018) and Margaretha Wewerinke-Singh, 'Climate Migrants' Right to Culture' in Avidan Kent and Simon Behrman (eds), *Climate Refugees: Beyond the Legal Impasse?* (Oxford, Routledge, 2018) on which parts of this chapter draw.

[2] Katja Frieler et al, 'High Noon for 2 degrees Celsius' (2009) Air Pollution & Climate Secretariat Sweden Environmental Fact Sheet 21, 2, available at www.airclim.org/acidnews/2009/AN3-09/high-noon-2°c. See also Carl-Friedrich Schleussner et al, 'Differential Climate Impacts for Policy-Relevant Limits to Global Warming: the Case of 1.5°C and 2°C' (2016) 7 *Earth System Dynamics* 327, 344.

[3] Republic of the Maldives, 'Submission to the Office of the UN High Commissioner for Human Rights under Resolution 7/23' (25 September 2008) 19, available at www.ohchr.org/Documents/Issues/ClimateChange/Submissions/Maldives_Submission.pdf ('Maldives Submission').

[4] The Montevideo Convention on the Rights and Duties of States (adopted 26 December 1933, entered into force 26 December 1934) 165 LNTS 19, Art 1, lists the following qualifications as prerequisite for statehood: (a) a permanent population; (b) a defined territory; (c) a government; (d) the capacity to enter into relations with other States.

parts or all of their territory also triggers a myriad of legal questions about the States ability to continue using the resources that are now within their Exclusive Economic Zones (EEZ's),[5] with associated consequences for the enjoyment of human rights.

We should note that according to projections many low-lying islands will become gradually uninhabitable well before they are completely inundated. Increased flooding and storm surges, stronger tropical cyclones and the destruction of freshwater resources and cultivable land are already forcing island communities to migrate from their traditional lands.[6] Furthermore, the threat of losing land is not unique to island nations: indigenous peoples and local communities in other regions are similarly faced with the degradation of the environments on which they depend for subsistence. The Inuit people in the Arctic, for example, are already experiencing dramatic social and cultural displacement and dangerous travel conditions as sea ice melts, while the wild animals on which they depend for subsistence are threatened with extinction.[7] In Africa, the cattle-farming Maasai are faced with higher temperatures, erratic rainfall and the disappearance of natural springs, resulting in water and food scarcity and the loss of livestock.[8] In the Andean highlands, indigenous peoples face water shortages and decreased crop yields due to critical levels of inter-tropical glacier retreat.[9] These examples illustrate how the effects of climate change have significant implications for the right of self-determination, with loss of statehood being the most extreme expression of these implications.

Under international law, all States have an obligation to respect and promote the right of self-determination. The right is widely accepted as customary international law,[10] and is cited by several highly qualified jurists as a norm of *jus cogens*.[11]

[5] United Nations Convention on the Law of the Sea (adopted 10 December 1982, entered into force 16 November 1994) 1833 UNTS 3, Arts 55–58. See also Lilian Yamamoto and Miguel Esteban, 'Atoll Island States and Climate Change: Sovereignty Implications', UNU-IAS Working Paper 166, October 2011, available at http://i.unu.edu/media/unu.edu/publication/20972/atoll-island-states-and-climate-change_unu-ias-working-paper-166.pdf.

[6] Yamamoto and Esteban (n 5) 41.

[7] Intergovernmental Panel on Climate Change (IPCC), 'Contribution of Working Group II to the IPCC Fifth Assessment Report' in CB Field et al (eds), *Climate Change 2014: Impacts, Adaptation and Vulnerability* (Geneva, IPCC, 2014) 765; Kevin Watkins et al, 'Human Development Report 2007/2008: Fighting Climate Change: Human Solidarity in a Divided World' (New York, United Nations Development Programme, 2007) 82.

[8] International Work Group for Indigenous Affairs, 'Country Technical Notes on Indigenous' Peoples Issues; The United Republic of Tanzania' (June 2012) 15, available at www.ifad.org/documents/10180/ce1a82cf-9a25-4405-b71e-e3e44394d003.

[9] Elizabeth Willetts, Lorenzo Guadagno and Ninni Ikkala, 'Addressing Climate Change: Issues and Solutions from Around the World' (International Union for the Conservation of Nature, 2010) 20.

[10] *Advisory Opinion on the Legal Consequences for States of the Continued Presence of South Africa in Namibia (South West Africa) Notwithstanding Security Council Resolution 276* [1970] ICJ Reports 1971, esp 31. See also Thomas M Franck, 'The Emerging Right to Democratic Governance' (1992) 86 *American Journal of Iinternational Law* 46.

[11] Ian Brownlie, *Principles of Public International Law*, 5th edn (Oxford, Oxford University Press, 1998) 513; Antonio Cassese, *International Law in a Divided World* (Oxford, Oxford University Press, 1986) 136; Alexandre Kiss, 'The Peoples' Right to Self-determination' (1986) 7 *Human Rights Law Journal* 174; Manfred Nowak, *U.N. Covenant on Civil and Political Rights: CCPR Commentary*, 2nd edn (Kehl am Rhein, NP Engel Publisher, 2004) 8.

As a principle of international law, self-determination has a prominent place in the Charter of the United Nations, which stipulates that one of the UN's goals is to 'develop friendly relations among nations based on respect for the principle of equal rights and self-determination of peoples'.[12] Furthermore, the right was expressed in the *Declaration on the Granting of Independence to Colonial Countries and Peoples*, which called for immediate steps to provide non-independent territories with complete independence and freedom.[13] The subsequent *Declaration on Principles of International Law Concerning Friendly Relations and Co-operation among States in Accordance with the Charter of the United Nations* reflects universal agreement that the right also applies outside the colonial context.[14] The right has also been reiterated in the resolutions of the UN Commission on Human Rights and its successor, the Human Rights Council.[15] The first treaty-based expression of self-determination as a legal right is contained in Article 1 common to the International Covenant on Civil and Political Rights (ICCPR),[16] and the International Covenant on Economic, Social and Cultural Rights (ICESCR)[17] with additional expressions contained in two separate articles of the African Charter on Human and Peoples' Rights (ACHPR or Banjul Charter).[18]

The right of self-determination is a right of peoples and applies, first, to all peoples in non-self-governing territories or territories that are 'geographically separate and … distinct ethnically and/or culturally from the country administering it'.[19] In the colonial context, the right of self-determination is understood as a right of peoples to be granted independence.[20] This was recognised by the International Court of Justice (ICJ) in its Advisory Opinion on Western Sahara,[21] and subsequently considered by the HRC as applicable to the Western Sahara.[22] The text of Article 1 of the ICCPR and ICESCR states, however, that the right extends to 'all peoples' and thus the HRC has clarified that it 'applies to all peoples,

[12] Charter of the United Nations (adopted 26 June 1945, entered into force 24 October 1945) 1 UNTS XVI, Arts 1(2), 55 and 73.

[13] *Declaration on the Granting of Independence to Colonial Countries and Peoples*, GA Res A/Res/1514(XV), (14 December 1960) (adopted by 89 votes to none; 9 abstentions).

[14] *Declaration on the Principles of International Law concerning Friendly Relations and Cooperation among States in accordance with the Charter of the United Nations*, GA Res A/Res/2625(XXV) (24 October 1970) 25 UN GAOR Supp (No 28), (adopted without vote), Annex at 121, UN Doc A/5217.

[15] This is particularly the case with regard to Palestine where an annual resolution on the Palestinians' right to self-determination is adopted.

[16] International Covenant on Civil and Political Rights (adopted 16 December 1966, entered into force 23 March 1976) 999 UNTS 171 (ICCPR).

[17] International Covenant on Economic, Social and Cultural Rights (adopted 16 December 1966, entered into force 3 January 1976) 993 UNTS 3 (ICESCR).

[18] African Charter on Human and Peoples' Rights (adopted 27 June 1981, entered into force 21 October 1986) (1982) 21 ILM 58 (ACHPR), Arts 20 and 21.

[19] GA Res A/Res/1541(XV) (15 December 1960) principle IV.

[20] Nowak (n 11) 23.

[21] *Western Sahara (Advisory Opinion)* [1975] ICJ Rep 12, 59.

[22] UN Human Rights Committee (UNHRC), 'Concluding Observations on Morocco' (1999) UN Doc CCPR/C/79/Add. 113, para 1.

and not merely to colonised peoples'.[23] Commentators consider that the term 'peoples' may be broadly defined as 'a group with a common racial or ethnic identity, or a cultural identity (which could incorporate political, religious, or linguistic elements) built up over a long period of time'.[24] Although the HRC has refrained from proposing a definition of 'peoples', its practice suggests that indigenous peoples may constitute 'peoples' in the sense of Article 1.[25]

In its General Comment No 12, the HRC clarifies that 'the obligations [under Article 1] exist irrespective of whether a people entitled to self-determination depends on a State party to the Covenant'.[26] This view is consistent with the objective nature of human rights obligations, which prohibits an interpretation of human rights law that restricts the scope of States' human rights obligations to particular categories of beneficiaries.[27] Reflecting this view, the OHCHR considers it 'clear' that 'insofar as climate change poses a threat to the right of peoples to self-determination, States have a duty to take positive action, individually and jointly, to address and avert this threat'.[28] Despite this, the OHCHR report on the relationship between climate change and human rights did not draw any conclusions about State responsibility. Instead, it states in rather cautious terms that 'The inundation and disappearance of small island States would have implications for the right to self-determination'.[29] The OHCHR's caution is in sharp contrast to the Maldives, which claims unequivocally that its people's right of self-determination will have been violated in a scenario of 'permanent loss of statehood, without a successor State to take its place'.[30] However, even the Maldives' submission is ambiguous on the question of which State, if any, is legally responsible for the violation. Moreover, it is unclear what impacts other than the loss of statehood, may amount to a violation of the right of self-determination. Answering these questions requires a closer examination of the legal norms that oblige each State to respect and promote this specific right.

We can distinguish three dimensions of the right of self-determination: a political dimension (paragraph 1); a resource dimension (paragraphs 2–4), and a solidarity dimension (paragraph 5).[31] The political dimension entails the right

[23] UNHRC, 'Concluding Comments on Azerbaijan' (1994) UN Doc CCPR/C/79/Add. 38, para 6.

[24] Sarah Joseph, Jenny Schultz and Melissa Castan, *The International Covenant on Civil and Political Rights: Cases, Materials, and Commentary*, 2nd edn (Oxford, Oxford University Press, 2005) 146.

[25] See the discussion below on the right to enjoy a distinct culture.

[26] UNHRC, 'CCPR General Comment No. 12: The Right to Self-Determination of Peoples (Art 1)' (13 March 1984) para 6.

[27] See above ch 2.

[28] Report of the Office of the United Nations High Commissioner for Human Rights on the Relationship between Climate Change and Human Rights (15 January 2009) UN Doc A/HRC/10/61 (OHCHR Report on Climate Change and Human Rights) para 41.

[29] Ibid.

[30] Maldives Submission (n 3) 40.

[31] Martin Scheinin, 'The Right of Self-Determination under the Covenant on Civil and Political Rights' in Pekka Aikio and Martin Scheinin (eds), *Operationalising the Right of Indigenous Peoples to Self-Determination* (Turku, Institute for Human Rights, Åbo Akademi University, 2000).

of all peoples to determine their political status free from national or external interference,[32] and imposes an obligation on States to take into account 'the freely expressed will of peoples'.[33] The right implies thus different levels of entitlement and political emancipation, depending on the circumstances.[34] Moreover, it 'implies that all peoples have the right to determine … their place in the international community based upon the principle of equal rights and exemplified by the liberation of peoples from colonialism and by the prohibition to alien subjugation, domination, and exploitation'.[35] The submission of the Maldives to the OHCHR highlights the importance of this dimension of the right when stating that for many peoples, 'the right to self-determination manifests [itself] in the formation of a sovereign State' which is 'the primary guarantor and source of protection for political, civil, economic, social and cultural freedoms'.[36] This point was subsequently incorporated by the OHCHR in its report on the relationship between climate change and human rights, which recognises that the implications of climate change for the right of self-determination extend to 'the full range of human rights for which individuals depend on the State for their protection'.[37]

The resource dimension of the right has also been referred to as 'economic, social and cultural self-determination'.[38] This entails the right of all peoples to pursue socio-economic and cultural development free from national or external interference, which may in some cases equate with a people's right to a given territory.[39] It is significant that the right to a given territory is conditional on the existence of a link between a people's culture and the territory concerned. This condition is clear in the HRC's jurisprudence on Article 1, which has emerged mainly through a systematic interpretation of the ICCPR in cases related to Article 27 (the right to enjoy one's culture) and Article 25 (the right to public participation). For an illustration of this condition see *Diergaardt v Namibia*,[40] where members of the Rehoboth Basters, an ethnic minority in Namibia, claimed a violation of Article 27 on the basis of the alleged expropriation of their communal land.[41] It was argued that this constituted a violation of Article 1, as the expropriation of land would prevent the Basters from pursuing their economic, social and cultural development, and did not allow them to freely dispose of the community's

[32] Nowak (n 11) 22.

[33] *Western Sahara* (Advisory Opinion) para 59.

[34] Joseph, Schultz and Castan (n 24) 149.

[35] *General Recommendation No. 21: The Right to Self-Determination* (48th session, 1996), UN Doc A/51/18, UN Committee on the Elimination of All Forms of Racial Discrimination (UN CERD), Annex VIII at 125, para 4.

[36] Maldives Submission (n 3) 40.

[37] OHCHR Report on Climate Change and Human Rights (n 28) para 41.

[38] Nowak (n 11) 24.

[39] Lea Brilmayer, 'Secession and Self-Determination: A Territorial Interpretation' (1991) 16 *Yale Journal of International Law* 177, 191.

[40] *J.G.A. Diergaardt (late Captain of the Rehoboth Baster Community) et al. v Namibia* (2000) Communication No 760/1997, UN Doc CCPR/C/69/D/760/1997.

[41] Ibid para 3.1.

wealth and resources.[42] In its views on the communication, the HRC found no violation of either provision based on complainants' failure to demonstrate that their relationship with the relevant lands was part of a distinctive culture.[43]

The case of the Rhoboth Basters can be compared with the situation of most indigenous peoples who are directly affected by the impacts of climate change, and whose close relationship with their territory or land is reflected in their indigenous cultures and languages. For example, in the Cook Islands Maori – a language spoken by inhabitants of some Pacific islands that face permanent inundation – 'enua' means 'land, country, territory, afterbirth'; in Futuna 'fanua' means 'country, land, the people of a place'; and in Tonga, 'fonua' means 'island, territory, estate, the people of the estate, placenta' and 'fonualoto', 'grave'.[44] In several other Polynesian languages 'pro-fanua is both the people and the territory that nourishes them, as a placenta nourishes a baby'.[45] The semi-nomadic Matses people of the Peruvian Amazon refer to the rainforest as Titá, or mother, and has distinct needs and powers.[46] In these cases, there is a clear indication of a close relationship between the people and their land.

The resource dimension of the right, and the ability of a people to enjoy the benefits of their natural wealth and resources, were also central to the decision of the African Commission on Human and Peoples' Rights (ACHPR) in *Social and Economic Rights Action Centre (Ogoni people) v Nigeria*,[47] where the Commission had received evidence that foreign investment had caused serious environmental degradation and interfered with a range of human rights, which were then found to constitute violations.[48] In finding a violation of Article 21 of the ACHPR (the right of peoples to freely dispose of their wealth and natural resources), the Commission noted that the development interfered with the substance of the right and did not create any material benefits for the local population.[49] In cases related to climate change, the large-scale activities causing climate change, and which are supported or permitted by a State, often do not create significant benefits for the peoples who are mostly affected by the adverse effects of climate change. This is particularly obvious in the case of small island nations, which have also contributed negligible amounts to the emissions that are the primary driver of climate change.

[42] Ibid para 3.2.

[43] Ibid para 10.6.

[44] Kalaveti Batibasaqa, John Overton and Peter Horsley, 'Vanua: Land, People and Culture in Fiji' in John Overton and Regina Scheyvens (eds), *Strategies for Sustainable Development: Experiences from the Pacific* (London, Zed Books, 1990) 100 (referring to W Pond, 'The Land with All Woods and Water' (Waitangi Tribunal Rangahaua Whanui Series, Waitangi Tribunal, 1997) 32.

[45] Ibid.

[46] Christian Lambrechts et al (eds), 'Vital Forest Graphics' (United Nations Environment Programme (UNEP), Food and Agriculture Organisation (FAO) and United Nations Forum on Forests (UNFF), 2009) 14.

[47] *Social and Economic Rights Action Centre (SERAC) and Another v Nigeria* (2001) African Commission on Human and Peoples' Rights (ACHPR), Communication 155/96, 15th Annual Activity Report AHRLR 60.

[48] Ibid para 4.

[49] Ibid para 55.

However, even peoples who form a minority within an industrialised State, such as the Inuit peoples of the Arctic, may not have benefited significantly from the development processes that led to the deterioration of the environment on which they depend for sustenance. The question of benefits needs to be examined on a case-by-case basis where violations of the right of self-determination relating to climate change are alleged.

The solidarity dimension of the right in Article 1 is essential in order to guarantee both the political and resource dimensions of the right. Recognising this, the HRC has consistently held that the obligations under Article 1 are imposed on 'all States and the international community',[50] and that 'all States parties to the Covenant should take positive action to facilitate the attainment of and respect for the right of peoples to self-determination'.[51] These entail obligations to ensure that peoples can participate in political processes, also at the international level.[52] The right also requires that States take account of the material benefits of resource exploitation in dealing with foreign actors, while refraining from wasting raw materials 'at the expense of the interests of the relevant peoples or [in transferring] control over natural resources to other States or foreign companies without corresponding compensation for the benefit of these peoples'.[53] The right could therefore create an entitlement and arguably an obligation on the part of States to rescind a treaty if it interferes with a people's right of free disposition over its natural resources for its own ends.[54] This is important in the light of the prominence of carbon trading and sequestration in the international climate change regime, which gives rise to an increasing number of agreements between States and foreign actors that affect the rights of indigenous peoples over their land. Equally important is the apparent duty of States to cooperate to guarantee the political dimension of the right of self-determination, which could involve a duty to make arrangements for safeguarding the political autonomy of peoples at risk of losing their territories.

Yet, arguably the most important implication of the right of self-determination is an obligation for all States to act, individually and jointly, to prevent levels of warming that would lead to the loss of traditional territories and means of subsistence for a people or peoples. The precise content of this preventive obligation remains unclear. However, the right of self-determination is intrinsically linked with all other human rights and has often been interpreted by human rights treaty bodies in conjunction with individual rights. The analysis of individual rights presented below – most notably the right to enjoy one's own culture – will shed more light on the meaning of States' prevention obligations relating to the right of self-determination. This will in turn help clarify in what circumstances a State or States may be found in violation of these obligations.

[50] UNHRC, *General Comment No. 12* (n 26) para 5.
[51] Ibid para 6.
[52] Nowak (n 11) 22.
[53] Ibid 26 (footnote omitted).
[54] Ibid 25. This observation is reinforced by Art 103 of the Charter of the United Nations.

The Right to Life

Human rights are meaningless without human life. Thus, the HRC has called the right to life 'the supreme right',[55] and has insisted that there can be no derogation even in times of national emergency.[56] The enjoyment of the right to life is affected by climate change because some of its effects are known to be life-threatening or fatal. Natural disasters linked to climate change such as tropical cyclones, hurricanes, heavy storms and heatwaves, are on the rise throughout the world and claim an increasing number of victims. The increased burden of disease, droughts and floods associated with climate change also results in loss of life. A report published by the Climate Vulnerable Forum estimates that every year climate change is responsible for the death of over 400,000 people.[57] Africa and Asia are the world regions worst affected by heat and cold-related illnesses linked to climate change, which are estimated to have caused 35,000 additional deaths in 2010.[58] The heatwave that struck Europe in 2003 – an event that scientists have attributed to global warming – is considered to be 'directly responsible for tens of thousands of deaths from cardiovascular and respiratory diseases'.[59]

Anecdotal evidence submitted by communities and nations to regional and international bodies sheds more light on the implications of climate change for the right to life. The December 2005 Inuit petition to the Inter-American Commission for Human Rights[60] described how climate change-induced alterations in ice and snow were jeopardising Inuit lives: as sea ice thins, freezes later in the year and thaws earlier, causing injury and loss of life. Fish and wildlife, which are the Inuit's primary food sources, become scarcer and more difficult to catch, and sudden, unpredictable storms increase the risk of fatal accidents for hunters. Furthermore, the melting summer ice has made the seas rougher, and threatens the lives of hunters in boats.[61] The Marshall Islands' submission to the OHCHR on the relationship between climate change and human rights explained how the increased scale, intensity and frequency of sea surges and other extreme weather events lead

[55] *General Comment No. 6: The right to life (Article 6)*, UN Doc HRI/GEN/1/Rev 6 (30 April 1982) 127, para 1; *General Comment No. 14: Nuclear Weapons and the Right to Life (Article 6)*, UN Doc HRI/GEN/1/Rev1 (9 November 1984) 18, para 1.

[56] UNHRC, General Comment No 6 (n 55) para 1. This follows also from Art 4(2) of the ICCPR, which lists Art 6 as one of the articles from which no derogation may be made.

[57] DARA, 'Climate Vulnerability Monitor: A Guide to the Cold Calculus of a Hot Planet', 2nd edn (Climate Vulnerable Forum, 2012).

[58] World Health Organization (WHO), 'Protecting Health from Climate Change: Connecting Science, Policy and People' (Geneva, WHO, 2009) 161.

[59] Daniel Bodansky, 'Climate Change and Human Rights: Unpacking the Issues' (2010) 38 *Georgia Journal of International and Comparative Law* 511, 581.

[60] *Petition to the Inter-American Commission on Human Rights Seeking Relief from Violations Resulting from Global Warming Caused by Acts and Omissions of the United States* (2005) Inter-American Commission on Human Rights, available at www.ciel.org/Publications/ICC_Petition_7Dec05.pdf, 90–91.

[61] Ibid.

to injury and loss of life.[62] In a statement to the High-Level Segment of the Paris Climate Conference, Vanuatu cited the suffering and devastation inflicted by category 5 Cyclone Pam in 2015 as evidence of the impact of climate change on the right to life.[63]

It is projected that climate change will become even deadlier as temperatures continue to rise. In its report on the relationship between climate change and human rights the OHCHR pointed out that 'Climate change will exacerbate weather-related disasters which already have devastating effects on people and their enjoyment of the right to life, particularly in the developing world'.[64] The World Health Organization (WHO) estimates that climate change will cause around 250,000 additional deaths per year between 2030 and 2050 from malnutrition, diarrhoea, malaria and heat stress alone.[65] And in its Fifth Assessment Report the Intergovernmental Panel on Climate Change (IPCC) expresses 'high confidence' that key risks associated with climate change that span sectors and regions include: (i) risk of death, injury, and disrupted livelihoods in low-lying coastal zones and SIDS, due to rising sea levels, coastal flooding, and storm surges; (ii) risk of food insecurity linked to warming, drought, flooding and precipitation variability, particularly for poorer populations; and (iii) risk of mortality, morbidity, and other physical harm during periods of extreme heat, particularly for vulnerable urban populations and those working outdoors.

The present and projected effects of climate change on the right to life call for an examination of State obligations under international law to respect and ensure this right. Some of the most prominent treaty obligations to respect the right to life are found in Article 6 of the ICCPR[66] and its Second Optional Protocol.[67]

[62] Republic of the Marshall Islands, 'National Communication regarding the Relationship Between Human Rights & The Impacts of Climate Change, Submitted by H.E. Mr. Phillip H. Muller to United Nations Human Rights Council' (31 December 2008) available at www.google.nl/url?sa=t&rct=j&q=&esrc=s&source=web&cd=1&ved=0ahUKEwji-rCCu7LQAhVGVRoKHYz_AgQQFggdMAA&url=http%3A%2F%2Fwww.ohchr.org%2FDocuments%2FIssues%2FClimateChange%2FSubmissions%2FRepublic_of_the_Marshall_Islands.doc&usg=AFQjCNH2Lu_A8RiQ9QI2I-pvD8kEm4vkfw2 ('Marshall Islands Submission').

[63] Republic of Vanuatu, 'Statement delivered by the Minister of Climate Change, Adaptation, Geo-Hazard, Environment and Energy, the Honourable Jerome Ludvaune at the High-Level Segment of the 21st Conference of the Parties to the United Nations Framework Convention on Climate Change' (8 December 2015) available at unfccc.int/files/meetings/paris_nov_2015/application/pdf-/cop21cmp11_hls_speech_vanuatu.pdf.

[64] OHCHR Report on Climate Change and Human Rights (n 28) 9.

[65] WHO, 'Quantitative Risk Assessment of the Effects of Climate Change on Selected Causes of Death, 2030s and 2050s' (Geneva, WHO, 2014) 13.

[66] Art 6 of the ICCPR provides that: 'Every human being has the inherent right to life. This right shall be protected by law. No one shall be arbitrarily deprived of his life.' Paras 2–6 oblige States that have not abolished the death penalty to limit its use and to abolish it for other than the 'most serious crimes'.

[67] Second Optional Protocol to the International Covenant on Civil and Political Rights, Aiming at the Abolition of the Death Penalty (adopted 15 December 1989, entered into force 11 July 1991) 1642 UNTS 414.

Additional provisions are in Article 4 of the American Convention on Human Rights (ACHR),[68] Article 4 of the ACHPR, Article 2 of the Convention for the Protection of Human Rights and Fundamental Freedoms (European Convention on Human Rights, ECHR) and its Sixth and Twelfth Protocols (ECHRP6 and ECHRP12),[69] Article 5 of the Arab Charter on Human Rights (Arab CHR),[70] and Article 6 of the Convention on the Rights of the Child (CRC).[71] It also appears in Article 3 of the UDHR,[72] and Article I of the American Declaration of the Rights and Duties of Man (ADRDM).[73] The right to life generally provides protection against arbitrary deprivation and requires that States take appropriate steps to protect the right to life. In the specific case of the protocols to the ICCPR and the ECHR, the death penalty is prohibited. The right to life has been singled out as a right that is part of customary international law and that creates obligations *erga omnes*.[74] The right has been considered by highly qualified jurists as having the character of a *jus cogens* norm under international law.[75] The beneficiaries of the right to life are human beings. Article 6 of the ICCPR, for example, stipulates that the right to life is an innate right of every human being.

In its General Comment No 6 on the Right to Life, the HRC states explicitly that the right to life 'is a right which should not be interpreted narrowly'.[76] This reflects the position of all regional and international human rights bodies with respect to the scope of the right to life. For example, the Inter-American Court of Human Rights (IACtHR) has stated that the 'fundamental right to life includes, not only the right of every human being not to be deprived of his life arbitrarily, but also the right that he will not be prevented from having access to the conditions that guarantee a dignified existence'.[77] The ACHPR has interpreted the right to life

[68] American Convention on Human Rights (adopted 22 November 1969, entered into force 21 October 1986) OAU Doc CAB/LEG/67/3 Rev 5, 21 ILM 58 (ACHR).

[69] Convention for the Protection of Human Rights and Fundamental Freedoms (adopted 4 November 1950, entered into force 3 September 1953) as amended by Protocol Nos 11 and 14 (entered into force 11 May 1994 and 1 June 2010 respectively) ETS 5; 213 UNTS 222 (ECHR).

[70] Arab Charter on Human Rights (adopted 22 May 2004, entered into force 15 March 2008) 12 IHRR 893 (Arab CHR).

[71] Convention on the Rights of the Child (adopted 20 November 1989, entered into force 2 September 1990) 1577 UNTS 3 (CRC).

[72] Universal Declaration of Human Rights (adopted 10 December 1948) UNGA Res 217 A(III), (UDHR).

[73] American Declaration of the Rights and Duties of Man, OAS Res XXX adopted by the Ninth International Conference of American States (1948) reprinted in Basic Documents Pertaining to Human Rights in the Inter-American System OEA/Ser L V/II.82 Doc 6 Rev 1 at 17 (1992), (ADRDM).

[74] WP Gormley, 'The Right to Life and the Rule of Non-Derogability: Peremptory Norms of Jus Cogens' in Bertrand G Ramcharan (ed), *The Right to Life in International Law* (Leiden, Martinus Nijhoff, 1995) 145.

[75] Rosalyn Higgins, 'Derogations Under Human Rights Treaties' (1977) 48 *British Yearbook of International Law* (1976–77) 281; Gormley (n 74) 143.

[76] UNHRC, General Comment No 6 (n 55) paras 1, 5 (quote from para 1).

[77] *Villagrán-Morales, et al., v Guatemala* (1999) Inter-American Court of Human Rights (IACtHR) Ser C No 63, para 144.

as requiring 'preventive steps to preserve and protect the natural environment'.[78] Numerous resolutions adopted by the UN Human Rights Council confirm that protection against the potentially deadly impact of climate change falls within the scope of the right to life.[79]

Article 6(1) of the ICCPR generates two categories of obligations: a prohibition of the arbitrary deprivation of life, and an obligation to take positive measures to ensure that right, including measures to ensure its protection in law.[80] As regards the obligation to take legislative measures, the HRC has found that the law's protection is required against a broad array of threats, ranging from infanticide committed to protect a woman's honour,[81] to the 'production, testing, possession, deployment and use of nuclear weapons'.[82] The ACHPR has stressed that States' legislation must 'protect beneficiaries … against political, economic and social interferences',[83] and found a violation of the right to life in *SERAC v Nigeria* as a result of on 'humanly unacceptable' levels of 'pollution and environmental degradation'.[84] At the European level, the ECtHR similarly holds that the States' legislative and administrative framework must protect against a wide variety of threats to human life,[85] including environmental damage.[86] It is safe to assume that in a similar vein, climate change-related threats must be mitigated through effective legislation in order to protect human life. As the Committee on the Rights of the Child (CRC) has emphasised, States' domestic legislation would need to be reviewed continuously through a process of impact assessment to ensure full compliance with this obligation.[87]

According to Manfred Nowak, a violation of the obligation to protect the right to life through law can generally be assumed 'when State legislation … is manifestly insufficient as measured against the actual threat'.[88] Moreover, a violation can be established when a State fails to uphold environmental legislation that indirectly

[78] *General Comment No. 3 on the African Charter on Human and Peoples' Rights: The Right to Life (Article 4)*, adopted during the 57th Ordinary Session of the ACHPR (4–18 November 2015) para 3.

[79] *Human Rights and Climate Change*, HRC Res 10/4 (March 2009), preambular recital 7, 18/22 (September 2011), preambular recital 13, 26/27 (July 2014), preambular recital 17, 29/15 (July 2015), preambular recital 8 and 32/22 (July 2016), preambular recital 10.

[80] UNHRC, General Comment No 6 (n 55) paras 3–5; Nowak (n 11) 105.

[81] UNHRC, 'Concluding Observations on Paraguay' (1995) UN Doc CCPR/79/Add 48, para 16.

[82] UNHRC, General Comment No 14 (n 55) paras 6–7.

[83] *SERAC and Another v Nigeria*, para 46.

[84] Ibid para 67. See also *Oneryildiz v Turkey* App no 48939/99 (ECtHR GC, 30 November 2004) 115.

[85] See, eg, *Osman v United Kingdom* ECHR 1998-VIII 3124, EHRR 245, para 115; *Ilhan v Turkey* App no 22277/93 (ECtHR, 20 December 2011) para 91; *Kilic v Turkey* App no 22492/93 (ECtHR, 28 March 2000) para 62; and *Mahmut Kaya v Turkey* App no 22535/93 (ECtHR, 19 February 1998) para 85.

[86] *Oneryildiz v Turkey*, para 79 (concerning the State's failure to prevent a possible explosion of methane gas from a garbage dump under the authority of the City Council).

[87] *General Comment No. 5: General Measures of Implementation of the Convention on the Rights of the Child (Arts. 4, 42 and 42, para. 6)* (27 November 2003) UN Doc. CRC/GC/2003/5, UN CRC, para 18.

[88] Nowak (n 11) 123. See also Bertrand G Ramcharan, 'The Concept and Dimension of the Right to Life' in Bertrand G Ramcharan (ed), *The Right to Life in International Law* (Leiden, Martinus Nijhoff, 1985) 20.

protects human life. This is particularly clear from the jurisprudence of the ECtHR on the right to life: the Court found violations of the right to life in virtually all cases where allegedly life-threatening environmental damage constituted a breach of the States' domestic environmental legislation.[89] The overwhelming evidence of the deadly impact of climate change means that States must also be similarly held to account for failing to abide by domestic legislation to reduce greenhouse gas emissions, including legislation adopted to give effect to the provisions of the UNFCCC, the Kyoto Protocol and the Paris Agreement, or a failure to adopt such legislation.

However, the positive obligations of States under the right to life go beyond an obligation to take legislative measures and uphold existing environmental standards.[90] For example, the HRC has taken the view that the right requires that States take 'measures to reduce infant mortality and to increase life expectancy, especially in adopting measures to eliminate malnutrition and epidemics'.[91] It has stressed that such obligations to ensure the right to life will only be fully met if States protect individuals against violations by its agents as well as violations committed by private persons or entities likely to prejudice the enjoyment of the right.[92] The obligation is triggered where threats to life are 'foreseeable'.[93] In a similar vein in the landmark case *Velásquez Radríguez v Honduras*[94] the IACtHR found that State responsibility for a violation of the right to life had arisen 'not because of the act [of abduction and killing] itself, but because of the lack of due diligence to prevent the violation or to respond to it as required by the Convention'.[95] In relation to climate change, foreseeable nature of climate change-related threats to life may arise from the reports of the IPCC and other scientific studies as well as from affected communities' efforts to draw attention to these risks.[96] The implication is that State responsibility can arise for failing to regulate or otherwise control private persons – from fossil fuel companies to consumers – to reduce the risks to human life associated with climate change.

The case of *Tatar C. v Roumanie*[97] illustrates that States' positive obligations to prevent human rights violations partly overlap with obligations arising from the precautionary principle as embodied in international environmental law,

[89] Dinah L Shelton, 'Litigating a Rights-Based Approach to Climate Change' (International Conference on Human Rights and the Environment, Tehran, 13–14 May 2009) 224 (with references).

[90] UNHRC, General Comment No 6 (n 55) para 5.

[91] Ibid.

[92] *General Comment No. 31: The Nature of the General Legal Obligation Imposed on States Parties to the Covenant* (29 March 2004) UN Doc CCPR/C/21/Rev1/Add 13, UNHRC, para 8.

[93] *Annakkarage Suranjini Sadamali Pathmini Peiris v Sri Lanka* (2011) UNHRC Communication No 1862/2009, UN Doc CCPR/C/103/D/1862, para 7.2.

[94] *Velásquez Radríguez v Honduras* IACtHR Series C no 4 (1988); 95 ILR 232.

[95] Ibid para 172. See also *Trail Smelter (United States v Canada)* [1941] 3 RIAA 1905, 1965 and the discussion of the 'no-harm rule' in ch 3.

[96] See ch 1.

[97] *Tatar C. Roumanie* App no 67021/01 (ECtHR, 5 July 2007).

including the UNFCCC.[98] In its ruling, the Court stressed that even in the absence of scientific probability regarding a causal link between the harm caused to the applicants and the State's conduct, the existence of a 'serious and substantial' risk to the health and well-being of the applicants imposed on the State 'a positive obligation to adopt adequate measures capable of protecting the rights of the applicants to respect for their private and family life and, more generally, to the enjoyment of a healthy and protected environment'.[99] The breach of this positive obligation was the basis on which the Court found a violation of the relevant right. The deadly effects of climate change already reported and linked to climate change suggest that the risks posed by climate change are indeed serious and substantial. This means that States are not only obliged to assess the risks to human life resulting from climate change, but must also respond to these risks with measures that are sufficiently ambitious and effective to protect human life.

ECtHR jurisprudence, starting with *Osman v UK*, suggests that the standard of care required in relation to a risk of which the State had actual or presumed knowledge is one of reasonableness: 'The Court does not accept … that the failure to perceive the risk to life in the circumstances known at the time or to take preventive measures to avoid that risk must be tantamount to gross negligence or wilful disregard of the duty to protect life. … Such a rigid standard must be considered to be incompatible with the requirements of [the right to life]. … [H]aving regard to the [fundamental] nature of [the right to life], it is sufficient for an applicant to show that the authorities did not do all that could be reasonably expected of them to avoid a real and immediate risk to life of which they have or ought to have knowledge'.[100] In relation to climate change-related risk to human life, the requirement to do 'all that could be reasonably expected of them' indicates that the standard of care may differ from one State to another. This is confirmed by the view of the IACtHR that States are required to take positive measures in response to foreseeable threats to life insofar as these measures do not impose an 'impossible or disproportionate burden' for the States.[101] As a result States' common but differentiated responsibilities and respective capabilities may be considered as part of an assessment of whether or not the State has met the standard of 'reasonableness'.

The Right to Enjoy One's Culture

Indigenous peoples and minority groups are amongst the worst affected by the impact of climate change. The close relationship of some indigenous peoples and

[98] UNFCCC Art 3(1). See also ch 3.

[99] *Tatar C. Roumanie*, paras 107–24.

[100] *Osman v United Kingdom*, paras 115–16. See also *Budayeva et al v Russia* App no 48939/99 (ECtHR, 30 November 2004) para 132.

[101] *Sawhoyamaxa Indigenous Community v Paraguay* (2003) IACtHR OEA/Ser.L/V/II.118 Doc 70 rev 2 378, para 155.

minorities with their traditional land makes them particularly vulnerable to the deterioration of the environment resulting from climate change. As already noted, entire nations face the prospect of losing some or all of their territory or land. Coastal features are already visibly changing in coastal areas around the world, with rising sea levels, higher king tides and storm surges, saltwater intrusion and changing weather patterns forcing a growing number of coastal and island communities to relocate from their traditional homelands. The effects of warming and drying, irregular weather patterns and the increase of extreme weather events similarly lead to involuntary migration and displacement in low-lying areas, drylands and high mountainous areas. It has been predicted that by 2050, 25 million to 1 billion people will have been forced to relocate as a result of climate change, with the highest number of migrants coming from sub-Saharan Africa.[102]

Many indigenous cultures – especially in the Pacific region – have a history of migration. One example is the village of Tabara in north-eastern Papua New Guinea, which has a history of fusion, division and migration extending over 130 kilometres.[103] The traditional knowledge of navigation and canoe-building possessed by indigenous peoples across the Pacific emphasises the historical importance of mobility in indigenous Pacific cultures.[104] At the same time, however, many Pacific migrants continue to feel a bond with their indigenous lands, even after having lived elsewhere for long periods of time.[105] The loss or uninhabitable character of an indigenous territory breaks these bonds and threatens the cultural identity of affected peoples and minorities. Indeed, some indigenous peoples principally reject migration as a form of adaptation to climate change because they consider their home territory as an essential part of their culture.[106] This indicates that despite the fact that migration and mobility are sometimes inherent in indigenous cultures, the projected loss of indigenous peoples' land that is forecast as a result of climate change still threatens to interfere with the cultural identity and related human rights of affected peoples and minorities.

These observations are confirmed by the submissions on the relationship between climate change and human rights made by SIDS to the OHCHR, which emphasise the links between the right of self-determination and traditional culture.

[102] International Organization for Migration (IOM), 'Migration, Climate Change and the Environment: A Complex Nexus' (2011).

[103] John Campbell, 'Climate-Induced Community Relocation in the Pacific: The Meaning and Importance of Land' in Jane McAdam (ed), *Climate Change and Displacement: Multidisciplinary Perspectives* (Oxford, Hart Publishing, 2010) 62 (citing JD Waiko, 'Na Minandere, Imo Averi? We Are Binandere, Who Are You?' (1985) 26 *Pacific Viewpoint* 9, 9).

[104] See generally Matt K Matsuda, *Pacific Worlds: A History of Seas, Peoples, and Cultures* (Cambridge, Cambridge University Press, 2012).

[105] Campbell (n 103) 9.

[106] For a discussion see Karen E McNamara and Chris Gibson, '"We do not want to leave our land": Pacific Ambassadors at the United Nations Resist the Category of "Climate Refugees"' (2009) 40 *Geoforum* 475. See also Chris Bramwell, 'Pacific Atolls "Could be Underwater by 2050"' (15 July 2016) RadioNZ, available at www.radionz.co.nz/news/political/308703/pacific-atolls-could-be-underwater-by-2050 (citing Kiribati's Minister of Foreign Affairs Murray McCullay as stating that the inhabitants of Kiribati's islands 'want to stay where they are, the traditions and cultures are everything').

For example, the submission made by the Republic of the Marshall Islands rejects the 'potential enforcement of an assertion that a low-lying, remote developing island nation can simply "adapt" to the physical loss of its homeland and nationhood by removing the population to a foreign nation' as 'perhaps, itself a violation of the fundamental human right to nationhood'.[107] The submission explains that the Marshallese are known for their strong emphasis on traditional culture which values cooperation and sharing, and that in accordance with its customary system of land tenure, land is 'not viewed as interchangeable real estate, but instead as a foundation of national, cultural and personal identity and spirit'.[108] The submission concludes that 'The reclassification of the Marshallese as a displaced nation or, loosely defined, as "climate refugees", is not only undesirable, but also unacceptable as an affront to self-determination and national dignity'.[109] The Maldives highlights that climate change-induced migration can lead to the division of communities or families, causing emotional distress and threatening 'the common culture of the community'.[110] It also mentions the risk that host populations 'will be resentful to the threat to its own resources or way of life, and respond with violence to the migrant population'.[111]

As noted above, the jurisprudence of the HRC reflects a strong link between the right of self-determination and the right to enjoy one's culture. This link was first recognised in the case of *Lubicon Lake Band v Canada*,[112] where the indigenous Lubicon Lake Band alleged that the permission for energy exploration by private corporations in the Band's territory entailed violations of its right of self-determination. Although the HRC considered the right of self-determination as not cognisable under the Optional Protocol, it then examined the communication under Article 27 of the ICCPR instead.[113] Article 27 has since provided an indirect way to invoke the provisions of Article 1 through the individual complaint procedure, and a significant part of the HRC jurisprudence on Article 27 now reflects the simultaneous expression of the right of self-determination.[114] Hence, the reasoning of the HRC in Article 27 cases helps us understand how the rights of peoples affected by climate change are protected under international law. The analysis of this right also highlights how indigenous peoples affected by climate change may be able to overcome the challenges relating to the justiciability

[107] Marshall Islands Submission (n 62) 9.
[108] Ibid 3.
[109] Ibid 10.
[110] Maldives Submission (n 3) 67.
[111] Ibid.
[112] *Ominayak and the Lubicon Lake Band v Canada* (1990) Communication No 167/1984, UN Doc CCPR/C/38/D/167/1984.
[113] Ibid para 13.4.
[114] See, eg: *Ivan Kitok v Sweden* (1988) Communication No 197/1985, UN Doc CCPR/C/33/D/197/1985, para 6.3; *Ominayak and the Lubicon Lake Band v Canada* (1990) Communication No 167/1984, UN Doc Supp No 40 (A/45/40) para 13.3; *Marshall v Canada* (1991) Communication No 205/1986, UN Doc CCCPR/C/43/D/205/1986) para 5.1; *Apirana Mahuika et al. v New Zealand* (1991) Communication No 547/1993, UN Doc CCPR/C/70/D/547/1993, para 9.2.

of the right of self-determination, and thus hold States accountable for the impact of climate change on their cultures, livelihoods and means of subsistence.

The right to enjoy one's culture was first codified in Article 27 of the UDHR, which provides that "everyone has the right to freely participate in the cultural life of the community".[115] Article 27 of the ICCPR provides a specific right of minorities to enjoy their own culture, while Article 15 of the ICESCR expresses the universal right 'to take part in cultural life'.[116] Furthermore, Article 13 of the American Declaration provides for the right to take part in the cultural life of the community,[117] while Article 14 of the Additional Protocol to the American Convention on Human Rights in the Area of Economic, Social and Cultural Rights (Protocol of San Salvador) provides for the universal right to take part in the cultural and artistic life of the community.[118] An almost identical provision is contained in Article 17 of the ACHPR.[119] The International Convention on the Elimination of All Forms of Racial Discrimination (ICERD) singles out 'the right to equal participation in cultural activities' as one of the rights that States must guarantee and which should be enjoyed without discrimination.[120] The CRC provides the right to participate in all aspects of social and cultural life.[121] The International Convention on the Protection of the Rights of All Migrant Workers and Members of their Families (CMW) provides for the right of access to, and participation in, cultural life,[122] and Article 13 of the CEDAW obliges States to guarantee the equal enjoyment between men and women to the right to participate in recreational activities, sports and all aspects of cultural life.[123] Finally, the Convention on the Rights of Persons with Disabilities (CRPD) provides for the right of persons with disabilities to take part on an equal basis with others in cultural life.[124]

The right to enjoy one's culture was intentionally formulated as an individual right, but the phrase 'in community with the other members of their group' was inserted in order to 'maintain the idea of a group'.[125] The CESCR stresses that the beneficiaries of the right are individuals, but that the right may be exercised either

[115] UDHR, Art 27(1).

[116] ICESCR, Art 15(1)(a).

[117] American Declaration, Art 13.

[118] Additional Protocol to the American Convention on Human Rights in the Area of Economic, Social and Cultural Rights (adopted 17 November 1988, entered into force 16 November 1999) OAS Treaty Series No 69 (Protocol of San Salvador) reprinted in Basic Documents Pertaining to Human Rights in the Inter-American System, OEA/Ser L V/II.82 Doc 6 Rev 1 at 67, Art 14(1).

[119] ACHPR, Art 17(2).

[120] International Convention on the Elimination of All Forms of Racial Discrimination (adopted 21 December 1965, entered into force 4 January 1969) 660 UNTS 195, Art 5.

[121] CRC, Art 31(2).

[122] International Convention on the Protection of the Rights of All Migrant Workers and Members of their Families (adopted 18 December 1990, entered into force 1 July 2003) 2220 UNTS 3, Art 43(1)(g).

[123] CEDAW, Art 13(c).

[124] Convention on the Rights of Persons with Disabilities (adopted 13 December 2006, entered into force 3 May 2008) 2515 UNTS 3 (CRPD) Art 30(1).

[125] Nowak (n 11) 655.

by a person as an individual, in association with others, or within a community or group.[126] The right to enjoy one's culture is therefore an individual right with a collective element,[127] protecting both group and individual interests in cultural integrity.[128] Perhaps it is not surprising that the meaning of the term 'minorities' partly overlaps with the term 'peoples' in Article 1 of the Covenant.[129] However, the two terms should be differentiated.[130] The term 'minorities' implies four things, namely: (1) numerical inferiority to the rest of the population; (2) being in a non-dominant position; (3) having ethnic, religious or linguistic characteristics that are distinct from those of the overall population of the State in question; and (4) showing, explicitly or implicitly, a sense of solidarity.[131] The term has been interpreted as including aliens; in other words, the term 'minorities' does not only relate to nationals of a particular State.[132] The HRC has gone as far as to state that just as beneficiaries of the right 'need not be nationals or citizens, they need not be permanent residents' and thus may include 'migrant workers or even visitors'.[133] Nowak also claims that the rights enjoyed by minorities 'should not be denied to immigrants, including migrant workers, who entered the country only recently'.[134] This indicates that people who are forced to migrate as a result of the adverse effects of climate change and who meet the definition of 'minorities' are entitled to protection of their right to culture in the receiving state, regardless of their legal status or citizenship.

The HRC has also made it clear that indigenous peoples may constitute a minority group as per the article.[135] It has upheld this view in several complaints submitted by representatives of indigenous peoples, which together make up most of the findings of the Committee under Article 27. In this context, it is important to note that even relatively small island nations are often composed of a myriad of culturally distinct groups. For example, the Republic of Vanuatu has about 80 inhabited islands, a population of about 283,000[136] and 138 indigenous languages

[126] *General Comment No. 21: Right of Everyone to Take Part in Cultural Life* (Art 15, para 1 (a), of the ICESCR) (21 December 2009) UN Doc E/C12/GC/21, UN CESCR, para 9.

[127] *General Comment No. 23: The Rights of Minorities (Art 27)* (8 April 1994) UN Doc CCPR/C/21/Rev1/Add5, UNHRC, para 16.

[128] James S Anaya, 'International Human Rights and Indigenous Peoples: the Move Toward the Multicultural State' (2004) 21 *Arizona Journal of International and Comparative Law* 13, 22.

[129] Nowak (n 11) 643.

[130] *Mikmaq Tribal Society v Canada* (Communication No 78/1980) UN Doc CCPR/C/22/D/78/1980, para 7.3.

[131] F Capotorti, 'Study by the Special Rapporteur of the United Nations Sub-Commission on Prevention of Discrimination and Protection of Minorities on the Rights of Persons Belonging to Ethnic, Religious and Linguistic Minorities' (6 March 1978) UN Doc E/CN.4/Sub.2/384/Rev.1, 96.

[132] Nowak (n 11) 645. Cf Capotorti (n 131) 12.

[133] UNHRC, General Comment No 23 (n 127) para 5.2.

[134] Nowak (n 11) 647.

[135] See UNHRC, General Comment No 23 (n 127) para 3.2.

[136] Website of Vanuatu National Statistics Office (VNSO), available at www.vnso.gov.vu. The website provides a 'live' counter of the population of Vanuatu. As of 18 November 2016, the total number was 289,324.

spoken by distinct cultural communities, each with its own traditions and social structures.[137] When speaking of the right to culture as protected under Article 27, it is the distinct 'micro' cultures of a nation that presumably attract entitlement to protection for each of its members. Insofar as an entire nation has a distinct culture, it may also be protected by virtue of parallel instruments and provisions that are not confined to minorities, including Article 1 of the ICCPR and ICESCR. Moreover, it would be protected where members of the nation migrate to a third country where they would effectively constitute a minority.

The substantive scope of the right to enjoy one's culture is comparatively wide: 'culture' is understood as a 'broad inclusive concept encompassing all manifestations of human existence' which includes 'natural and man-made environments' and the 'arts, customs and traditions through which individuals, groups of individuals and communities express their humanity and the meaning they give to their existence'.[138] In *Ilmari Länsman v Finland*[139] the HRC clarified that under Article 27, minorities or indigenous groups have the right to the protection of traditional activities such as hunting, fishing or reindeer husbandry.[140] It noted the 'spiritual significance' to the complainants' culture of Mount Riutusvaara (where the activities that allegedly interfered with the complainants' right were carried out), as well as the potential negative effects of a disturbed environment on the quality of slaughtered reindeer.[141] At the same time, it found that Article 27 does not only protect *traditional* means of livelihood of national minorities: the fact that a minority uses modern technology to adapt its traditional means of livelihood to a modern way of life does not prevent it from invoking Article 27 to protect those means. The HRC reaffirmed these findings in *Apirana Mahuika v New Zealand*, where it clarified that economic activities may come within the ambit of Article 27, if they are an essential element of the culture of a community.[142] It thus found that the Maoris' right to enjoy the benefits of commercial fishing came within the scope of Article 27.[143] This broad conception of culture is important for communities and peoples affected by climate change: as Jessie Hohmann notes, the process of identifying the victims of human rights violations comes with the risk that the culture of potential victims is presented as static.[144] The HRC's insistence that the right to enjoy one's culture cannot be determined *in abstracto*, but has to be

[137] Alexandre François et al, 'The Languages of Vanuatu: Unity and Diversity' (Asia Pacific Linguistics Studies in the Languages of Island Melanesia, College of Asia and the Pacific, Australian National University, 2015) 2, available at alex.francois.free.fr/data/Francois-et-al_2015_Languages-of-Vanuatu_SLIM.pdf.

[138] UN CESCR, General Comment No 21 (n 126) paras 11 and 13.

[139] *Ilmari Länsman et al. v Finland* (1994) Communication No 511/1992) UN Doc CCPR/C/52/D/511/1992.

[140] Ibid para 9.3.

[141] Ibid.

[142] *Mahuika et al v New Zealand*, para 9.3.

[143] Ibid para 9.4.

[144] Jessie Hohmann, 'Igloo as Icon: A Human Rights Approach to Climate Change for the Inuit?' (2009) 18 *Transnational Law and Contemporary Problems* 295, 315–16.

placed in context,[145] prevents human rights-based climate litigation or policy from becoming an obstacle to innovation and change, which would have potentially detrimental effects on the adaptive capacity of peoples and minorities.

When considering the obligations of States in relation to the right to culture, a first point to note is that Article 27 is the only right protected under the ICCPR that is negatively formulated in the treaty text. However, the HRC has consistently held that Article 27 imposes positive obligations on States. More precisely, it prescribes 'Positive measures of protection … not only against the acts of the State party itself, whether through its legislative, judicial or administrative authorities, but also against the acts of other persons within the State party'.[146] The interpretation of the right as giving rise to negative and positive obligations mirrors the interpretation of parallel rights protected under other human rights treaties. The Committee on the Rights of the Child has identified a close linkage between Article 30 CRC and Article 27 ICCPR in its *General Comment on Indigenous Children and Their Rights under the Convention*.[147] The Committee has declared that States must refrain from interfering with the right and instead take positive measures to protect it against the acts of public authorities and against the acts of other persons within the State party.[148] The protective measures themselves must be participatory.[149] Along the same lines, the CESCR has interpreted the right to take part in cultural life as requiring 'both abstention (ie non-interference with the exercise of cultural practices and with access to cultural goods and services), and positive action (ensuring preconditions for participation, facilitation and promotion of cultural life, and access and preservation of cultural goods)'.[150]

The HRC's assessment of States' compliance with obligations has focused on both the impact of a State's acts or omissions on the complainants' culture and the decision-making process through which the alleged violation materialised. In *Apirana Mahuika v New Zealand*, the HRC clarified that 'the acceptability of measures that affect or interfere with the culturally significant economic activities of a minority depends on whether the members of the minority in question have had the opportunity to participate in the decision-making process in relation to these measures and whether they will continue to benefit from their traditional economy'.[151] Martin Scheinin describes the test applied by the HRC as a 'combined test of participation by the group and sustainability of the indigenous economy'.[152]

[145] UNHRC, General Comment No 23 (n 127) para 9.3; *Apirana Mahuika et al. v New Zealand*, para 9.4.
[146] UNHRC, General Comment No 23 (n 127) para 6.1.
[147] General Comment No 11: Indigenous Children and Their Rights under the Convention (12 February 2009) UN Doc CRC/C/GC/11, CRC, para 16.
[148] Ibid.
[149] Ibid para 20.
[150] UN CESCR, General Comment No 21 (n 126) para 6.
[151] *Apirana Mahuika et al. v New Zealand*, para 9.5.
[152] Martin Scheinin, 'Advocating the Right to Development through Complaint Procedures under Human Rights Treaties' in Bard A Andreassen and Stephen P Marks (eds), *Development as a Human Right: Legal, Political and Economic Dimensions*, 2nd edn (Antwerp, Intersentia, 2010) 343.

Examples of the application of this test are found in the HRC's views on a series of cases against Finland brought by members of the indigenous Sami people, concerning the impact of extractive activities on their traditional reindeer herding culture.[153] In *Ilmari Länsman v Finland*, the HRC confirmed that the right contains a substantive aspect that States are obliged to protect against interferences by private actors:

> A State may understandably wish to encourage development or allow economic activity by enterprises. The scope of its freedom to do so is not to be assessed by reference to a margin of appreciation, but by reference to the obligations it has undertaken under Article 27. Article 27 requires that a member of a minority shall not be denied his right to enjoy his own culture. Thus, measures whose impact amount to a denial of the right will not be compatible with the obligations under Article 27.[154]

In considering whether or not the right to enjoy one's culture had been denied, the HRC examined the impacts of post-extractive activity and future activities that had been approved by the authorities. In relation to both past and future activities, it considered whether the activities were 'of such proportions as to deny the authors the right to enjoy their culture in that area'.[155] The exact same question was asked in *Jouni Länsman v Finland*,[156] another case dealing with the impact of extractive activities in reindeer herding alleging violation of Article 27. In both *Länsman* cases the HRC was unable to find a violation of Article 27 based on the impact of past and approved activities alone: it found that the authors had failed to present clear evidence that the extractive activities had adversely affected the complainants' means of subsistence, or that the complainants' rights would be denied as a result of approved activities.[157] However, it warned that if the extractive activities were approved on a large scale and significantly expanded, then this might constitute a violation of the complainants' rights under Article 27.[158]

As regards the procedural part of the test, the HRC first considered whether and how the communities to which the complainants belonged had been consulted in the relevant proceedings. In both cases the communities had been consulted and their interests had been considered before the activities were approved.[159] Moreover, in *Ilmari Länsman v Finland* the HRC deemed that reindeer herding activity was protected by national legislation,[160] while noting in *Jouni Länsman v*

[153] These cases include *O.Sarea v Finland* (1994) Communication No 431/1990, UN Doc CCPR/C/50/D/431/1990; *Anni Äärelä and Jouni Näkkäläjärvi v Finland* (1997) Communication No 779/1997, UN Doc CCPR/C/73/D/779/1997, and the cases discussed below.

[154] *Ilmari Länsman et al. v Finland*, para 9.4.

[155] Ibid para 10.4.

[156] *Jouni E. Länsman et al. v Finland* (1996) Communication No 671/1995, UN Doc CCPR/C/58/D/58/D/671/1995.

[157] Ibid paras 10.5–10.6; *Ilmari Länsman et al. v Finland*, paras 9.6–9.7.

[158] *Ilmari Länsman et al. v Finland*, para 9.8. See also *Jouni E. Länsman et al. v Finland*, para 10.7.

[159] *Ilmari Länsman et al. v Finland*, para 9.6; *Jouni E. Länsman et al. v Finland*, para 10.5.

[160] *Ilmari Länsman et al. v Finland*, para 9.7.

Finland that the authorities had completed the process of 'weighing the authors' interests and the general economic interests in the area specified in the complaint'.[161] In the latter case, it was also significant that the national courts had specifically examined whether the proposed activities constituted a denial of the complainants' rights under Article 27 without misinterpreting or misapplying the article.[162] In conjunction with the HRC's findings on the substantive part of the test, these considerations resulted in findings of no violation of Article 27 in both cases.

In relation to climate change, the HRC's jurisprudence implies that States have some discretion to permit polluting activities, as long as the harm does not deprive minorities of their means of subsistence and members of those minorities are able to participate in relevant decision-making processes. A wide range of factors need to be considered in determining whether or not the State has exceeded its discretion, including the impact of the disputed activities on the minorities' traditional culture, details of consultation processes, national legislation and available judicial remedies. In the absence of jurisprudence to clarify the obligations of States to respect and ensure the right to culture extraterritorially, it is unclear exactly what forms of consultations, legislation and remedies are required to meet the participation part of the test in relation to the transboundary impacts of climate change. However, it is clear that States' discretion to permit activities that contribute to further climate change will be limited in practice given that climate change has already reached levels where peoples and minorities around the world are gradually being deprived of their means of subsistence. In other words, activities that contribute to climate change may be considered unacceptable due to the imminent threat that climate change poses to the sustainability of peoples' and minorities' traditional economies. The precise form of State discretion may need to be examined in the light of its respective contribution to climate change and capacities to mitigate the adverse effects on minorities within and outside their territories. This argument is discussed in more detail at the end of this chapter.

The Right to the Highest Attainable Standard of Health

Some of the impacts of climate change are deadly. Rising temperatures and sea levels, drought, desertification, more intense heatwaves, extreme weather events and the spread of tropical and vector-borne diseases all have significant impact on human life and health. However, climate change also acts as a threat multiplier and undermines the underlying determinants of health. Globally, an estimated 4 billion people already face severe water scarcity, and this number is expected to increase as temperatures continue to rise.[163] Farming societies at lower lati-

[161] *Jouni E. Länsman et al. v Finland*, para 10.5.
[162] Ibid.
[163] Mesfin M Mekonnen and Arjen Y Hoekstra, 'Four Billion People Facing Severe Water Scarcity' (2016) 2 *Science Advances* 1.

tudes will face lower crop yields even with small local temperature increases. Africa is generally recognised as the world's most vulnerable region in terms of climate change impacts on agricultural produce and fishery losses.[164] Droughts in sub-Saharan Africa are already occurring more frequently and lasting longer and crop yields could drop by as much as 50 per cent across large regions of sub-Saharan Africa by 2020, exposing tens of millions more individuals to malnutrition.[165] Water-borne and vector-borne diseases such as cholera, malaria, hantavirus, dengue fever, scrub typhus and schistosomiasis are all expected to increase as a result of temperature rise and geographic and ecological changes associated with climate change.[166] The population at risk of malaria in Africa is projected to grow by 170 million by 2030,[167] and vulnerable groups such as children,[168] the elderly, and pregnant women[169] will be hardest hit.

In its report on the relationship between climate change and human rights, the OHCHR notes that 'Non-climate related factors, such as education, health care [and] public health initiatives are critical in determining how global warming will affect the health of populations. Protecting the right to health in the face of climate change will require comprehensive measures, including mitigating the adverse impacts of global warming on underlying determinants of health and giving priority to protecting vulnerable individuals and communities'.[170] In his capacity of Special Rapporteur on the Right of Everyone to the Enjoyment of Physical and Mental Health; a post created by the UN Commission on Human Rights in 2002, Paul Hunt has also drawn attention to the impact of climate change on the right to health.[171] In his report to the 62nd General Assembly he lists several impacts of climate change on the right to health, including a decline in dependable access to water, disruption of natural ecosystems, increases in the range and season of disease-spreading vectors, and various harmful health impacts of drought and flooding.[172] He claims that 'The failure of the international community to take the health impact of global warming seriously will endanger the lives of millions of people across the world'.[173]

[164] DARA (n 57) 178.
[165] WHO (n 58) 20.
[166] WHO and World Meteorological Organization (WMO), 'Atlas of Health and Climate' (Geneva, WHO, 2012) 14; IPCC, 'Contribution of Working Group I to the IPCC Fourth Assessment Report' in S Solomon et al (eds), *Climate Change 2007: The Physical Science Basis* (Cambridge, Cambridge University Press, 2007) 48; WHO (n 58) 7.
[167] IPCC (n 166) 439.
[168] WHO (n 58) 16.
[169] IPCC (n 166) 446.
[170] OHCHR Report on Climate Change and Human Rights (n 31) para 34 (footnotes omitted).
[171] *The Right of Everyone to the Enjoyment of the Highest Attainable Standard of Physical and Mental Health*, UNCHR Res 2002/31 (2002).
[172] Paul Hunt, 'Report of the Special Rapporteur on the Right of Everyone to the Enjoyment of the Highest Attainable Standard of Physical and Mental Health' (8 August 2007) UN Doc A/62/214, 22, paras 100–01.
[173] Ibid para 102.

In July 2015, the Human Rights Council adopted a resolution calling for a detailed analytical study from the OHCHR on the relationship between climate change and the right to the highest attainable standard of health.[174] The OHCHR published its study in May 2016, after collecting written submissions from stakeholders and convening a panel discussion on the topic.[175] The report observes that in the panel discussion and written submissions, 'stakeholders overwhelmingly agreed that climate change posed a grave threat to human health, including the social and environmental determinants of health such as clean air, safe drinking water, sufficient food and secure shelter'.[176] It then outlines these threats in detail, with specific attention for disproportionate impacts on persons and groups in vulnerable situations.[177] The report concludes with a call for 'rights-based climate action' and mobilisation of 'the human rights machinery' to 'monitor climate commitments'.[178] However, the report throws no light on the circumstances in which States may incur international responsibility for violations of the right to health associated with climate change. Again, an examination of States' obligations connected with the right to health is needed to understand in what circumstances such responsibility may arise.

The Preamble to the WHO Constitution adopted in 1946 recognises that the 'enjoyment of the highest attainable standard of health is one of the fundamental rights of every human being'.[179] A more frequently cited expression of the human right to health is found in Article 12 of the ICESCR,[180] and in special human rights treaties such as the ICERD,[181] the CEDAW,[182] the CRC,[183] the ILO Convention No 169 concerning Indigenous and Tribal Peoples in Independent Countries (1989),[184] the CMW,[185] and the CRPD.[186] At the regional level, the right to health is contained in Article 16 of the ACHPR,[187] and reiterated in an ACHOR Protocol on Violence Against Women,[188] and the African Charter on the Rights and Welfare

[174] *Human Rights and Climate Change*, Res 29/15 (2 July 2015) UN Doc A/HRC/RES/29/15, UNHRC.

[175] OHCHR, 'Analytical Study on the Relationship between Climate Change and the Human Right of Everyone to the Enjoyment of the Highest Attainable Standard of Physical and Mental Health' (6 May 2016) UN Doc A/HRC/32/23.

[176] Ibid 5.

[177] Ibid 5–10.

[178] Ibid 18.

[179] Constitution of the World Health Organization (adopted 22 July 1946, entered into force 7 April 1948) 14 UNTS 185 (Constitution of the WHO).

[180] ICESCR, Art 12.

[181] ICERD, Art 5(e)(iv).

[182] CEDAW, Arts 11(1)(f), 12 and 14(2)(b).

[183] CRC, Art 24.

[184] ILO Convention No 169 (adopted 27 June 1989, entered into force 5 September 1991) 1650 UNTS 384, Arts 7, 20, 25, and 30.

[185] CMW, Art 28.

[186] CPRD, Arts 25 and 26.

[187] ACHPR, Art 16.

[188] Protocol to the ACHPR on the Rights of Women in Africa (adopted 13 September 2000, entered into force 25 November 2005) AU Doc CAB/LEG/66.6, Art 14.

of the Child.[189] In the Inter-American context the right is contained in Article 10 of the Protocol of San Salvador,[190] and in the European context both the European Social Charter (ESC)[191] of the Council of Europe and the Charter of Fundamental Rights (CFR) of the European Union[192] contain the right to health. The Arab CHR of the League of Arab States also recognises the right to health.[193] Finally, the Organization of Islamic States (OIC) has endorsed the human right to health in the Cairo Declaration on Human Rights in Islam.[194] This right is now generally accepted as part of customary international law.[195] This conclusion is based on the widespread ratification of human rights treaties and other instruments containing the right to health, and on the commitment of governments to the provision of health care services pursuant to national legislation.

The right to health is a right that States are obliged to realise progressively. The CESCR has emphasised that although 'the right to health is not to be understood as a right to be *healthy*',[196] it nonetheless creates States' obligations.[197] The text of Article 12 of the CESCR (and Article 24 of the CRC) make it clear that the general scope of the right extends beyond the provision of health care, and includes provision for the general conditions conducive to health such as an 'adequate supply of safe and potable water and basic sanitation; the prevention and reduction of the population's exposure to harmful substances such as radiation and harmful chemicals or other detrimental environmental conditions that directly or indirectly impact upon human health'.[198] Mirroring the language of Article 25(1) of the UDHR, the right to health is defined in Article 12(1) of the ICESCR as a right of 'everyone'. The CESCR has confirmed that the right is 'the right of everyone'.[199] In accordance with Article 2(2) and (3) of the ICESCR the enjoyment of the right

[189] African Charter on the Rights and Welfare of the Child (adopted 11 July 1990, entered into force 29 November 1999) OAU Doc CAB/LEG/24.9/49, Arts 14, 11(2)(h).

[190] Protocol of San Salvador, Art 10.

[191] European Social Charter (adopted 18 October 1961, entered into force 26 February 1965) 529 UNTS 89; revised and adopted as European Social Charter (entered into force 7 January 1999) ETS No 163 (ESC), Arts 11 and 13.

[192] Charter of Fundamental Rights of the European Union (adopted 7 December 2000, entered into force 1 December 2009) reprinted in Official Journal of the European Communities, 18 December 2000 (OJ C 364/01) (CFR), Art 35.

[193] Arab CHR, Arts 38–39.

[194] See Art 17 of the Cairo Declaration on Human Rights in Islam, adopted at the 14th Islamic Conference of Foreign Ministers, Res No 49/19-P (1990). See also Art 15 of the Covenant on the Rights of the Child in Islam (adopted in June 2005 at the 32nd Islamic Conference of Foreign Ministers in Sana'a, Republic of Yemen, not yet in force) OIC Doc OIC/9-IGGE/HRI/2004/Rep. Final (2004).

[195] ED Kinney, 'The International Human Right to Health: What Does This Mean For Our Nation and World?' (2001) 34 *Indiana Law Review* 1457, 1464–67 and 1475.

[196] *General Comment No 14: The Right to the Highest Attainable Standard of Health (Article 12)* (11 August 2000) UN Doc E/C 12/2000/4, CESCR, para 8.

[197] Ibid paras 30–45.

[198] Ibid para 15.

[199] Ibid.

is non-discriminatory. Significantly, this may mean 'providing equal opportunities when past developments have caused serious inequalities to arise'.[200]

The obligations arising from the right to health are understood as including 'immediate obligations ... [to] ... guarantee that the right will be exercised without discrimination of any kind' and to take steps that 'must be deliberate, concrete and targeted towards the full realisation of the right to health'.[201] To clarify the content of States' obligations, the CESCR has used a respect-protect-fulfil model of obligations that arise from the right to health.[202] It interprets the obligation to 'respect' the right as 'an obligation of States to respect the freedom of individuals and groups to preserve and to make use of their existing entitlements'.[203] States are thus obliged to ensure 'the effective implementation of the obligations arising from other human rights provisions: the right to property, the right to work with an adequate income, and/or the right to social security',[204] and to guarantee and uphold the collective land rights of indigenous peoples.[205] For the CESCR the right to health requires respect for the right to health of a people within a State's territory and in other States,[206] entailing an obligation 'to refrain from unlawfully polluting air, water and soil, e.g. through industrial waste from State-owned facilities'.[207] Hence, the right could be violated by State activities that are a direct cause of environmental degradation, including activities that contribute to climate change. Moreover, the CESCR explicitly states that the right to health obliges States to ensure that international instruments, presumably including climate change-related agreements, 'do not adversely impact upon the right to health'.[208]

The obligation to protect the right to health means 'the preservation of existing entitlements or resource bases', also through regulation and legal and political means,[209] in accordance with the UN Charter and applicable international law.[210] This means preventing encroachment on the land of indigenous peoples,[211] ensuring food availability, regulating food prices and subsidies,[212] and preventing

[200] Asbjørn Eide, 'The Right to an Adequate Standard of Living Including the Right to Food' in Asbjørn Eide, Catarina Krause and Allan Rosas (eds), *Eonomic, Social and Cultural Rights* (Leiden, Martinus Nijhoff, 2001) 144.

[201] UNHRC, General Comment No 14 (n 55) para 30.

[202] Ibid para 15. This typology is based on the work of the former Special Rapporteur on the Right to Food, Asbjørn Eide. See Asbjørn Eide, 'Economic, Social and Cultural Rights as Human Rights' in Asbjørn Eide, Catarina Krause and Allan Rosas (eds), *Economic, Social and Cultural Rights,* 2nd edn (Leiden, Martinus Nijhoff, 2001) 23–25.

[203] Ibid 142.

[204] Ibid.

[205] Ibid.

[206] UN CESCR 'General Comment No 14' (n 196) para 39.

[207] Ibid para 34.

[208] Ibid para 39.

[209] See Eide (n 202) 143. See also UN CESCR, General Comment No 14 (n 196) para 35.

[210] UN CESCR, General Comment No 14 (n 196) para 39.

[211] Eide (n 202) 143.

[212] Ibid 144.

private enterprises from engaging in environmental pollution.[213] More specifically, States must adopt measures against environmental health hazards and formulate and implement national policies to reduce and eliminate air, water and soil pollution.[214] In the context of climate change, the right to health thus seems to imply an obligation to regulate private actors in order to achieve and uphold emission limitation and reduction standards, and to adopt and implement 'laws, plans, policies, programmes and projects that tackle the adverse effects of climate change'.[215] The result of these regulations and measures must be that the underlying determinants of health such, as food and nutrition, safe drinking water and a healthy environment remain, or become, available and accessible to all.[216]

Part of States' obligations relating to the right to health is to ensure that health and environmental impact assessments are made available to potentially affected communities where private actors propose activities that could undermine the right to health. This is illustrated by the ACHPR's decision in *SERAC v Nigeria*, where the State's failure to produce basic health and environmental impact assessments was a significant factor in the Commission's finding that the right to health had been violated.[217] The requirement to provide beneficiaries of the right with information about serious health risks relates both to the prevention of environmental harm and to the ability of beneficiaries to protect themselves against associated health risks. The latter dimension is closely related to what the CESCR describes as the obligations to 'fulfil' the right to health; a positive obligation that is triggered 'whenever an individual or group is unable, for reasons beyond their control' to enjoy the right 'by the means at their disposal'.[218] It basically requires that the State 'be the provider', which 'can range anywhere from a minimum safety net, providing that it keeps everyone above the poverty line appropriate to the level of development of that country, to a full comprehensive welfare model'.[219] According to the CESCR, States must give 'sufficient recognition to the right to health in the national political and legal systems, preferably by way of legislative implementation',[220] and must allocate a sufficient percentage of a State's budget earmarked for the right to health.[221] The right to health must also be given 'due attention in international agreements' and may require, in the

[213] UN CESCR, 'Concluding Observations on the Russian Federation' (1997) UN Doc E/1998/22, para 124.

[214] UN CESCR, General Comment No 14 (n 196) paras 36–37.

[215] Paul H Hunt and Rajat Khosla, 'Climate Change and the Right to the Highest Attainable Standard of Health' in Stephen Humphreys (ed), *Climate Change and Human Rights* (Cambridge, Cambridge University Press, 2009) 252.

[216] UN CESCR, General Comment No 14 (n 196) paras 4, 12.

[217] *SERAC v Nigeria*, paras 5, 53, 70.

[218] UN CESCR, General Comment No 14 (n 196) para 37.

[219] Eide (n 200) 145.

[220] UN CESCR, General Comment No 14 (n 199) para 36.

[221] See, eg, UN CESCR, 'Concluding Observations on Chile' (1988) UN Doc E/C.12/1988/SR.13, para 12 and UN CESCR, 'Concluding Observations on North Korea' (1987) UN Doc E/C.12/1987/SR.22, paras 5 and 17.

view of the CESCR, 'the development of further legal instruments'.[222] States are also required to 'facilitate access to essential health facilities, goods and services in other countries, wherever possible and [to] provide the necessary aid when required'.[223] This is interpreted as an obligation on high-income States to facilitate access to essential health service as well as assistance to adapt to climate change in low-income States.[224]

The parallel obligations of developed States contained in Article 4 of the UNFCCC and reaffirmed in the Paris Agreement[225] can be taken as a bottom line when it comes to interpreting these obligations. The procedural framework established under the Paris Agreement could also shed light on compliance with these obligations. Indeed, the Agreement specifically requires developed States to communicate information related to the fulfilment of their finance obligations, while other States providing resources are encouraged to communicate such information.[226] This information is to inform the global stocktaking process aimed at reviewing States' 'collective progress towards achieving the purpose of [the Agreement] and its long-term goals',[227] including the goals of 'Making finance flows consistent with a pathway towards low greenhouse gas emissions and climate-resilient development' and 'Increasing the ability to adapt to the adverse impacts of climate change and foster climate resilience and low greenhouse gas emissions development, in a manner that does not threaten food production'.[228] To meet these goals, and fulfil parallel obligations under international human rights law, developed States will need to scale-up funding to assist developing States in taking the resilience-building and adaptation actions required to ensure the realisation of the right to health.[229]

Conflict between Rights

The analysis of rights has confirmed what has long been observed in the analysis of human rights jurisprudence, namely that the human rights obligations of States are more wide-ranging than is apparent from the treaty texts. Even negatively formulated rights trigger obligations to take measures that are 'deliberate, concrete and targeted as clearly as possible towards meeting human rights obligations'.[230]

[222] UN CESCR, General Comment No 14 (n 199) para 39.

[223] Ibid. See also Curtis Doebbler and Flavia Bustreo, 'Making Health an Imperative of Foreign Policy: The Value of a Human Rights Approach' (2010) 12 *Health and Human Rights Journal* 47, 53.

[224] Hunt and Khosla (n 218) 252.

[225] Paris Agreement, Art 9(1).

[226] Paris Agreement, Art 9(5).

[227] Paris Agreement, Art 14(1).

[228] Paris Agreement, Art 2(1)(c) and (b).

[229] See also Margaretha Wewerinke-Singh and Curtis Doebbler, 'The Paris Agreement: Some Critical Reflections on Process and Substance' (2016) 39 *University of New South Wales Law Journal* 1486; fn 135 and accompanying text.

[230] UN CESCR, *General Comment No 3: The Nature of States Parties' Obligations (Art. 2, Para. 1, of the Covenant)* (14 December 1990) UN Doc E/1991/23, para 2.

These broad obligations come with a risk that rights will conflict. This is particularly so in relation to climate change; a problem that is entwined with virtually all aspects of economies, societies and cultures across the globe. Perhaps the most pressing case of potential clashes between rights are developing countries with limited access to renewable energy technologies, for whom aggressive mitigation action to prevent human rights violations may compromise the realisation of the economic and social rights of their own people. Cases of conflicting rights may also emerge where economic rights-holders invoke the right to property or peaceful enjoyment of their possessions in order to hamper climate change action within their own State.[231] The prospect of these potential clashes make it important to examine how the content of States' human rights obligations should be determined in cases of conflicting rights.

A first point to note is that treaty texts and jurisprudence provide guidance on how to deal with situations of conflicting rights. The general principle for limitations of rights is contained in Article 29(2) of the UDHR, which states that 'In the exercise of his rights and freedoms, everyone shall be subject only to such limitations as are determined by law solely for the purpose of securing due recognition and respect for the rights and freedoms of others and of meeting the just requirements of morality, public order and the general welfare in a democratic society'. Other limitations are rights-specific. For example, Article 47 of the ICCPR and Article 35 of the ICESCR provide that nothing in the two Covenants 'shall be interpreted as impairing the inherent right of all peoples to enjoy and utilise fully and freely their natural wealth and resources'. The jurisprudence of the HRC also suggests that States' obligations under Article 1 common to the two Covenants can influence the interpretation of other Covenant provisions; the HRC case of *Gillot v France* demonstrating that Article 1 may be invoked not just to reinforce other rights, but also to justify limitations to the exercise of the rights of individuals where the limitation is a reasonable measure to promote the collective right to self-determination.[232] The HRC has also insisted that 'positive action [required to promote the right of self-determination] must be consistent with the States' obligations under the Charter of the United Nations and under international law: in particular, States must refrain from interfering in the internal affairs of other States and thereby adversely affecting the exercise of the right to self-determination'.[233] These interpretations indicate that the right of self-determination is only limited to the extent that it enables the right of self-determination of different peoples to be exercised 'as fully as possible in the circumstances'.[234]

[231] See also Stephen Humphreys, *Climate Change and Human Rights: A Rough Guide* (International Council on Human Rights Policy, 2008) 5.

[232] *Marie-Hélène Gillot et al. v France* (2002) Communication No 932/2000, UN Doc A/57/40, para 3.16.

[233] UN HRC, General Comment No 12 (n 26) para 6.

[234] Robert McCorquodale, 'Group Rights' in Daniel Moeckli, Sangeeta Shah and Sandesh Sivakumaran (eds), *International Human Rights Law*, 2nd edn (Oxford, Oxford University Press, 2014) 345.

In contrast with the right of self-determination, some individual rights have limitations that are specifically spelt out in treaty texts or identified in jurisprudence. These limitations shed light on the substantive scope of the rights, which define the contours of States' obligations. For example, imposing the death penalty in certain cases, killing during armed conflicts and the use of reasonable force by law enforcement agents are widely recognised as the only possibly lawful limitations on the right to life. These specific limitations contrast with the much broader limitations permitted in relation to some economic and social rights. The right to property has possibly the widest range of potentially permitted limitations of all human rights.[235] In the context of climate change, apparent conflicts between rights seem to be easily resolvable where it is clear from the context that one right (eg the right to property) is subject to broad permitted limitations, whereas another right (eg the right of self-determination or the right to life) is not. Naturally, the discretion of States to restrict the enjoyment of a right with broad permitted limitations will be more limited in cases where the restriction simultaneously restricts the enjoyment of a right that has more narrow permitted limitations.

Human rights jurisprudence offers numerous examples of how established limitations of human rights affect States' obligations in cases where rights appear to conflict. See, for example, the case of *Mastromatteo v Italy*,[236] where the ECtHR considered the compatibility of a prisoner release scheme with Article 2 of the ECHR (protecting the right to life). The case arose from the murder of the applicant's son by a violent prisoner who was released early under the scheme. Although the case involved the prisoner's right to liberty, it was decided solely with reference to the States' obligation to protect the right to life: the Court scrutinised the key features of the scheme – considering, amongst other things, statistical evidence on the behaviour of prisoners granted early release – and extrapolated that the authorities could not have foreseen that the release of this particular prisoner would pose a real threat to life. The Court's apparent lack of consideration for the right to liberty appears to be based on the understanding that the right to liberty can be limited through criminal law which, in the light of the evidence, would have made the continued detention of the prisoner lawful.[237] In terms of conflicting rights, the question before the Court was therefore to what extent interference with the right to liberty was *required* to protect the right to life. *Mastromatteo v Italy* also demonstrates how risks assessments can be used to clarify the content of States' positive obligations to protect human rights. The risks posed by climate

[235] eg Art 21(2) of the ACHR provides that 'No one shall be deprived of his property except upon payment of just compensation, for reasons of public utility or social interest, and in the cases and according to the forms established by law'.

[236] *Mastromatteo v Italy* App no 37703/99 (ECtHR, 24 October 2002).

[237] The case of Tim de Christopher illustrates, however, that criminal law can also be abused to restrict the right to liberty of peaceful protestors who seek to protect the Earth's climate system. On this case see 'Tim's Story' (2011) Peaceful Uprising, available at www.peacefuluprising.org.

change may similarly require States to limit the exercise of certain rights (such as the right to property) to prevent the violation of other human rights.

In more complex situations of potentially conflicting rights we often need to consider the principle of non-discrimination. This basically prescribes that a State may have to treat right-holders who are in different positions in different ways, if treating them in the same way would perpetuate inequalities. In other words, international human rights law permits and sometimes requires 'some sort of privileged treatment … in order to achieve real equality'.[238] States' positive obligations to take affirmative measures towards substantive equality are perhaps most pronounced in cases concerning minorities and indigenous peoples. The obligations are based on the rationale that equality 'cannot be achieved by mere State obligations of non-interference, since experience shows that minorities, and indigenous peoples in particular, are not only threatened by government action but equally by other, more dominant … groups, by businesses and similarly powerful private actors'.[239] Thus, in the case of *Lubicon Lake Band v Canada*, the HRC found a violation of the right to enjoy one's culture where Canada allowed a provincial government to expropriate the territory of an indigenous community for the benefit of oil and gas companies. It explicitly stipulated that the violation involved 'historical inequities and certain more recent developments'.[240] The CESCR has also emphasised that the non-discrimination principle entails an obligation for States to take affirmative measures to protect the rights of disadvantaged groups including women, children and adolescents, the elderly, persons with disabilities and indigenous peoples.[241]

The decision of the European Committee on Social Rights (the Committee) on a complaint against France in a discrimination case is a useful illustration of how compliance with obligations that arise from the overarching prohibition of discrimination can be assessed in cases where the realisation of the right places a considerable burden on a State's resources. The case, *Autism-Europe v France*, arose from a complaint that France was failing to take sufficient measures to guarantee equality in access to education for those suffering from autism, in violation of the right of persons with disabilities to independence, social integration and participation in the life of the community (Article 15 of the ESC), the right of children to education and training (Article 17(1)), and the prohibition of discrimination (Article E, Part V). After noting that discrimination may arise by failing to take account of all relevant differences or by 'failing to take adequate steps to ensure that the rights and collective advantages that are open to all are genuinely accessible by and to all',[242] the Committee emphasised that the substantive rights protected in

[238] Nowak (n 11) 662.
[239] Ibid.
[240] *Ominayak and the Lubicon Lake Band v Canada*, para 33.
[241] UN CESCR, General Comment No 14 (n 196) paras 21–27.
[242] *Autism-Europe v France* European Committee on Social Rights (ECSR) Complaint No 13/2002 (4 November 2003) para 52.

the Charter and the prohibition of discrimination were 'so intertwined as to be inseparable'.[243] It found a violation of the three provisions in question based on the *ratio* that the Charter required States

> to take not merely legal action but also practical action to give full effect to the rights recognised in the Charter. When the achievement of one of the rights in question is exceptionally complex and particularly expensive to resolve, a State Party must take measures that allows it to achieve the objectives of the Charter within a reasonable time, with measurable progress and to an extent consistent with the maximum use of resources. States Parties must be particularly mindful of the impact that their choices will have for groups with heightened vulnerabilities.[244]

The decision in *Autism-Europe v France* illustrates an important point, namely that the right not to be discriminated against in the enjoyment of rights can be violated 'when States without an objective and reasonable justification fail to treat differently persons whose situations are significantly different'.[245] Moreover, it shows that positive obligations arising from the prohibition of discrimination can be exercised in a way that reconciles the immediate nature of those obligations with concurring obligations to realise economic, social and cultural rights progressively. This reflects an approach that could be meaningfully used to reconcile States' immediate obligations to protect peoples and individuals against the adverse effects of climate change with co-existing obligations to progressively realise the rights of those who have obtained negligible benefits from emission-producing activities. At the global level, for example, the estimated 1.2 billion individuals without access to electricity and the 2.7 billion without hygienic cooking conditions,[246] could be considered as particularly disadvantaged groups entitled to positive measures in international cooperation on climate change.

Yet evidential complexities inevitably arise in determining the scope of States' obligations when conflicts between rights involve beneficiaries within the State's territory as well as a potentially never-ending number of beneficiaries abroad. Part of the answer lies in acknowledging that it is 'for the national authorities to make the initial assessment both of the existence of a problem of public concern warranting measures … and of the remedial action to be taken'.[247] To some extent, these initial assessments have been carried out in connection with climate change, and several States have presented evidence of the adverse effects of climate change on the enjoyment of human rights within their territories to multilateral forums while suggesting specific mitigation, adaptation and compensation actions to

[243] Ibid para 47.
[244] Ibid para 53.
[245] *Autism-Europe v France*, para 52, quoting from *Thlimmenos v Greece* App no 34369/97 (ECtHR, 6 April 2000) ECHR 2000-IV, para 44.
[246] International Energy Agency (IEA), 'World Energy Outlook 2016' (Organisation for Economic Co-operation and Development and IEA, 2016) 2.
[247] *Case of James et al. v United Kingdom* (1986) Series A no 98, para 46. See also: *Handyside v UK* (1996) Series A no 24, 1 EHRR 737, para 48.

remedy those effects. The suggested actions primarily concern mitigation and support to be provided by other States. This raises the question to what extent other States may need to restrict the enjoyment of selected rights within their own territory to prevent the violation of rights in the States whose populations are most severely affected by climate change. The significance of 'systemic integration' is perhaps most apparent in relation to this question, as the content of a State's otherwise non-specific human rights obligations vis-a-vis beneficiaries of human rights everywhere may be usefully illuminated by reference to existing rules and principles of international climate change law. The principle of CBDRRC and the provisions of the UNFCCC, the Kyoto Protocol and the Paris Agreement which operationalise it are particularly important in this regard.

The principle of CBDRRC ensures that the UNFCCC's objective of preventing dangerous climate change is met without exacerbating existing inequalities. Although the principle applies exclusively to relations between States, it shares with international human rights law the objective of achieving substantive equality.[248] Consequently, CBDRRC could function as an application of the human rights principle of non-discrimination in inter-State relations, making it a form of affirmative action to correct historical inequities to ensure the equal enjoyment of rights at the global level. This application is consistent with the express prohibition of discrimination based on nationality under international human rights law and its interpretation as requiring States to take positive steps to eradicate discrimination.[249] This was highlighted by the Special Rapporteur on the Right to Housing, Raquel Rolnik, when she stated that as a result of the principle of non-discrimination, 'Industrialized countries must lead in reducing emissions levels and support developing countries in pursuing low-carbon development paths'.[250] In much the same way, commentators have argued that in the light of developed and developing countries' differing responsibilities and capacities developed States have 'a human rights duty, arising from non-discrimination and equality, to take reasonable steps to stop and reverse climate change'.[251] Although the principle of CBDRRC and related obligations do not answer all questions related to the content of States' obligations vis-a-vis beneficiaries within and outside their territories, these obligations do provide minimum standards that can be usefully applied in determining whether or not a State has complied with its human rights obligations

[248] On CBDRRC generally, see Marie-Claire Cordonier Segger et al, 'Prospects for Principles of International Sustainable Development Law after the WSSD: Common but Differentiated Responsibilities, Precaution and Participation' (2003) 12 *Review of European Community and International Environemntal Law* 54, 57.

[249] See also United Nations Development Programme (n 7) 147 (suggesting that developed States that do not respect the CBDRRC principle are acting contrary to their international commitments on poverty reduction).

[250] Raquel Rolnik, 'Report of the Special Rapporteur on Adequate Housing as a Component of the Right to an Adequate Standard of Living, and on the Right to Non-Discrimination in This Context' (6 August 2009) UN Doc A/64/255, para 70.

[251] Hunt and Khosla (n 215) 250.

relating to climate change. These minimum standards could significantly ease the burden on actors responsible for interpreting human rights norms who are faced with climate change-related claims involving alleged breaches of extraterritorial obligations.

Conclusion

As a result of human rights obligations, States have limited discretion when it comes to responding to climate change. First of all, States are obliged to take measures to prevent harm to human life, health and cultures resulting from climate change. These obligations cover beneficiaries both within and outside the State's territory. Through these prevention obligations, international human rights law sets a bottom line for climate action: States must ensure that the Earth's climate system does not deteriorate to the point where the enjoyment of human rights can no longer be guaranteed. Prevention obligations are important not only to prevent or mitigate a range of adverse effects of climate change that would affect the enjoyment of human rights, but also to create accountability for climate change-related human rights violations that might already be occurring. In part, these prevention obligations overlap with the obligations of States to ensure the progressive realisation of economic, social and cultural rights, which for high-income States means an obligation to assist low-income States with measures to respond to the adverse effects of climate change on the enjoyment of human rights within their territories. While taking measures to prevent and respond to climate harm, States must also ensure that human rights are not undermined or violated in the process. This means ensuring that climate policies and actions do not perpetuate existing inequalities. Finally, States must ensure that those whose human rights are affected by climate change have access to adequate and effective remedies.

Human rights bodies and courts have a key role to play when it comes to providing adequate and effective remedies for climate change-related human rights violations. However, assessing State compliance with human rights obligations relating to climate change is an evidentiary complex task. This is particularly the case in instances of alleged violations involving a State's obligation to prevent future harm, either through mitigation action or through financial assistance for mitigation, adaptation and disaster risk reduction in third States. To enable human rights bodies to deal with such cases with due regard for equity and non-discrimination, sophisticated analyses are needed not only to assess how direct impacts of climate change affect the enjoyment of relevant human rights, but also to determine, as the OHCHR puts it, 'how a given distribution of burden affects the enjoyment of human rights'.[252] This may mean integrating human rights indicators

[252] OHCHR Report on Climate Change and Human Rights (n 28) para 88.

into forecasting models.[253] New forecasting models may also need to be developed to give us a better understanding of the consequences of specific response measures such as reforestation, biofuel substitution, carbon trading and adaptation for the enjoyment of human rights. These models could draw on existing frameworks for human rights impact analysis, based on benchmarks and indicators,[254] and use data collected through other processes, such as data related to health, food security and human development.[255] New methodologies also need to be developed to link macro-level trends with micro-level observations, including anecdotal evidence or judicial decisions that reveal human rights violations connected with response measures.[256] Finally, in the light of the differentiated impacts of climate change there is a pressing need for further data, in particular disaggregated data, to help provide a better insight into the consequences of mitigation and adaptation scenarios for the enjoyment of rights by minorities and other potentially disadvantaged groups.[257]

Yet even without additional data and improved forecasting models we can, in principle, establish State responsibility for human rights violations associated with climate change. Anecdotal evidence of impacts coupled with existing scientific evidence of global trends and States' contributions to those trends may be sufficient to establish that a particular right has been violated as a result of a State's action or inaction on climate change. Detailed information on the conduct of individual States is available as a result of States' reporting obligations under the UNFCCC and the Kyoto Protocol, while even more detailed information will become available as States start to report on their Nationally Determined Contributions (NDCs) submitted under the Paris Agreement. Both past and present conduct can be considered in assessing whether or not a State has complied with its human rights obligations to prevent climate harm. In this context, it is important to recall that States' positive obligations to protect against threats to selected human rights – such as the rights to life, health and culture – include obligations to establish a legislative and administrative framework that provides effective protection against climate change-related threats. These obligations open the door to an integrative approach premised on the assumption that compliance with human rights obligations involves, at a minimum, upholding existing laws that offer legal

[253] Humphreys (n 231) 7.

[254] UN Office of the High Commissioner for Human Rights, 'Human Rights Indicators: A Guide to Measurement and Implementation' UN Doc HR/Pub/12/5 (New York, 2012).

[255] For a similar discussion, see Olivier de Schutter et al, 'Foreign Direct Investment, Human Development and Human Rights: Framing the Issues' (2009) 3 *Human Rights and International Legal Discourse* 137.

[256] See, eg, Joanne Scott and Lavanya Rajamani, 'EU Climate Change Unilateralism' (2012) 23 *European Journal of International Law* 469, 469ff (highlighting potentially detrimental impacts of EU aviation tax policies on vulnerable people in developing countries).

[257] See also UN Committee on the Elimination of All Forms of Discrimination Against Women (CEDAW) 'Statement of the CEDAW Committee on Gender and Climate Change' (44th session New York, 20 July–7 August 2009).

protection against serious and substantial risks to the enjoyment of human rights. In other words, open-textured provisions of human rights law can be interpreted in a way that holds States to account for non-compliance with the standards they have set for themselves in domestic and international legal frameworks related to climate change and the environment.

At the domestic level, States' own climate, energy and environmental laws can provide useful benchmarks for their compliance with human rights obligations. This is illustrated in particular by ECtHR jurisprudence on the right to life, where violations were established in virtually all cases where a State failed to uphold its domestic environmental legislation. At the international level, compliance benchmarks could be derived from the UNFCCC, the Kyoto Protocol and the Paris Agreement. The ECtHR's approach to the Hague Convention on the Civil Aspects of International Child Abduction (Hague Convention) illustrates the operation of an integrative approach where legal protection against human rights harm is indirectly provided by another international treaty: the ECtHR has systematically considered States' compliance with relevant provisions of the Hague Convention in child abduction cases related to Article 8 of the ECHR.[258] The most interesting element of this approach is that apparent violations of the Hague Convention almost automatically lead to a violation of Article 8 of the ECHR. As one scholar observed, 'the Court looks so closely into the Hague Convention that it is sometimes difficult to tell whether the judges are applying the European Convention on Human Rights or the Hague Convention'.[259] It is possible that a breach of the substantive provisions of the UNFCCC, or one of its associated instruments, could be read as coinciding with a violation of internationally protected human rights. The application of the principle of effectiveness – which features prominently in international human rights jurisprudence – may make it imperative to consider international climate change law as providing minimum standards of protection in connection with climate change and its adverse effects on human rights.

Conversely, the *lex specialis* on climate change must be interpreted in accordance with international human rights law. This follows from the premise that substantive human rights obligations are binding on all States as 'horizontal' norms that influence the interpretation of other treaties and even invalidate instruments that are not in line with those obligations. International human rights obligations may thus be understood as creating thresholds of minimum acceptability,[260] or as 'levels of protection for individual rights which can be regarded as the

[258] See, eg, *Carlson v Switzerland*, App no 49492/06 (ECtHR, November 2008) para 76.

[259] Daniel Rietiker, 'The Principle of "Effectiveness" in the Recent Jurisprudence of the European Court of Human Rights: Its Different Dimensions and Its Consistency with Public International Law – No Need for the Concept of Treaty Sui Generis' (2010) 79 *Nordic Journal of International Law* 245, 273.

[260] Simon Caney, 'Climate Change, Human Rights and Moral Thresholds' in Stephen Humphreys (ed), *Human Rights and Climate Change* (Cambridge, Cambridge University Press, 2009) 69ff.

minimum acceptable outcome'[261] in the interpretation and operationalisation of the UNFCCC, the Kyoto Protocol and the Paris Agreement. For example, the right of self-determination presses in favour of interpreting the Paris Agreement as requiring all States to prevent more than 1.5°C global temperature rise, as higher levels of warming are associated with near certainty that peoples inhabiting the most vulnerable small island States would permanently lose their territories and means of subsistence.[262] The increasing risks to human life, health, well-being and indigenous cultures associated with further warming also call for an interpretation of long-term temperature goal that draw the line at 1.5°C warming.[263] Other provisions, such as the global goal of enhancing adaptive capacity, strengthening resilience and reducing vulnerability to climate change,[264] must also be interpreted in terms of a minimum requirement; that is, the continuing protection of human rights. Human rights law not only demands an ambitious interpretation of such provisions, but also provides legal back-up for provisions that are not legally binding per se.

This brings us back to the key point of this chapter, namely that it is possible, at least in principle, to establish State responsibility for human rights violations associated with climate change. In practice, some form of litigation is normally needed to ensure that State responsibility leads to actual remedies for victims of the violation. However, as a matter of international law, State responsibility is established '*as immediately as* between the two [or more] States'.[265] In other words, the legal consequences of State responsibility are automatic when the wrongful conduct occurs, irrespective of whether any victim of the violation actively seeks a remedy. The legal consequences of human rights violations associated with climate change are spelt out in chapter eight, while chapter nine sets out how individuals, communities and States affected by climate change can invoke State responsibility before human rights bodies, courts and tribunals.

[261] OHCHR Report on Climate Change and Human Rights (n 28) 28.
[262] See Frieler et al (n 2); Schleussner et al (n 2).
[263] In a 2015 report, UN Human Rights Council Special Procedure mandate holders highlighted the greater risk of human rights harm associated with more than 1.5°C warming. See report by Special Procedures of the Human Rights Council, 'The Effects of Climate Change on the Full Enjoyment of Human Rights' (30 April 2015) available at www.thecvf.org/wp-content/uploads/2015/05/humanrightsSRHRE.pdf, 3ff.
[264] Paris Agreement, Art 7(1).
[265] *Phosphates in Morocco (Italy v France)* [1938] PCIJ Ser A/B No 74 10, para 48.

8

Remedies for Climate Change-Related Human Rights Violations

Introduction

As demonstrated in the previous chapters, international human rights law can provide an exclusive or complementary basis for State responsibility claims related to climate change. A key feature of international human rights law is that it creates *erga omnes* obligations, based on the 'legitimate interest' of the international community as a whole in compliance with these obligations. In a similar vein, the substantive obligations derived from the United Nations Framework Convention on Climate Change (UNFCCC), the Kyoto Protocol and the Paris Agreement (and parallel customary norms, such as the no-harm rule) are most appropriately characterised as obligations to the international community as a whole. The characterisation of these obligations as *erga omnes* affects the legal consequences when they are breached, including the rights of States to invoke responsibility and the content of 'secondary' obligations incurred by the responsible State as a result of the breach.

This chapter will explore the legal consequences of internationally wrongful conduct relating to climate change and its adverse effects. It first sets out the range of 'secondary obligations' that arise automatically on the occurrence of an internationally wrongful act, using international jurisprudence to unpack the meaning of these obligations in the context of climate change and human rights. It specifically considers questions of legal causation which, although not arising in assessing attribution, do arise in relation to reparations for injury. It proceeds to consider the proposed international law obligation known as aggravated State responsibility,[1] which is particularly relevant for addressing the human rights implications of climate change. Finally, it discusses how the legal consequences of State responsibility can gain practical force through the formal invocation of State responsibility by one or several States. This discussion will set the stage for chapter nine, which discusses avenues for the enforcement of relevant obligations.

[1] James Crawford, *State Responsibility: The General Part* (Cambridge, Cambridge University Press, 2013) 365.

Cessation of Wrongful Conduct and Guarantees of Non-repetition

In relation to the legal consequences of wrongful conduct (or what the International Law Commission (ILC)'s Articles on the Responsibility of States for Internationally Wrongful Acts (ILC ARS) call the 'content' of State responsibility), the first point to note is that legal consequences will arise even if the breach has not caused any verifiable injury, or if the link with injury cannot be approximated or proven.[2] This follows from the basic principle that a State that commits an internationally wrongful act 'must, so far as possible, wipe-out all the consequences of the illegal act and re-establish the situation which would, in all probability, have existed had that act not been committed'.[3] The emphasis on restoring the situation to what it was before the wrongful act was committed reflects the broader objective of compliance with obligations, which is emphasised in the ILC ARS through the codification of the continued duty of performance,[4] and of the duty to cease the wrongful act (if it is ongoing)[5] in two separate articles. Together, these provisions make it clear that the law of State responsibility is not a liability system with the primary or exclusive goal of providing injured persons with compensation. In this respect, the law of State responsibility differs substantially from private law systems which tend to impose more stringent evidentiary requirements on victims seeking to recover damages. Indeed, compliance with the obligation to end wrongful conduct does not even require the identification of victims: for example, a State's violation of an obligation to prevent harm could be ceased by taking adequate measures in accordance with the original obligation. The Commentaries emphasise that compliance with existing obligations is a prerequisite to the restoration and repair of the legal relationships affected by the breach.[6] The duty of cessation further comprises an obligation to offer appropriate assurances and guarantees of non-repetition where the circumstances require, which may be described as a positive reinforcement of future performance.[7] International human rights law similarly recognises that adequate and effective remedies for violations 'serve to

[2] See also Margaretha Wewerinke-Singh, 'State Responsibility for Human Rights Violations Associated with Climate Change' in Sébastien Jodoin, Sébastien Duyck and Alyssa Johl (eds), *Routledge Handbook of Human Rights and Climate Governance* (Abingdon, Routledge, 2018) ch 6, on which this chapter partly draws.

[3] *Case Concerning the Factory at Chorzów (Germany v Poland)* [1927] PCIJ Rep Series A no 17, 47.

[4] International Law Commission (ILC)'s Articles on the Responsibility of States for Internationally Wrongful Acts (ILC ARS), Art 29.

[5] ILC ARS, Art 30(a). The treatment of cessation as a distinct legal consequence of an internationally wrongful acts is a relatively novel development: previously cessation was considered as part of the remedy of satisfaction. See also James Crawford, *The International Law Commission's Articles on State Responsibility: Introduction, Text, Commentaries* (Cambridge, Cambridge University Press, 2002) 68, para 114; and James Crawford, *Brownlie's Principles of Public International Law* (Oxford, Oxford University Press, 2012) 567.

[6] ILC ARS, Commentary to Art 30, para 1.

[7] ILC ARS, Art 30(b) and Commentary to Art 30, para 1.

deter violations and uphold the legal order that the treaties create'.[8] The duty of cessation is therefore an important part of remedies for human rights violations and characterised by the HRC as 'an essential element of the human right to a remedy' that entails an obligation 'to take measures to prevent the recurrence of a violation', including through changes in the State Party's laws or practice if necessary.[9]

The consequences for States that incur these types of obligations based on climate change-related wrongful conduct could be drastic, particularly where the violation involves a series of wrongful acts and omissions or 'practice'. To meet its obligation of cessation, a State may need to make changes to significant parts of its laws, regulatory system and levels of assistance requested from, or provided to, other States in order to restore compliance with the violated obligations. The ACHPR's findings in *SERAC v Nigeria* illustrates that in the human rights context, the duty to offer appropriate assurances and guarantees of non-repetition may reinforce existing procedural rights: when violating a range of human rights, Nigeria had incurred 'secondary' obligations to provide 'information on health and environmental risks and meaningful access to regulatory and decision-making bodies to communities likely to be affected by oil operations'.[10] In the context of climate change, the duty of cessation could involve withdrawing fossil fuel subsidies, adopting new regulations and policies to phase out fossil fuels, and bringing all relevant existing regulations and policies in line with the goals of the Paris Agreement and the objective and principles of the Convention.[11] In a similar vein, a developed State might be under an immediate obligation to scale-up funding for mitigation, adaptation and capacity-building actions in developing States to restore compliance with its human rights obligations. The duty to offer appropriate assurances and guarantees of non-repetition also reinforces procedural obligations to provide information about the risks and consequences of climate change while ensuring the rights of individuals and communities to participate meaningfully in the design and implementation of responses to climate change.

Duty to Make Reparations

The second set of obligations arising from an internationally wrongful act centre around an obligation to make full reparations for the injury caused by the

[8] Dinah Shelton, *Remedies in International Human Rights Law*, 2nd edn (Oxford, Oxford University Press, 2010) 99.

[9] *General Comment No. 31*: Nature of the General Legal Obligation on states Parties to the Covenant (29 March 2004) HRC paras 16–17.

[10] *SERAC and Another v Nigeria* (2001) Communication 155/96, 15th Annual Activity Report AHRLR 60, para 69.

[11] This requirement matches the procedural obligation under the Paris Agreement of submitting 'nationally determined contributions' that reflect these objectives. See Paris Agreement, Art 4(3).

wrongful act.[12] The duty to make full reparations is closely related to the question of causation: it requires the identification of victims and triggers evidentiary questions related to the scope of injury for which reparations must be made. Article 33(1) clarifies that the duty to make reparations may be owed to the international community as a whole, while Article 33(2) specifically acknowledges that the content of responsibility 'is without prejudice to any right, arising from the international responsibility of a State, which may accrue directly to any person or entity other than a State'.[13] Injury is understood as including any material or moral damage caused by the act[14] and includes 'the injury resulting from and ascribable to the wrongful act' rather than 'any and all consequences' flowing from it.[15] This makes it clear that there must be a causal link between the wrongful act and some form of injury in order for there to be an obligation of reparation. The causal requirement is however not the same in relation to every breach and may depend, for example, on the specific right that was violated.[16]

Where the obligation breached relates to the prevention of harm, the link between injury and the breach is likely to involve consideration of the extent to which the harm was a reasonably foreseeable consequence of the action taken.[17] Based on the reports of the Intergovernmental Panel on Climate Change (IPCC), input from affected communities and the definition of 'climate change' in Article 1 of the UNFCCC, a broad range of climate change-related harm could be considered as reasonably foreseeable consequences of climate change and the human activities that are known to cause it. Cases such as *United States Diplomatic and Consular Staff in Tehran* demonstrate that causation can be established even when the wrongful conduct was only one of several factors that contributed to the injury.[18] In addition, the principle of effectiveness may require shifting at least part of the risk of uncertainty to the State where it can be established with a reasonable degree of certainty that specific injury has occurred as a result of global warming.[19] This supports the suggestion of Werkman that the correlation between greenhouse gas emissions, atmospheric chemistry and global warming has probably 'been demonstrated with sufficient confidence that it seems unlikely that an adjudicator would require a complainant, in order to obtain relief, to demonstrate what would

[12] ILC ARS, Art 31(1).

[13] These provisions mark a significant breakthrough in the general law of State responsibility, signalling a departure from the traditional principle that injuries suffered by individuals are legally suffered by the State of nationality, and it is the State that claims reparations for these injuries. See, eg, *Corfu Channel Case (United Kingdom v Albania)* [1949] ICJ Reports 4. See also *General Comment No. 31* (n 9) para 16; and *Sergio Euben Lopez Burgos v Uruguay*, para 14.

[14] ILC ARS, Commentary to Art 31, para 5.

[15] Ibid para 10.

[16] Ibid.

[17] Shelton, *Remedies in International Human Rights Law* (n 8) 99, 89.

[18] See, eg, *United States Diplomatic and Consular Staff in Tehran (Judgement)* [1980] ICJ Reports 3.

[19] Ibid 50, 317 (stating that the burden of uncertainty or lack of proof may sometimes shift to the State to uphold the deterrent function of remedies for human rights violations).

not be possible – that a specific emission of greenhouse gases by [the allegedly responsible State] directly caused the specific impact in [the State that claims to be injured]'.[20] As the science of attribution evolves, the chances that the victims of climate change will be able to ascertain their entitlement to reparations should further increase.

Once the duty to make full reparations has been triggered, the scope of the injury caused by the wrongful act has to be established. This will be a fact-sensitive exercise which will require significant interpretation of complex evidence related to risks and probabilities. However, the law of State responsibility does provide some clear road signs for determining the nature and amount of reparations due. The first is the principle that no reduction or attenuation of reparation will be made for any concurrent causes.[21] The duty to make reparations is similarly unaffected by a responsible State's ability to pay,[22] or by a claimant's inability to determine the quantity and value of the losses suffered.[23] In other words, the duty of the responsible State to make full reparations for the injury is unqualified in general international law.[24] In light of the principle that the beneficiaries of human rights obligations are the ultimate holders of the right to 'full reparations', the unqualified nature of the duty to make those reparations then means that the general law of State responsibility accommodates States' obligations to ensure the right to a remedy. The understanding of this right as a substantive human right implies that the focus of the duty to make reparations for a breach of international human rights law lies squarely on restoring the rights of victims, insofar as victims of the violation can be identified. Where it is not certain whether an individual qualifies as a victim of the breach, uncertainty could be addressed in accordance with the human rights principle *in dubio pro libertate et dignitate*. Furthermore, irrespective of whether or not victims can be identified, the content of the obligation must reflect the aim of re-establishing the *status quo ante*.[25]

[20] Jacob David Werksman, 'Could a Small Island Successfully Sue a Big Emitter? Pursuing a Legal Theory and a Venue for Climate Justice' in Michael B Gerrard and Gregory E Wannier (eds), *Threatened Island Nations: Legal Implications of Rising Seas and a Changing Climate* (Cambridge, Cambridge University Press, 2012) 412.

[21] See, eg, *United States Diplomatic and Consular Staff in Tehran (Judgement)* [1980] ICJ Reports 3.

[22] See Crawford (n 1) 481.

[23] *Mentes et al. v Turkey (Judgement)* App nos 58/1996/677/867, (ECtHR, 24 July 1998) para 106 (stating that there should be some pecuniary remedy, but 'since the applicants have not substantiated their claims as to the quantity and value of their lost property with any documentary or other evidence, the Government have not provided any detailed documents, and the Commission has made no findings of fact in this respect, the Court's assessment of amounts to be awarded must, by necessity, be speculative and based on principles of equity').

[24] ILC ARS, Commentary to Art 31, para 12 (stating that 'international practice and the decisions of international tribunals do not support the reduction or attenuation of reparation for concurrent causes'). See also Crawford (n 1) 496.

[25] *Case Concerning Application of the Convention on the Prevention and Punishment of the Crime of Genocide (Bosnia and Herzegovina v Serbia and Montenegro)* [2007] ICJ Reports 43; *Ahmadou Sadio Diallo (Guinea v DRC) (Judgment)* [2010] ICJ Reports 639; *Velásquez Radríguez v Honduras* (1988) IACtHR (Ser C) no 4.

Perhaps the most pressing legal question raised by States' duties to make full reparations for wrongful conduct connected with climate change concerns the likelihood that the consequences of a duty to make full reparations exceed what the responsible State can bear on its own. This possibility is clear from the cases discussed in chapter five, all of which involved multiple States to which the same injury could be ascribed and one State (potentially) incurring responsibility to make reparations for the entire injury: in *Corfu Channel*, the establishment of Albania's responsibility led to an unqualified obligation to make full reparations for the damage caused by the presence of mines in its waters, despite the fact that it was acknowledged that another State had probably laid the mines. In other words, Albania was held fully responsible for repairing the damage that appeared to be caused in part by the wrongful conduct of another State. In a similar vein, in *Soering* the United Kingdom incurred an unqualified obligation to make full reparations for damage done to the applicant by the United States, a non-party to the European Convention on Human Rights (ECHR). And in *Certain Phosphate Lands in Nauru* the dispute was settled with Australia paying for the full settlement; however, the two other States that were allegedly responsible for the same wrongful act agreed to pay Australia a contribution to the settlement.[26]

The latter example of burden-sharing reflects good practice rather than an existing rule: as noted in chapter five, a rule or principle for apportioning responsibility for reparations between responsible States is currently lacking (except for the basic principle of equity, quoted in Article 47(2) of the ILC ARS, that an injured State may not recover, by way of compensation, more than the damage it has suffered).[27] The principle of effectiveness is particularly relevant in this case: the duty to make reparations may be interpreted accordingly as requiring that where States incur a seemingly unbearable burden of reparations, they proactively take steps to try to meet their obligations towards victims. The most obvious avenue for doing so is negotiations or cooperation with other responsible States, as in *Certain Phosphate Lands in Nauru*. For example, States could agree to set up a mechanism to provide reparations to victims based on effective burden-sharing between responsible States. Innovative mechanisms such as fossil fuel and aviation levies could be used to generate additional funds to compensate victims. However, the continuing controversy around liability and compensation at the international climate change negotiations suggest that negotiations on reparations may fail to produce meaningful results. If no collaborative solutions are found, a more confrontational approach may be necessary: one responsible State could then invoke the responsibility of other States to try to enforce the parallel obligations of those States to make reparations for the same injury. The advantage of the rule contained in Article 47 of the ILC ARS is that it entitles the first responsible State

[26] UK Agreement, 24 March 1994, in UKMIL (1994) 65 BY 625.
[27] ILC ARS, Art 47(2) and Commentary to Art 47, para 3.

(as a non-injured State) to invoke the responsibility of other responsible States for wrongful conduct contributing to injury. This invocation of responsibility of third States will in turn shed light on each of those States' obligations to make reparations to victims of climate change. We can speculate that reliance on this rule by one responsible State could trigger a 'race to the top', where States' respective obligations relating to climate change and human rights are clarified and progressively start influencing State conduct. This may even occur if claims are triggered by a responsible State's motivation to share an otherwise massive burden for reparations (capped at the amount of injury actually suffered), as any subsequent claim against other States would entail the task of ascertaining whether or not the allegedly wrongful conduct had been stopped and, if it is ongoing, articulating duties of cessation. This process would help consolidate the limits of States' discretion in areas that affect the Earth and its habitability for human beings.

We can observe that States' obligations towards victims could create a new situation of potentially conflicting rights, especially where these obligations involve making reparations for significant damage that has already been done. This case could be addressed through the application of the substantive norms and principles that are routinely applied in human rights cases to reconcile the rights of victims with those of other beneficiaries.[28] The nature of this exercise has led commentators to characterise the practice of human rights bodies of resorting to remedies as 'the area of judicial activity that most clearly embodies the tension between the ideal and the real'.[29] The wide range of remedies awarded for human rights violations (including restitution, compensation, rehabilitation, and measures of satisfaction such as public apologies, public memorials, guarantees of non-repetition and, perhaps most importantly, changes in relevant laws or practices) reflect the potential for constructing remedies that are consistent with the object and purpose of international human rights law.[30] It is not the nature of climate change-induced human rights' violations but the potential scale of injury ascribable to climate change-related wrongs that creates the most significant legal, evidential and practical questions regarding reparations for those violations. The severity and scale of damage and, in the human rights context, the virtually limitless number of potential victims of any established violation, means that the effectiveness of international laws pertaining to climate change is hinged on the extent to which States exercise their right to invoke responsibility (as injured or non-injured States) and cooperate to give effect to the victims' right to a remedy and to restore the rule of law.

In this regard, we should note that wrongful conduct that amounts to 'serious breaches of obligations under peremptory norms of general international law' has specific legal consequences that go beyond the rights of invocation and

[28] Shelton (n 8) 99.
[29] Paul Gewirtz, 'Remedies and Resistance' (1983) 92 *Yale Law Journal* 585.
[30] *General Comment No. 31* (n 10) para 16.

obligations to cease the wrongful act and make full reparations for the injury.[31] These consequences include a duty not to recognise the situation created by the breach as lawful;[32] a duty not to provide aid or assistance in maintaining the unlawful situation;[33] and a duty of all States to cooperate to bring the breach to an end through lawful means.[34] It is significant that in its *Wall* Advisory Opinion the International Court of Justice (ICJ) not only recognised the duties of cooperation and non-recognition as customary international law, but also implied that these obligations extend to all serious breaches of *erga omnes* obligations.[35] Given the potentially catastrophic consequences of climate change for the enjoyment of human rights, it is conceivable that wrongful conduct that is one of the concurrent causes of climate change will trigger obligations of non-recognition and cooperation for all other States. We should emphasise that whether or not a State's

[31] ILC ARS, Arts 40 and 41. Art 40(1) defines a 'serious breach' of an obligation under a peremptory norm as involving 'a gross or systematic failure by the responsible State to fulfil the obligation'. A peremptory norm can be understood in accordance with Arts 53 and 64 of the VCLT as norms that are 'mandatory and imperative in any circumstances'. See Gerald Fitzmaurice, 'Third Report on the Law of Treaties' (1958) II *Yearbook of the International Law Commission* 40. Some have argued that the scholarly attention for the *jus cogens* concept has been disproportionate to its actual influence. See: Prosper Weil, 'Towards Relative Normativity in International Law?' (1983) 77 *The American Journal of International Law* 413, 432; and Christian Tomuschat, 'Reconceptualizing the Debate on Jus Cogens and Obligations Erga Omnes: Concluding Observations' in Christian Tomuschat and Jean-Marc Thouvenin (eds), *The Fundamental Rules of the International Legal Order: Jus Cogens and Obligations Erga Omnes* (Leiden, Martinus Nijhoff, 2006) 436.

[32] The Commentaries to Art 41 stipulate that 'waiver or recognition induced from the injured State by the responsible State cannot preclude the international community interest in ensuring a just and appropriate settlement'.

[33] ILC ARS, Art 40. See also James Crawford, *The International Law Commission's Articles on State Responsibility: Introduction, Text, Commentaries* (Cambridge, Cambridge University Press, 2002) Commentary to Art 41, paras 4, 9 (explaining that the second para of Art 40 provides for an obligation of abstention which comprises two obligations, namely not to recognise the situations created by the serious breaches as lawful and, secondly, not to render aid or assistance in maintaining that situation).

[34] ILC ARS, Commentary to Art 40, para 3 (explaining that the obligation arises from substantive rules of conduct that prohibit what has come to be seen as intolerable because of the threat that it presents to the survival of States and their peoples and the most basic human values).

[35] *Legal Consequences of the Construction of a Wall in the Occupied Palestinian Territory* [2004] ICJ Reports 2004, para 159 ('Given the character and the importance of the rights and obligations involved, the Court is of the view that all States are under an obligation not to recognise the illegal situation resulting from the construction of the wall in the Occupied Palestinian Territory … They are also under an obligation not to render aid or assistance in maintaining the situation created by such construction. It is also for all States, while respecting the United Nations Charter and international law, to see to it that any impediment, resulting from the construction of the wall, to the exercise by the Palestinian people of its right to self-determination is brought to an end'). Cf ILC ARS, Commentary to Art 41(1), para 3 (stating that 'paragraph 1 … may reflect the progressive development of international law', but adds that 'in fact such cooperation, especially in the framework of international organizations, is carried out already in response to the gravest breaches of international law and is often the only way of providing an effective remedy'). In particular, commentators have argued that the rule contained in Art 41(1) has been construed too narrowly by the ILC, given that under customary international law 'the same consequences follow from any serious breach of any customary international law obligation designed to protect fundamental values of the international community as a whole'. See Antonio Cassese, 'The Character of the Violated Obligation' in James Crawford, Alain Pellet and Simon Olleson (eds), *The Law of International Responsibility* (Oxford, Oxford University Press, 2010) 416.

conduct amounts to a 'serious breach' depends on substantive obligations which are, as highlighted in previous chapters, differentiated. Furthermore, it must be stressed that international law, including substantive human rights norms, limits States' discretion in responding to serious violations.[36] Maintaining these limits is important because the wrongful conduct could be of such scope and quality that non-recognition would have severe economic and political consequences for the recalcitrant State or States, thus creating a risk of knock-on effects on the enjoyment of human rights.[37] The existence of these risks reinforces the importance of the duty to cooperate to realise human rights, which in the context of aggravated State responsibility requires 'a joint and coordinated effort by all States to counteract the effects of [serious breaches of relevant human rights obligations], [possibly] in the framework of a competent international organization, in particular the United Nations'.[38] In relation to climate change, cooperation designed to bring an ongoing serious violation to an end could take place under the auspices of the Conference of the Parties to the UNFCCC (COP), Conference of the Parties serving as the Meeting of the Parties to the Kyoto Protocol (CMP) or Conference of the Parties serving as the meeting of the Parties to the Paris Agreement (CMA), given that the wrongful conduct would almost certainly constitute a violation of international climate change law. Another appropriate forum for the required cooperation could be the UN Human Rights Council. One potential role for quasi-judicial human rights treaty bodies could be to deduce specific standards from existing human rights principles to ensure that the potentially massive burden of reparations for human rights violations related to climate change is shared equitably between responsible States. This could be done, either at their own initiative or in response to a claim (under one of the inter-State complaint procedures) by a State that has incurred responsibility against another State that allegedly contributed to the same injury through the same or related wrongful conduct.

The wide range of remedies awarded for human rights violations (including restitution, compensation, rehabilitation, and measures of satisfaction such as public apologies, public memorials, guarantees of non-repetition and, more importantly, changes in relevant laws or practices) reflect the potential for constructing

[36] See, eg, ICCPR, Art 1 and ICESCR, Art 1. See also Margo Kaplan, 'Using Collective Interests to Ensure Human Rights: an Analysis of the Articles of State Responsibility' (2004) 79 *New York University Law Review* 1902. See also ILC ARS, Commentary to Art 40, which refers to the ICJ's Namibia Advisory Opinion where the Court stressed that 'The non-recognition of South Africa's administration of the Territory should not result in depriving the people of Namibia of any advantages derived from international cooperation'; and ILC ARS, Commentary to Art 41(1), para 10.

[37] Some members of the HRC have suggested that States' obligations under Art 1(3) of the ICCPR to promote the right to self-determination may include the termination of diplomatic relations with States that violate this right. See Dominic McGoldrick, *The Human Rights Committee* (Oxford, Oxford University Press, 1991) 251–52 (noting instances where individual HRC members questioned governments with regard to their diplomatic relations with Israel (in the context of its occupation of Palestinian territories) and with South Africa (in the context of the apartheid regime).

[38] ILC ARS, Commentary to Art 41(1), para 2.

remedies for climate change damage that are consistent with human rights objectives.[39] These remedies should materialise through bottom-up processes: individuals and communities affected by climate change themselves are in the best position to identify and develop suitable remedies for violations of their human rights. Thus, in cases where a State plans to invoke the law of State responsibility on behalf of affected communities, consultative processes will be needed to ensure that reparation claims accurately reflect the demands of those communities.

Invocation of Responsibility

As noted previously, State responsibility is established '*as immediately as* between the two [or more] States'[40] whenever a State violates its international obligations. This rule indicates that the legal consequences of State responsibility arise automatically once a State violates an international obligation through conduct relating to climate change. Indeed, legal consequences of wrongful conduct arise even if other States do not (immediately) realise or recognise that the State in question has acted contrary to its international obligations. However, the formal legal consequences of State responsibility are unlikely to have practical effect unless and until either a State or a victim of the violation seeks to invoke the responsibility of the State in question, either bilaterally or through a judicial or quasi-judicial body.

The ILC ARS codify the entitlement of a State that is specifically affected by the breach of an *erga omnes* obligation to invoke the responsibility of the violating State. The ILC's interpretation of this entitlement confirms that States with populations whose human rights have been violated as a result of wrongful conduct contributing to climate change could, in principle, invoke the responsibility of the violating State or States. The ILC ARS make it clear that when there is a plurality of injured States, each is entitled to invoke responsibility.[41] However, the claim of a wrongful act connected with climate change specifically affecting a particular State or States necessarily raises questions about the attribution of specific impacts to anthropogenic climate change. The evidence reviewed in chapter one suggests that States whose populations are affected by long-term effects of climate change, such as rising sea levels and the melting of permafrost, would have no difficulty in establishing that they were specifically affected by wrongful conduct that contributed to climate change. Yet meeting the 'specifically affected' standard may be more difficult for States whose populations are primarily affected by the amplification of pre-existing risks or vulnerabilities. These may be the increased risk of drought, disease or extreme weather events. The extent to which States are specifically affected by the breach depends on the evidence and interpretation of the 'specifically affected' criterion in the context of the alleged violation.

[39] *General Comment No. 31* (n 9) para 16.
[40] *Phosphates in Morocco (Italy v France)* [1938] PCIJ Ser A/B, No 74 at 10, para 48.
[41] ILC ARS, Art 46 and Commentary. See also Crawford (n 1) 545ff.

The ILC ARS recognise, however, that States with a 'wider, more diffuse interest in performance of the [*erga omnes*] obligation'[42] could also be 'injured States' as regards the right to invoke responsibility. This is the case when the breach is 'of such a character as to radically change the position of all the other States to which the obligation is owed with regard to the further performance of the obligation'.[43] It is worth noting that the rule does not apply automatically to any breach of obligations owed to the international community as a whole: as Crawford points out, it is restricted to breaches which affect the 'structure of the whole regime'.[44] A breach of obligations to prevent dangerous climate change derived from the UNFCCC or international human rights law almost certainly comes into this category: the irreversibility of the changes to the Earth's climate system resulting from the breach means that the objective of preventing dangerous climate change will become more difficult to achieve, and perhaps even unachievable, as a result of the breach. It therefore appears that at least all State Parties to the UNFCCC would be able to invoke the responsibility of another State or States for such a breach as 'injured States'. In a similar vein, one State's breach of its own obligations to prevent climate change-induced human rights violations will affect the capacity of virtually all other States to guarantee minimum levels of human rights protection, thus arguably entitling those States to invoke the responsibility of the violating State as 'injured States'.

The right to invoke responsibility for wrongful conduct related to climate change is, presumably, not even confined to 'injured States' in this broader sense: the ILC ARS suggest that where the obligation breached is of an *erga omnes* nature, all States could invoke responsibility based on the presumption that in light of the nature of the obligation, invocation will be in the collective interest.[45] This mirrors the view of the HRC in its General Comment 31, in which it not only commends that violations of Covenant rights by any State Party 'deserve the attention' of all other State Parties, but also stresses that drawing attention to possible breaches of Covenant obligations and calling on other State Parties to comply with their obligations should 'far from being regarded as an unfriendly act, be considered as a reflection of legitimate community interests'.[46] In the context of climate change,

[42] Crawford (n 1) 546.

[43] ILC ARS, Art 42 (suggesting that if the obligation breached is not owed to the State itself but to the international community as a whole, a State is entitled to invoke the responsibility of another State if the violation specifically affects that State or 'is of such a character as radically to change the position of all the other States to which the obligation is owed with respect to the further performance of the obligation').

[44] Crawford (n 1) 547.

[45] ILC ARS, Art 48. See also WP Gormley, 'The Right to Life and the Rule of Non-Derogability: Peremptory Norms of Jus Cogens' in Bertrand G Ramcharan (ed), *The Right to Life in International Law* (Leiden, Martinus Nijhoff, 1995) 146. See also Malgosia Fitzmaurice, 'International Responsibility and Liability' in Daniel Bodansky, Jutta Brunnée and Ellen Hey (eds), *The Oxford Handbook of International Environmental Law* (Oxford, Oxford University Press, 2007) 1021.

[46] *General Comment No. 31* (n 9) para 2. Cf Christian Tomuschat, 'Global Warming and State Responsibility' in Holger Hestermeyer and others, *Law of the Sea in Dialogue* (Saint Paul, Springer, 2011)

the implication is that any State could possibly invoke the responsibility of another State that fails to comply with its obligations under international human rights law and/or international climate change law to protect individuals, communities and cultures from the adverse effects of climate change.

Conclusion

Once a breach of obligations has occurred, the responsible State must first and foremost restore compliance with the obligations that were violated. In other words, a State whose legislative framework or conduct is not in accordance with a human rights obligation incurs an obligation to bring its laws and practices in line with the relevant obligation. Moreover, the State must take measures to prevent future breaches of the obligation. And where the unlawful conduct – such as a State's failure to take adequate measures to prevent loss of life associated with the adverse effects of climate change – has actually caused harm, the State also incurs an obligation to make full reparations for the injury. These reparations must be directed to the beneficiaries of the obligation, which usually means the victims of the human rights violation.

The scope and nature of appropriate remedies might be relatively easy to establish where the violation concerns localised damage to individuals or communities, such as harm resulting from land grabbing or the exclusion of vulnerable communities from adaptation programmes. However, where the unlawful conduct relates to the impact of climate change per se on the enjoyment of human rights, the severity and scale of damage and the virtually limitless number of potential victims will trigger difficult questions related to causation, proof and victimhood. These questions will be complicated by the fact that multiple States might be responsible for the same damage. In such cases, the effectiveness of the law of State responsibility is hinged on the extent to which States cooperate to give effect to the victims' right to a remedy and to restore the rule of law. With liability and compensation excluded, at least for now, from the scope of the Warsaw Mechanism on Loss and Damage Associated with Climate Change,[47] it would seem opportune to explore the role of human rights bodies in facilitating such cooperation. Meanwhile, the human rights community could work with affected communities to develop guidance on the types of remedies that might be appropriate for various climate change-related human rights violations.

14 (suggesting that recognising the *erga omnes* nature of the obligations contained in the UNFCCC 'would mean that every individual State could possibly bring a claim against every other State' which he considers to be 'not a sensible proposition').

[47] COP Decision 1/CP.21, para 52. See further MJ Mace and Roda Verheyen, 'Loss, Damage and Responsibility After COP21: All Options Open for the Paris Agreement' (2016) 25 *Review of European Community & International Environmental Law* 197.

9

Litigating Climate Change before Human Rights Bodies, Courts and Tribunals

Introduction

The previous chapters have described how human rights violations resulting from climate change can be established. In a nutshell, States' acts and omissions that contribute to climate change can be characterised as a breach of human rights obligations (such as the obligation to take all necessary measures to protect against serious risks to human life). State responsibility arises automatically upon the occurrence of a breach of such obligations. However, as suggested previously, the legal consequences of a breach are unlikely to have practical effect unless the responsibility of the violating State is formally invoked. In principle, all it takes to do so is an announcement from an authorised representative from another State indicating the same. Yet there is a good chance that the allegedly responsible State will simply refute the allegations or ignore the claim, in which case the invoking State may wish to resort to litigation. Against this backdrop, this chapter looks at potential avenues for pursuing rights-based State responsibility claims at the domestic, regional and international levels. It reviews emerging practice and jurisprudence in rights-based climate litigation, but also evaluates avenues for rights-based climate litigation that have not yet been tried and tested.

It is important to note at the outset that while rights-based climate litigation against States has a certain appeal, alternative approaches (litigious or non-litigious) may sometimes be preferable. First of all, inter-State cases carry a risk of undermining relationships with the defendant State or States in question (which may well be important donors of foreign aid). Second, litigation usually requires significant technical expertise and financial resources, which may not be available to climate vulnerable individuals, communities and nations. There are also significant legal and technical obstacles to rights-based climate litigation, as discussed in previous chapters and elaborated in the present one. Finally, litigation at the international level is often less accessible to plaintiffs and witnesses due to the location of international human rights bodies.

On the positive side, rights-based climate litigation can serve to highlight the adverse consequences of climate change for individuals and societies. It can also give climate vulnerable States important bargaining power in international climate change negotiations. Perhaps most importantly from a human rights perspective, litigation can serve to deliver on a key promise embedded in human rights law and discourse: victims' access to effective remedies for human rights violations.

When thinking about potential rights-based climate cases, an initial question is who potential plaintiffs in rights-based climate lawsuits could be. In light of the vast scale of the losses and damages resulting from climate change, lawsuits by local or national governments on behalf of those whose rights are implicated by these losses and damages appear to be the most efficient way of seeking redress for the human rights implications of climate change. At the same time, individuals and communities may want to seek recourse to justice for climate change-related human rights violations where their governments are unwilling or unable to act on their behalf. This chapter therefore considers litigation avenues that could be pursued by individuals and communities, as well as avenues that could be pursued by local or national governments. The chapter discusses constitutional claims before domestic courts and national human rights institutions; regional human rights bodies; the complaint procedures related to the Special Procedure mechanisms of the UN Human Rights Council; and the individual and inter-State complaint procedures of human rights treaty bodies. Potential litigation before the International Court of Justice (ICJ) is discussed in relation to Convention on the Elimination of All Forms of Discrimination Against Women (CEDAW) and in general, adding to existing scholarship on the ICJ's potential to address climate change.

Domestic Courts

Most rights-based climate litigation to date has been brought before domestic courts. At the time of writing there are 17 ongoing or completed rights-based climate cases in 14 different jurisdictions, including Belgium, Colombia, Ireland, the Netherlands, Nigeria, Norway, Pakistan, the Philippines, South Africa, Sweden, Switzerland, the United Kingdom, the United States and the European Union.[1] Numerous additional cases are being prepared or contemplated.[2] Most of these cases draw on constitutional rights, which are generally coupled with the right to a remedy for their violation, available through the courts. Reference is also frequently made to regional and international human rights law, as well as to the UNFCCC, the Kyoto Protocol and the Paris Agreement. Naturally, the extent to which international law is enforceable before domestic courts depends on the nature of the legal system in question.

[1] The cases can be accessed through the Sabin Center for Climate Change Law's Climate Change Litigation Databases: US cases (2) and non-US cases (15), available at www.climatecasechart.com.

[2] See United Nations Environment Programme (UNEP), *The Status of Climate Change Litigation: a Global Review* (UNEP, 2017). 'Rights-based climate litigation' is defined here as litigation where the plaintiff(s) seeks to hold one or more governments or corporations to account for climate action or inaction based wholly or in part on the adverse effects of climate change on the enjoyment of human rights.

One of the first hurdles plaintiffs in rights-based climate cases must overcome is to establish what is often called 'standing' or *locus standi*. In other words, plaintiffs must show some direct interest in the matter at dispute in order to bring a case.[3] In rights-based climate cases, individuals or communities who are directly affected by the adverse effects of climate change might be able to establish standing based on the damage suffered to their legal rights. Establishing standing in these cases will likely turn primarily on the quality of the evidence that establishes the attribution of specific harms to climate change (discussed below). Another category of potential claimants are public interest organisations: the Dutch NGO Urgenda, for example, successfully established standing in its case against the Dutch government based on its mission to strive for a more sustainable society.[4] Similarly, the African NGO Earthlife was found to have standing when it sued the South African government based on its mission to mobilise civil society around environmental issues.[5] Finally, national or local governments representing climate vulnerable individuals and communities might fulfill the requirement of standing. In the latter case, inspiration could be drawn from the reasoning of the US Supreme Court in *Massachusetts v EPA*[6] where standing was granted to several states based on their sovereign capacity 'to have the last word as to whether its mountains shall be stripped of their forests and its inhabitants shall breathe pure air'.[7] In a case based on human rights, however, the emphasis is on the State's right and obligation to protect the rights of its people against infringements by public and private actors. These obligations were recognised in broad terms by the Hague District Court in *Urgenda v the Netherlands*,[8] where the court stated that the existence of 'a high risk of dangerous climate change with severe and life-threatening consequences for man and the environment' triggered an obligation on the State 'to protect its citizens from it by taking appropriate and effective measures'.[9] It can be argued that litigation against major polluters is amongst the most appropriate and effective measures climate vulnerable States could take to protect the rights of their people against the threats posed by climate change, especially if international climate change negotiations continue to fail to address questions of liability and compensation.

Where a domestic court considers the merits of a rights-based climate case, the plaintiffs would need to establish some kind of relationship between the conduct of a State on the one hand and infringements with rights on the other. It remains

[3] Jennifer Corrin and David Newton Bamford, *Courts and Civil Procedure in the South Pacific*, 2nd edn (Antwerp, Intersentia 2016) 53.

[4] *The Urgenda Foundation v Kingdom of the Netherlands* [2015] District Court of the Hague, HAZA c/09/00456689, June 2015.

[5] *Earthlife Africa v Minister of Environmental Affairs*, Case no 65662/16 (judgment of 6 March 2017), High Court of South Africa (Gauteng Division) para 3.

[6] *Massachusetts v EPA* 549 US SC 497 (2007).

[7] Ibid para 14 (quoting from *Georgia v Tennessee Copper Co.* 206 US SC 230 (1907)).

[8] *The Urgenda Foundation v Kingdom of the Netherlands.*

[9] Ibid para 4.74.

an open-ended question what kind of test the courts would apply on this point. As noted earlier, international and regional human rights bodies have highlighted that human rights violations can be established even in the absence of scientific probability regarding a causal link. This approach is based on the positive obligations of States to protect human rights, which essentially shifts part of the burden of uncertainty about environmental impacts to the State, in line with the precautionary principle.[10] Nonetheless, defendants can – and often do – argue that the emissions for which they are responsible are only a fraction of the global total and hence cannot be found to have caused a particular harm.[11] In *EPA v Massachusetts*, for example, the Environmental Protection Agency (EPA) of the United States argued that its decision not to regulate greenhouse gases contributed so insignificantly to the plaintiffs' injuries that there was no realistic possibility that the relief sought would mitigate climate change and remedy the plaintiffs' injuries.[12] However, the Supreme Court found that the EPA overstated its case on this point and that its refusal to regulate greenhouse gas emissions 'contributed' to Massachusetts' injuries.[13] Similarly, in *Urgenda v the Netherlands* the court held that the fact that the amount of Dutch emissions is small compared to other countries did not affect the State's obligation to take precautionary measures to address climate change.[14] As for evidence on causation, plaintiffs can increasingly rely on a growing body of 'attribution research' which links contributions of majors polluters to specific climate impacts.[15] This evidence, coupled with anecdotal evidence about the damaging impact of climate change already experienced around the world, might be sufficient to establish causation, especially if the court in question takes due account of victims' right to a remedy for human rights violations.

One major advantage of climate litigation before domestic and regional courts – as compared to litigation before quasi-judicial human rights bodies – is that it has the potential to result in a binding judgment. Specifically, plaintiffs could obtain an order for equitable relief to prevent future harm as well as compensatory damages, including the means for as full rehabilitation as possible.[16]

[10] See also Dinah Shelton, *Remedies in International Human Rights Law*, 2nd edn (Oxford, Oxford University Press, 2010) 50, 317.

[11] See also Jacqueline Peel, 'Issues in Climate Change Litigation' (2011) 5(1) *Carbon & Climate Law Review* 15, 16.

[12] *Massachusetts v EPA*, 20.

[13] *Massachusetts v EPA*, 21.

[14] *The Urgenda Foundation v Kingdom of the Netherlands*, para 4.79.

[15] Brenda Ekwurzel et al, 'The Rise in Global Atmospheric CO2, Surface Temperature, and Sea Level from Emissions traced to Major Carbon Producers' (2017) 144(4) *Climatic Change* 579. According to the study, the carbon majors are responsible for 50 per cent of global surface temperature rise, 57 per cent of the increase in carbon dioxide in the atmosphere and between 26 and 32 per cent of global sea level rise.

[16] The right to rehabilitation as part of redress is found in several international instruments, with perhaps the strongest formulation in the Convention Against Torture and Other Cruel, Inhuman or Degrading Treatment or Punishment (adopted 10 December 1984, entered into force 26 June 1987) 1465 UNTS 85, Art 14.

The litigation could thus result in tangible remedies for victims in case of a court victory. Another significant benefit of rights-based climate litigation before a domestic court is that it offers tremendous opportunities for involving civil society, the private sector, academia and the local media in the legal action. If a rights-based climate case is brought before a domestic court in a country where the alleged climate harms are suffered, those whose rights are implicated by the harm could relatively easily serve as witnesses, which would likely be more cumbersome and expensive in international or transnational-level litigation. The bottom-up nature of rights-based climate litigation at the domestic level also ensures that lawyers and members of the judiciary in jurisdictions where the case is brought become crucial players in the global climate law movement.

Rights-based climate litigation before domestic courts also has limitations. First of all, in some jurisdictions, it may not be sensible or desirable for individuals or communities affected by climate change to attempt to hold their own government to account for human rights violations resulting from climate change. For example, Pacific Island nations are at the forefront of climate change, but the region as a whole contributes no more than 0.03 per cent to global greenhouse gas emissions.[17] In light of this fact, it would not only seem futile but also contrary to 'climate justice'[18] to bring a claim against Pacific Island States for human rights violations associated with the adverse effects of climate change. Indeed, some foreign States are not only responsible for much larger shares of global emissions, but also have greater capacities to decarbonise their economies.[19] In these cases, rather than trying to sue their own government, individuals and communities may wish to take legal action against a foreign State or States. However, claims against foreign States before domestic courts are likely barred by legal doctrines of State immunity. Innovative transnational litigation may offer some recourse to justice where victims are unable to access meaningful redress within their jurisdiction of domicile. Alternatively, individuals, communities or governments may use domestic courts or quasi-judicial bodies to file human rights claims against private actors, as has been done in the innovative petition filed before the Commission of Human Rights of the Philippines (discussed below). Another option in these cases is to directly approach regional (where available) or international human rights bodies with claims, where the requirement that domestic remedies be exhausted may be lifted based on the non-availability of such remedies in the circumstances.

[17] Lifou, Loyalty Islands and New Caledonia, 'Paris 2015: Save Oceania!' (3rd Oceania 21 Summit, 2015) available at www.sprep.org/attachments/VirLib/New_Caledonia/Lifou_Declaration_2015.pdf.

[18] 'Climate justice' is understood here as requiring not only that every effort is made to address climate change, but also that its uneven burdens are corrected.

[19] For precise figures on historical responsibility of States and a proposal for the equitable division of the remaining carbon budget see Tim Crosland, Aubrey Meyer and Margaretha Wewerinke-Singh, 'The Paris Agreement Implementation Blueprint: A Practical Guide to Bridging the Gap between Actions and Goal and Closing the Accountability Deficit (Part 1)' (2017) 25(2) *Environmental Liability* 114.

National Human Rights Institutions

National Human Rights Institutions (NHRIs) have similar advantages to domestic courts in terms of their accessibility to plaintiffs, witnesses, local media and the general public, proximity to the experienced impacts of climate change, and capacity building opportunities. Jurisdictional requirements of NHRIs may be less stringent than those of domestic courts, depending on the mandate of the NHRI. In the first (and so far, only) rights-based climate case before an NHRI, the Commission on Human Rights of the Philippines assumed jurisdiction over a petition against 50 multinational fossil fuel companies based on its broad constitutional mandate 'to investigate and monitor all matters concerning the human rights of the Filipino people'.[20] The 'carbon majors' petition also illustrates the potential of quasi-judicial procedures – in this case an inquiry – to enhance accountability of major polluters for the human rights impact of climate change, as well as the potential for rights-based claims against private actors.[21] And despite the fact that NHRIs themselves are incapable of making binding judgments, some NHRIs do have a mandate to make an application to a domestic court to provide victims with redress. NHRIs could therefore serve as a useful starting point in victims' quests for tangible remedies, in addition to their awareness-raising function.

Regional Human Rights Bodies

Regional human rights bodies have unique qualities that make them particularly suitable as forums for litigating rights-based climate change cases. First of all, they have developed significant jurisprudence on environmental protection through the specific lens of human rights. Second, experts and judges who serve on regional human rights bodies tend to have a better understanding of national and regional concerns than international bodies. Third, these bodies are geographically closer to plaintiffs than international bodies while offering a wider range of potential defendant States than domestic courts. The potential of the three regional human rights systems that currently exist – in the Americas, Europe and Africa – to consider climate change cases is discussed below.[22]

[20] Republic of the Philippines Commission on Human Rights, 'Press Release: National Inquiry on the Impact of Climate Change on the Human Rights of the Filipino People' available at chr.gov.ph/wp-content/uploads/2018/03/Press-Release_CHR-to-hold-1st-NICC-hearing-26-March-18.pdf.

[21] As the focus of this book is on State responsibility, claims against private actors fall outside the scope of this chapter.

[22] While several human rights declarations have been adopted in Asia and the region has two human rights bodies – the Asian Human Rights Commission and the ASEAN Intergovernmental Commission on Human Rights – there is currently no mechanism with the power to receive individual complaints. Similarly, the Arab Charter on Human Rights protects a range of human rights and establishes an Arab Human Rights Committee, but the Committee's mandate does not include consideration of individual petitions. The Pacific Islands region has discussed the possibility of a regional human rights mechanism for decades but has so far not taken any concrete steps to let it materialise.

The Americas

The American Convention on Human Rights established two human rights bodies, both of which are operational: The Inter-American Commission on Human Rights and the Inter-American Court on Human Rights. The Commission has jurisdiction over cases brought by individuals, groups of individuals or NGOs against any State Party to the American Convention on Human Rights.[23] Under the American Convention only the Commission and State Parties can refer cases to the Court.

The Inter-American Court is renowned for its considerable jurisprudence on environmental rights and the rights of indigenous peoples. It was also the first human rights body to be confronted with a climate change case: as early as 2005 it received a petition brought by members of the Inuit community alleging that the United States had violated its obligations under the American Declaration of Human Rights based on its acts and omissions that contributed to climate change.[24] The petition described and documented in detail how the enjoyment of a range of human rights is affected by climate change impacts such as changes to sea ice and snowfall and unpredictable weather patterns. It sought the following remedies: a fact-finding mission; a report finding the United States responsible for violations of the rights protected in the American Declaration of Rights and Duties of Man; recommendations that the United States adopt mandatory emission reduction targets; establish and implement a plan, in coordination with affected Inuit, to protect Inuit culture and resources and provide adaptation assistance; and 'any other relief that the Commission considers appropriate and just'.[25] However, the petition was not even considered on admissibility: The Commission merely wrote a letter to the Petitioners advising them that it 'will not be able to process your petition at present … The information provided does not enable us to determine whether the alleged facts would tend to characterize a violation of rights protected by the American Declaration'.[26] The petition did succeed in triggering significant public and scholarly attention, and the Commission later went on to hold a hearing on the impacts of climate change on human rights.[27]

[23] See further T Burguenthal, 'The Evolving International Human Rights System' 100 *American Journal of International Law* (2006) 783, 729ff.

[24] Inter-American Commission for Human Rights 'IACHR Concludes Its 141st Regular Session' available at www.cidh.oas.org/Comunicados/English/2011/28-11eng.htm; Petition to the Inter American Commission on Human Rights Seeking Relief from Violations Resulting from Global Warming Caused by Acts and Omissions of the United States, availabe at www.earthjustice.org.

[25] Ibid 7–8.

[26] AC Revkin, 'World Briefing Americas: Inuit Climate Change Petition Rejected' *New York Times* (16 December 2006) 9.

[27] See Earthjustice 'Inter-American Commission on Human Rights to Hold Hearing on Global Warming' available at www.earthjustice.org; Elisabeth Caesens and Maritere Padilla Rodriguez, *Climate Change and the Right to Food: A Comprehensive Study*, vol 8 (Berlin, Heinrich Boll Stiftung Publications Series on Ecology, 2009) 92 (calling the Commission's rejection of the petition a 'missed opportunity to bridge the gap' between the climate change and human rights regimes) and Stephen Humphreys, *Climate Change and Human Rights: A Rough Guide* (Versoix, International Council on

Eight years later a similar petition was filed before the Commission, this time concerning the impact of black carbon pollution from Canada on the human rights of the Athabaskan peoples from the Artic.[28] Like the *Inuit* petition, the *Athabaskan* petition did not explicitly call for compensation for climate harm but rather sought declaratory relief, cessation and some corrective measures: it asked the Commission to carry out fact-finding regarding the harm suffered by the Athabaskans affected by Arctic warming and melting; to prepare a report declaring that Canada's failure to substantially reduce its black carbon emissions violates rights affirmed in the American Declaration; and recommend that Canada takes steps to limit black carbon emissions and protect Arctic Athabaskan culture and resources from the effects of accelerated Arctic warming and melting.[29] At the time of writing the petition is still under consideration by the Commission. The Inter-American Court has so far not addressed climate change but could presumably do so either through an inter-State complaint or through the referral of a case by the Inter-American Commission.

Europe

The European Court of Human Rights (ECtHR) constitutes another potential forum for rights-based climate action. The Court began operating in 1950, first as complementary to the European Commission on Human Rights which was eventually abolished in 1998. The Court has jurisdiction to hear both inter-State and individual applications, although inter-State complaints remain rare, especially

Human Rights Policy, 2008) 43 (arguing that '[p]ioneering cases such as the Inuit case will play an important part in creating space for innovation, assisted by a widening understanding of the reality of anthropogenic climate change and its potential to injure'). See similar arguments in Hari M Osofsky, 'The Inuit Petition as a Bridge? Beyond the Dialectics of Climate Change and Indigenous Peoples' Rights' (2005) 31 *American Indian Law Review* 675; Marguerite Middaugh, 'Linking Global Warming to Inuit Human Rights' (2007) 8 *San Diego International Law Journal* 179; Hari M Osofsky, 'The Geography of Climate Change Litigation: Implications for Transnational Regulatory Governance' (2006) 83 *Washington University Law Quarterly* 1789; and Sara C Aminzadeh, 'A Moral Imperative: The Human Rights Implications of Climate Change' (2006) 30 *Hastings International & Comparative Law Review* 231. Cf Jessie Hohmann, 'Igloo as Icon: A Human Rights Approach to Climate Change for the Inuit?' (2009) 18 *Transnational Law & Contemporary Problems* 295 (discussing the risk of creating simplistic images of a traditional culture); and Joanna Harrington, 'Climate Change, Human Rights, and the Right to Be Cold' (2007) 18 *Fordham Environmental Law Review* 513, 526 (arguing that 'The Commission's decision to reject the [Inuit] Petition on preliminary grounds is admirable, because although there is no doubt that human activities are contributing to global warming, it is not clear that the State bears all responsibility for these activities').

[28] Arctic Athabaskan Council, '*Petition to the Inter-American Commission on Human Rights Seeking Relief from the Violations of Rights of Arctic Athabaskan Peoples Resulting from Rapid Arctic Warming and Melting Caused by Emissions of Black Carbon from Canada*' (2013), available at earthjustice.org/sites/default/files/AAC_PETITION_13-04-23a.pdf [Athabaskan petition]. See further Sabaa A Khan, 'Connecting Human Rights and Short-Lived Climate Pollutants: the Arctic Angle' in Sébastien Duyck, Sébastien Jodoin and Alyssa Johl, *Routledge Handbook of Human Rights and Climate Governance* (Oxford, Routledge, 2018).

[29] Ibid Request for Relief.

in comparison with the enormous volume of individual applications made to the Court today.

Despite the absence of a specific right to a healthy environment from the European Convention on Human Rights (ECHR), the ECtHR has developed a significant body of jurisprudence on environmental protection.[30] While no rights-based climate case has, as yet, been filed before the ECtHR, the growing number of such cases brought before domestic courts in Europe suggests that chances of such cases reaching the ECtHR in the near future are high. Indeed, in 2017, a group of Portuguese schoolchildren from an area affected by forest fires announced their intention to sue 47 European States for alleged violations of their right to life resulting from the States' failure to address climate change before the ECtHR.[31] If this case goes ahead, it would be the first rights-based climate case brought against multiple States at once.

Perhaps surprisingly, it is not the ECtHR but the Court of Justice of the European Union (CJEU) that has become the first European court to be confronted with a rights-based climate case. In a case against the European Union institutions – dubbed the 'People's Climate Case' – plaintiffs from Fiji and Kenya joined plaintiffs from across Europe in seeking redress for the impact of climate change on the enjoyment of their fundamental rights.[32] While the plaintiffs face significant jurisdictional and legal obstacles, the sheer media attention around the case has already succeeded in underscoring the possibility that industrialised States will be held to account for human rights violations resulting from the adverse effects of climate change in developing States. A similar effect could be achieved through transnational litigation before domestic courts in industrialised States involving plaintiffs from developing States (discussed above).

Africa

The African Commission on Human and Peoples' Rights, established in 1987, is the main human rights body of the African continent. An African Court on Human and Peoples' Rights was established in 1998.[33] The Commission is mandated to receive inter-State complaints as well as individual complaints concerning alleged

[30] These include the cases discussed in ch 7.

[31] See Sandra Laville, 'Portuguese Children to Crowdfund European Climate Case' *The Guardian* (Portugal, 25 September 2017) available at www.theguardian.com/world/2017/sep/25/portuguese-children-crowdfund-european-climate-change-case-sue-47-countries.

[32] *Armando Ferrao Carvalho and others v the European Parliament and the Council*, Application for annulment pursuant to Article 263 TFEU, Application/ claim for non-contractual liability pursuant to article 268 and 340 TFEU and Application for Measures of Inquiry pursuant to articles 88 and 91 of the Rules of Procedure of the General Court (2018), available at peoplesclimatecase.caneurope.org/wp-content/uploads/2018/05/application-delivered-to-european-general-court-1.pdf.

[33] Protocol to the African Charter on Human and Peoples' Rights on the Establishment of an African Court on Human and Peoples' Rights (adopted June 1998, entered into force January 2005) Art 1.

violations of the African Charter committed by any State Party. The Court may receive cases filed by the Commission, State Parties to the Protocol that establishes the Court or African intergovernmental organisations. NGOs with observer status before the Commission and individuals can also bring cases before the Court provided that the defendant State has recognised the jurisdiction of the Court to receive individual complaints. The African Charter on Human and Peoples' Rights codifies a specific right to a healthy environment,[34] which the Commission has interpreted as creating a range of obligations on State Parties.[35]

Neither the Commission nor the Court has so far dealt with cases that specifically address States' obligations to prevent and address climate change. However, in *Ogoniland* the Commission did establish human rights violations based on the State's failure to protect against the environmentally devastating consequences of 'gas flaring'.[36] The Commission's interpretation of the right to a healthy environment as a justiciable right also suggests that climate change does fall within the scope of the Charter. Indeed, the Commission has already adopted three resolutions on Climate Change and Human Rights in Africa in which it has expressed commitment to conduct a study on the impact of climate change on human rights in Africa.[37] The Commission (and presumably the Court) therefore have significant potential to entertain State responsibility claims concerning the consequences of climate change for the enjoyment of human rights in Africa. The outcome of a case before the Commission would not be binding; however, the Commission now has the possibility of referring cases to the Court where a binding judgment could be obtained. And individuals and communities affected by climate change can directly petition the Court in some cases. When it comes to establishing State responsibility for human rights violations associated with climate change, perhaps the greatest limitation of the African human rights system is its regional character: this makes it is difficult, if not impossible to consider claims concerning the responsibility of non-African States for such violations.[38] Rights-based climate litigation before the African human rights bodies is therefore unlikely to correct the uneven burdens of climate change at the global level. However, it would seem to be well-placed for addressing more localised human rights issues associated with climate change, including adaptation and land issues related to response measures.

[34] African Charter on Human and Peoples' Rights (ACHPR), Art 24.

[35] See, eg, African Commission on Human and Peoples' Rights, *The Social and Economic Rights Action Center and the Center for Economic and Social Rights v Nigeria* (*Ogoniland*), para 52.

[36] See ch 7.

[37] African Commission on Human and Peoples' Rights, 'Climate Change and the Need to Study Its Impacts on Africa', ACHPR/ Res153 (XLVI)09, adopted at the 46th Ordinary Session (25 November 2009); African Commission on Human and Peoples' Rights, 'Climate Change in Africa', ACHPR/ Res271, adopted at the 55th Ordinary Session (12 May 2014); African Commission on Human and Peoples' Rights, 'Climate Change and Human Rights in Africa', ACHPR/Res342 (LVIII), adopted at the 58th Ordinary Session (20 April 2016).

[38] Such cases would need to be based on the complicity of at least one African State in the alleged violation and could not address the responsibility of the non-African State head-on given that membership to the Charter is limited to African States.

The United Nations Human Rights Council

The Human Rights Council (HRC) is the primary intergovernmental human rights body of the United Nations (UN) and mandated to promote the effective coordination and mainstreaming of human rights within the UN system.[39] Members of the HRC are elected directly and individually by a majority of the members of the General Assembly to three-year terms.[40] Climate change has featured on the agenda of the HRC since 2008, when the HRC adopted its first resolution on human rights and climate change at the initiative of Small Island Developing States (SIDS) led by the Maldives.[41] Since then the Council has adopted an additional seven resolutions,[42] requested and received four analytical reports on various aspects of the relationship between climate change and human rights from the Office of the UN High Commissioner for Human Rights (OHCHR), and held several seminars and panel discussions on the topic, including three thematic panel discussions on the impacts of climate change on the enjoyment of the right to health, the rights of the child, and the rights of migrants and persons displaced across international borders.[43] At its forty-first session the Council will hold a panel discussion on women and climate change.[44] Climate change has also been discussed as part of the Universal Period Review (UPR) process, and some developing States have used the process to raise concerns about the adverse effects of climate change on the enjoyment of human rights within their own territories[45] and to recommend that industrialised States cut their emissions in order to comply with their human rights obligations.[46] This in itself signals a shift away from the paradigm of States being primarily responsible for the realisation of human rights within their own territories, towards a paradigm of responsibility based on the consequences of a State's acts or omissions on the realisation of human rights irrespective of the location of the rights-holders.[47]

[39] *Human Rights Council* GA Res A/RES/60/251, 72nd mtg (3 April 2006) para 3.

[40] Ibid paras 7 and 14. No Pacific Island State is currently a member of the Human Rights Council.

[41] Human Rights Council Resolution 7/23, Human Rights and Climate Change (UN Doc A/HRC/7/23, 28 March 2008).

[42] Human Rights Council Resolutions 10/4 (UN Doc A/HRC/10/L.11, 12 May 2009); 18/22 (UN Doc A/HRC/18/22, 28 September 2011); 26/27 (UN Doc A/HRC/26/27, 23 June 2014); 29/15 (UN Doc A/HRC/29/15, 30 June 2015); 32/33 (UN Doc HRC/32/33, 28 June 2016); 35/20 (UN Doc A/HRC/35/20, 19 June 2017) and 38/4 (UN Doc A/HRC/38/4, 2 July 2018), all titled 'Human Rights and Climate Change'.

[43] See website of UN OHCHR, available at www.ohchr.org/EN/Issues/HRAndClimateChange/Pages/HRClimateChangeIndex.aspx.

[44] Pursuant to its resolution 38/4 (n 42).

[45] See, eg, the documentation on the reviews of Tuvalu, Kiribati, Vanuatu, Nauru, Micronesia, Palau, Papua New Guinea, Solomon Islands and Fiji, available at www.upr-info.org/database.

[46] See, eg, the documentation on the reviews of Australia and the United States available at www.upr-info.org/database.

[47] See ch 2.

Although the Council itself is an intergovernmental body premised on international collaboration, it has a number of Special Procedures – including Special Rapporteurs, Independent Experts and Working Groups – with quasi-judicial mandates to report and advise on human rights issues. Amongst other things, Special Procedures undertake country visits, conduct studies, convene expert consultations, contribute to the development of international human rights standards, engage in advocacy and advise governments.[48] Many existing Special Procedure mandate holders have already considered climate change under their respective mandates through reports, country visits, statements and press releases and contributions to HRC debates, seminars and panel discussions.[49] Many Special Procedures also have a mandate to consider individual cases of alleged human rights violations,[50] which have so far not been used to address climate change. These complaint procedures are amongst the most flexible of all human rights complaint procedures: victims' ability to complain does not depend on the ratification of human rights treaties by their own State; there are usually no jurisdictional restrictions on the scope of complaints; complaints could refer to past, ongoing as well as potential future violations; and victims may identify any State or non-State actor as the alleged perpetrators of the violation. There is no requirement that domestic remedies be exhausted. These features make the Special Procedures particularly suitable for filing innovative human rights complaints relating to climate change. Essentially, all it takes to use the procedure is filling out a two-page questionnaire available on the OHCHR website and sending it to a dedicated email address. Although the questionnaire asks for 'identification of the person(s) or organization(s) submitting the communication, if different from the victim', the flexible and discretionary nature of the procedure makes it unlikely that information would not be considered if it were to be submitted by a State on behalf of its people. Indeed, States could generate global attention even by attempting to use the procedure to hold foreign States to account for the human rights implications of climate change.

Perhaps the greatest drawback of the procedure is that the powers of mandate holders do not go beyond diplomacy and 'naming and shaming': If a mandate

[48] See website of UN OHCHR, available at www.ohchr.org/EN/HRBodies/SP/Pages/Welcomepage.aspx.

[49] For Pacific Island States, most notable has been a visit of the Special Rapporteur on the Right to Water and Sanitation, Catarina de Albuquerque, to Kiribati and Tuvalu in July 2012. The visit involved consultations with communities and resulted in reports highlighting the adverse effects of climate change on the enjoyment of rights related to water and sanitation. See Human Rights Council Resolution 24/44, Report of the Special Rapporteur on the human right to safe drinking water and sanitation, Cartarina de Albuquerque- Addendum- Mission to Kiribati (23–29 July 2012) (UN Doc A/HRC/24/44/Add.1, 28 June 2013) and Human Rights Council Resolution 24/44, Report of the Special Rapporteur on the human right to safe drinking water and sanitation, Cartarina de Albuquerque – Addendum – Mission to Tuvalu (17–19 July 2012) (A/HRC/24/44/Add.2, 1 July 2013).

[50] See website of UN OHCHR, available at www.ohchr.org/EN/HRBodies/SP/Pages/Welcomepage.aspx.

holder decides to act on a particular complaint (a decision which is made at her or his discretion), the most likely intervention is a letter to the allegedly responsible State(s) identifying 'the facts of the allegation, applicable international human rights norms and standards, the concerns and questions of the mandate-holder(s), and a request for follow-up action'.[51] The text of the communications sent by mandate holders and any replies received would be reported to the HRC and made publicly available.[52] If the purpose of the action is to achieve tangible redress for the human rights implications of climate change, perhaps the most sensible strategy would be to combine legal action before a domestic court with political pressure that could be generated through the existing Special Procedures. At the same time, governments and civil society could continue to advocate for a dedicated Special Procedure on Human Rights and Climate Justice,[53] which could be created at any session of the Council through the adoption of a resolution. A dedicated Climate Justice mandate could contribute to norm-development on human rights and climate change, including on complex legal questions such as the status of those who lose their traditional land as a result of climate change, and support ongoing advocacy for systemic change to safeguard human rights in the face of climate change.

United Nations Human Rights Treaty Bodies

Individual Complaints

As noted in chapter two, the international human rights system has several quasi-judicial procedures that allow individuals (and, in some cases, groups of individuals) to submit complaints about alleged human rights violations to human rights treaty bodies. Most of these individual complaint procedures are established under Optional Protocols to the core human rights treaties. Not all States whose populations are particularly affected by climate change have ratified these Protocols, which means that the possibilities for submitting complaints before human rights treaty bodies about human rights violations allegedly committed by those States are limited. However, individuals or communities whose State of domicile has not ratified a relevant Protocol could, instead of trying to hold their own State to account, take an innovative transnational approach and submit a

[51] See website of UN OHCHR, available at www.ohchr.org/EN/HRBodies/SP/Pages/Communications.aspx.

[52] See website of UN OHCHR, available at www.ohchr.org/EN/HRBodies/SP/Pages/CommunicationsreportsSP.aspx.

[53] See, eg, Statement by Penelisa Alofa, National Coordinator for the Kiribati Climate Action Network, at the full-day panel discussion of the UN Human Rights Council in March 2015, available at webtv.un.org/watch/general-segment-10th-meeting-28th-regular-session-human-rights-council/4095103978001# (at 1:40:56).

communication about human rights violations allegedly attributable to third States based on their respective contributions to climate change. In this regard, it is worth noting that most high-income States that are responsible for a significant portion of greenhouse gases stocked in the global atmosphere have recognised the competency of at least some human rights treaty bodies to consider complaints from individuals or groups of individuals.

States confronted with a complaint from alleged victims of climate change-related human rights violations in third States would almost certainly refer to jurisdictional clauses contained in most human rights treaties and Optional Protocols, which arguably limit the territorial scope of States' human rights obligations, and/ or bar treaty bodies from considering complaints from individuals or groups of individuals outside a State's territory. However, as noted in chapter two, the practice of human rights treaty bodies generally emphasises individuals' right to an adequate and effective remedy for human rights violations, which in turn leads to a broad interpretation of the scope of States' human rights obligations and treaty bodies' own mandate to consider alleged breaches of those obligations. For example, claims about the extraterritorial human rights implications of climate change could build on the reasoning of the UN Human Rights Committee that a State should not be allowed 'to perpetrate violations of the Covenant on the territory of another State, which violations it could not perpetrate on its own territory'.[54]

Another hurdle facing individuals or groups of individuals submitting complaints before UN human rights treaty bodies is the requirement to demonstrate that they are 'victims' of the alleged violation or that they are acting on behalf of an alleged victim.[55] Meeting this requirement in a climate change case would probably involve providing proof of a link between State conduct relating to climate change on the one hand and the specific impacts of climate change on the alleged victims on the other. As noted above in relation to litigation at the national level, victims (or those acting on their behalf) could rely on a growing body of evidence about the attribution of specific impacts to global climate change. Whether or not the evidence will be sufficient to establish 'victim' status would depend mostly on the extent to which the particular impacts in question can be attributed to factors other than climate change.

Finally, using the individual complaint procedures is only possible where domestic remedies are exhausted, unreasonably prolonged or unlikely to bring effective relief.[56] Arguably this requirement will be met in many cases, given the comparatively small contributions of some States to global emissions and the

[54] *Sergio Euben Lopez Burgos v Uruguay* (Communication no R12/52) para 12.3.

[55] See, eg, Optional Protocol to the International Covenant on Economic, Social and Cultural Rights (adopted 10 December 2008, entered into force 5 May 2013) 14531 UNTS (OP-ICESCR) art 2.

[56] See, eg, Optional Protocol to the Convention on the Elimination of All Forms of Discrimination against Women (adopted 6 October 1999, entered into force 22 December 2000) 20378 UNTS (OP-CEDAW) Art 4(1); OP-ICESCR, Art 3.

doctrine of State immunity barring claims against foreign States responsible for the lion's share of global emissions before domestic courts. Taking all these factors into account, the chances of success for individuals or communities in an innovative case against a foreign State or States before an international human rights body are potentially significant.

Inter-State Complaints

As an alternative to action by individuals or groups of individuals, States could bring a complaint about the human rights implications of climate change before a human rights treaty body on behalf of their people. The International Covenant on Civil and Political Rights (ICCPR) and International Convention on the Elimination of All Forms of Racial Discrimination (ICERD) both establish inter-State complaints procedures, while a complaint procedure for the International Covenant on Economic, Social and Cultural Rights (ICESCR) is established as part of its Optional Protocol. CEDAW allows State parties to submit a dispute with another party concerning the interpretation or application of the treaty to arbitration or – when the parties are unable to agree on the organisation of the arbitration within six months – referral of the dispute to the ICJ.[57] None of these procedures would require a State to represent or even identify 'victims' of human rights violations: the focus is on alleged non-compliance with treaty obligations or (in case of CEDAW) the interpretation or application of the treaty, which presumably makes it easier to complain about a State's alleged failure to prevent future impacts of climate change. However, the ICCPR's complaints procedure applies only to State Parties who have made a declaration recognising the competence of the Committee to consider inter-State complaints, which – as noted in chapter two – only a minority of State Parties has done so far. This seems like a missed opportunity for some of the climate vulnerable States, as making the declaration (and ratifying the ICCPR if they have not already done so) would allow those States to bring a claim before an international body against some of the major historical polluters that have refused to recognise the jurisdiction of most other international bodies.[58] The inter-State complaint procedure under the ICESCR is currently not accessible to many States due to a lack of ratifications of the Optional Protocol. The one inter-State complaint procedure that is readily available to most States is that established under ICERD, which in theory allows States that have ratified ICERD to claim that another State Party has breached its obligations under the treaty by failing to take measures to correct the disproportionate impacts of climate change on specific

[57] CEDAW, Art 29. Although State Parties to CEDAW can opt out of this possibility, neither Pacific Island States nor Annex I States that have ratified CEDAW have done so.

[58] The most prominent example is the United States, which made the declaration upon ratification in 1992.

categories of people. The promises and pitfalls of this course of action remain somewhat uncertain, as the inter-State complaint procedures of international human rights bodies have remained unused until very recently (when Palestine filed an inter-State complaint against Israel for alleged breaches of its obligations under ICERD) and this recent attempt has not yet produced an outcome.[59]

What is clear in any event, however, is that treaty bodies do not have the power to make binding judgments that would provide tangible remedies to victims of climate change in case of a victory. This is true irrespective of whether it is an individual, a community or a State that files the complaint. The only opportunity for a binding judgment consists in the dispute settlement provisions of CEDAW, which provide a rare opportunity to bring climate change before the ICJ. However, the scope of the procedure seems somewhat limited, both in terms of substance (requiring a narrow focus on the allegedly discriminatory impacts of climate change on women) and in terms of procedure (focusing on disputes concerning the interpretation or application of CEDAW rather than on alleged non-compliance with treaty obligations). Even if a State succeeded in getting the dispute beyond the admissibility stage at the ICJ, it remains to be seen whether the Court would be amenable to accepting an invitation to interpret CEDAW in a way that would probably be mind-boggling to its original drafters. Perhaps the greatest chances of influential litigation consist in the individual complaint procedures under the ICCPR, ICESCR and CRC which – despite their non-binding nature – could help shape climate policies in States whose politicians and judiciary maintain a degree of deference to international human rights bodies.

The International Court of Justice

The ICJ is the principal judicial organ of the United Nations. It has a mandate to settle legal disputes submitted to it by States and provide advisory opinions on legal questions referred to it by authorised UN organs and agencies. Individuals and communities cannot submit cases to the Court. The ICJ has jurisdiction in all areas of international law and could therefore, at least in principle, deal with legal questions and disputes concerning human rights violations resulting from climate change. Indeed, it has relied upon the provisions of international human rights treaties and pronouncements of the UN human rights treaty bodies in several judgments and advisory opinions[60] and developed a significant body of jurisprudence

[59] Oliver Holmes, 'Palestine Files Complaint Against Israel under Anti-Racism Treaty' *The Guardian* (Jerusalem, 23 April 2018) available at www.theguardian.com/world/2018/apr/23/palestinians-file-complaint-against-israel-under-anti-racism-treaty.

[60] See, eg, *Legal Consequences of the Construction of a Wall in the Occupied Palestinian Territory* [2004] ICJ Rep 136; *Case Concerning Ahmadou Sadio Diallo (Republic of Guinea v Democratic Republic of Congo)* [2010] ICJ Rep 639. See further Ghandhi, 'Human Rights and the International Court of Justice: The *Ahmadou Sadio Diallo Case*' (2011) 11 *Human Rights Law Review* 527.

on environmental protection.[61] If a case concerning climate change and human rights were to be considered by the Court, this would provide an excellent opportunity for overcoming some of the challenges concerning the fragmentation of international law in this area.

Although no State has so far actually attempted to bring climate change before the ICJ, the idea has been discussed in scholarship and practice for almost three decades.[62] This debate reached a first peak when some small island States publicly started to show an interest in confronting the Court with climate change, starting in 2002 with Tuvalu's expression of interest in bringing a case against the United States for failure to act on climate change.[63] This was followed by Palau's suggestion to obtain an Advisory Opinion from the ICJ about the applicability of the no-harm rule to climate change through a request from the UN General Assembly.[64] Neither of these initiatives actually materialised. Nonetheless, a vivid debate on the role of the ICJ in addressing climate change continues in scholarly and activist circles and between governments and their advisors. This ongoing debate has received new impetus with the announcement of the Trump administration that the United States would withdraw from the Paris Agreement.[65] The idea of seeking an advisory opinion on climate change from the ICJ was revived at the International Union for Conservation of Nature 2016 World Conservation Congress in Hawaii, where a resolution on the same was adopted.[66]

Much of the literature is devoted to discussing the jurisdictional and substantive legal obstacles to bringing a contentious case on climate change before the ICJ.[67] At the core of the debate is the concept of State consent, which is the basis for the ICJ's jurisdiction over disputes between two or more States. Some scholars have asserted that bringing a contentious case concerning climate change before the ICJ seems 'a rather remote possibility' because States that are most obviously responsible for climate change and its adverse consequences are unlikely to submit themselves voluntarily to the jurisdiction of the ICJ over such a case.[68]

[61] For a discussion see Philippe Sands, 'Climate Change and the Rule of Law: Adjudicating the Future in International Law' (2016) 28 *Environmental Law* 19, 23.

[62] See, eg, Durwood Zaelke and James Cameron, 'Global Warming and Climate Change: An Overview of the International Legal Process' (1990) 5(2) *American University International Law* Review 249.

[63] See Rebecca Elizabeth Jacobs, 'Treading Deep Waters: Substantive Law Issues in Tuvalu's Threat to Sue the United States in the International Court of Justice' (2005) 14(1) *Pacific Rim Law & Policy Journal* 104.

[64] 'Palau Seeks UN World Court Opinion on Damage Caused by Greenhouse Gases' *UN News* (22 September 2011) available at www.un.org/apps/news/story.asp?NewsID=39710.

[65] See, eg, Daniel Bodansky, 'The Role of the International Court of Justice in Addressing Climate Change: Some Preliminary Reflections' (2017) 49(1) *Arizona State Law Journal* 1.

[66] Ibid.

[67] See, eg, Jacobs (n 61); Andrew Strauss, 'Climate Change Litigation: Opening the Door to the International Court of Justice' in William CG Burns and Hari M Osofsky (eds), *Adjudicating Climate Change: State, National, and International Approaches* (Cambridge, Cambridge University Press, 2009); Jacob Werksman, 'Could a Small Island Successfully Sue a Big Emitter?' in Michael Gerrard and Gregory Wannier (eds), *Threatened Island Nations: Legal Implications of Rising Seas and a Changing Climate* (Cambridge, Cambridge University Press, 2013); Sumudu Atapattu, *Human Rights Approaches to Climate Change: Challenges and Opportunities* (Oxford, Routledge, 2016) 288.

[68] See, eg, Atapattu (n 67) 288.

However, jurisdiction could be established over a dispute between States that have both (or all, if the dispute involves three or more States) accepted the jurisdiction of the court as compulsory.[69] Perhaps the most pressing jurisdictional question in this scenario is whether the *Monetary Gold* principle bars the Court from exercising jurisdiction over cases involving potentially responsible States that are not parties to the litigation.[70] The ICJ's ruling on admissibility in *Certain Phosphate Lands in Nauru*[71] suggests this is not the case. In this case, Australia had challenged the admissibility of the claim against it based on the argument that its alleged international responsibility was inseparably linked with the responsibility of two other States, the United Kingdom and New Zealand, over which the Court had no jurisdiction. The ICJ rejected Australia's argument and was willing to consider the case on its merits, emphasising the principle of independent responsibility.[72] It therefore appears that there is a real possibility that the Court would consider a case concerning human rights violations associated with climate change on the merits, as long as the case focuses on a violation of international law allegedly committed by at least one State that has accepted the jurisdiction of the Court as compulsory. If this were indeed to happen, the Court would need to grapple with many of the substantive legal questions discussed in this book. A judgment of the Court on the merits of a rights-based climate case could include an order to bring domestic laws, policies and practices in line with States' human rights obligations, as well as an order to make full reparations for injuries suffered. As highlighted in chapter eight, reparations will be owed to the beneficiaries of the obligations: in this case, individuals and communities who suffered human rights violations resulting from climate change. It should be recalled however that the duty to make full reparations is only enforceable to the extent that the invoking State or States are able to establish that the injury suffered was caused by the internationally wrongful act of the defendant State or States.[73]

An Advisory Opinion would similarly offer the Court an opportunity to pronounce itself on the science of climate change and applicable areas of international law.[74] Although an opinion is not binding, it does carry incomparable

[69] See 'Declarations recognizing the jurisdiction of the Court as compulsory' available at www.icj-cij.org/en/declarations, for a list of States that have made declarations recognising the jurisdiction of the Court as compulsory.

[70] *Monetary Gold Removed from Rome in 1943 (Italy v France, United Kingdom of Great Britain and Northern Ireland and United States of America) (Preliminary Question)* [1954] ICJ Reports 19, 32.

[71] *Corfu Channel Case (United Kingdom v Albania)* [1949] ICJ Reports 4.

[72] *Certain Phosphate Lands in Nauru (Nauru v Australia) (Preliminary Objections)* [1992] ICJ Rep 240, 258–59; ibid 301.

[73] See ch 8.

[74] See further Douglas A Kysar, 'Climate Change and the International Court of Justice' (Public Research Paper No 315, Yale Law School, 2013); Tracey Skillington, 'Climate Change and the Human Rights Challenge: Extending Justice beyond the Borders of the Nation State' (2012) 16 *The International Journal of Human Rights* 1196; and Anmol Gulechha, 'Not an Exclusive Sovereign Issue: Advisory Opinion from the International Court of Justice for Global Warming' (2018) *The World Journal on Juristic Polity* 2394.

persuasive authority.[75] As Bodansky highlights, it could serve both 'as a prod to the negotiations and [help] to shape and stabilise normative expectations among the wider set of public and private actors engaged in climate-related work'.[76] Like other litigation options considered in this chapter, it would not solve the climate problem on its own. However, it does stand out as one of the most powerful top-down responses international law has to offer to the injustices and human suffering connected with climate change.

Conclusion

This chapter has analysed several litigation options that could be pursued by States, individuals or groups against those most responsible for anthropogenic climate change. Some of these options appear to be mutually exclusive: for example, the requirement that domestic remedies must be exhausted before individuals or communities can bring a case before a regional or international human rights body seems to prescribe a sequential approach to litigation, starting at the domestic level. At the same time, the doctrine of State immunity bars claims against foreign States before domestic courts, which makes regional human rights bodies, international human rights bodies or the ICJ appropriate forums for such claims. Claims by individuals or communities against local and national governments could be entertained by domestic courts and Special Procedure mandate holders but not by human rights treaty bodies unless domestic remedies are exhausted. Special Procedure mandate holders will not require that the alleged victim has exhausted domestic remedies in order to consider a communication, which opens the door to simultaneous action at the national and international levels.

The options for rights-based climate litigation to seek redress for the adverse effects of climate change on human life, livelihoods and cultures are ultimately innumerable. Individuals, communities and governments across regions could pursue litigation jointly or in parallel. Bottom-up, community-led action is particularly appropriate for cases seeking to highlight the impacts of climate change through the lens of human rights. States could at the same time initiate action against foreign States through regional or international human rights bodies or the ICJ, with available litigation options depending on the ratifications and declarations made by the States involved. No one option can guarantee even incremental progress towards climate justice. However, a 'let a thousand flowers bloom' approach to litigating human rights violations resulting from the impacts of climate change is likely to have significant impact in terms of both awareness-raising and chances of obtaining actual remedies for victims.

[75] See Kenneth Keith, 'The Advisory Jurisdiction of the International Court of Justice: Some Comparative Reflections' (1996) 17 *Australian Yearbook of International Law* 39, 41.
[76] Bodansky (n 65) 4.

10

Conclusion

This book used an integrated analysis of three legal regimes – climate change, human rights and State responsibility – to explain the potential of innovative rights-based climate litigation that could shape climate and energy policies around the world. Its purpose was to fill the gaps in our understanding of the role of international human rights law in enhancing accountability for actions related to climate change. While accountability is central to human rights law and practice, in the context of climate change it has been undermined by a lack of clarity regarding a series of legal and practical questions. At the heart of the conundrum is the question of who bears which obligations in relation to the impact of climate change on human rights. Other pressing questions are the relationship between international human rights law and the United Nations Framework Convention on Climate Change regime, and to what extent human rights bodies are competent to deal with cases related to climate change. As the Paris Agreement has shifted the focus of the climate change regime towards voluntary action, and the prospect of irreversible large-scale impacts has grown, accountability has become an increasingly salient issue.

Against this backdrop, this book offered a comprehensive analysis of the issues related to accountability for the human rights impact of climate change, drawing on the State responsibility regime. Part I presented a legal framework designed to serve as a contextual structure for potential State responsibility claims linked to the impact of climate change on the enjoyment of human rights. Based on a wealth of examples and case analysis, it demonstrated that a holistic approach to the three legal regimes – climate change, human rights and State responsibility – enhances both the integrity and the effectiveness of each regime. In bringing these three areas of international law together, the book captured the emerging international trend of linking climate change with human rights from the perspective of the general law of State responsibility. Part II used the integrated framework to explain how State conduct related to climate change may qualify as unlawful under international human rights law, depending on location and circumstances. It then discussed how State responsibility claims can be pursued before international, regional or domestic judicial or quasi-judicial bodies. The analysis here demonstrated that international courts and human rights bodies can play a significant role in establishing State responsibility for climate change-related violations of human rights law when provided with sufficient and relevant evidence. The analysis also showed how an integrated approach to the three legal regimes enhances the potential of international law to govern State behaviour in a way that reduces the risks to human beings posed by climate change.

While the writing of this book was in progress, a trend of rights-based climate litigation before domestic courts started to emerge. This trend was discussed in chapter nine, which assessed the challenges and opportunities in pursuing rights-based climate litigation against one or more States at various levels. The book also noted at several points that no rights-based State responsibility claims have so far been pursued at the international level. The analysis in chapters seven and eight reveal the sweeping impact that the increasing currency of rights-based climate litigation could have on societies globally, based on the legal consequences that arise from State responsibility for human rights violations associated with climate change. However, as the methodology relied upon in this book was doctrinal, the focus was on explaining these consequences from the perspective of international law. Many interesting questions relating to State responsibility, climate change and human rights were not unpacked in this book as a result of this focus. As more rights-based climate cases are brought in courts and quasi-judicial bodies around the world, new questions arise – both legal and extra-legal – which beg for new inquiries. Three lines of inquiry that could be pursued in this context deserve special attention.

A first line of inquiry relates to the integration of human rights standards in forecasting about climate change and development. This book has demonstrated that the strengths of the human rights and climate change regimes can be combined to produce a normative framework geared towards fairer burden-sharing arrangements and inclusive, sustainable development. However, the analysis also highlighted that the legal norms discussed in this book remain open-textured. International lawyers are therefore unable to say in a precise fashion what exactly is required of each State in terms of energy and development policies, unless evidence is provided which shows the implications of certain policy choices for the enjoyment of human rights. Interdisciplinary collaboration between legal scholars, climate scientists, development economists and social scientists could aim to produce such evidence, perhaps building on the work of Office of the UN High Commissioner of Human Rights on human rights indicators.[1] Predictive forecasting of human rights outcomes in different scenarios could enhance compliance with States' human rights obligations in mitigation and adaptation actions. At the same time, the availability of such evidence could make it easier to establish State responsibility for human rights violations relating to climate change after the fact, based in part on States' decisions to either ignore or act upon the evidence.[2]

A second line of inquiry concerns victims' right to a remedy. As highlighted at several points in this book, the right to a remedy is at the heart of a human

[1] Office of the High Commissioner of Human Rights (OHCHR), 'Human Rights Indicators: A Guide to Measurement and Implementation' (Geneva, OHCHR, 2012).

[2] Cf Stephen Humphreys, 'Conceiving Justice' in Stephen Humphreys (ed), *Human Rights and Climate Change* (New York, Cambridge University Press, 2010) 313–15.

rights approach to climate change. Given the global nature of climate change and the uneven ways in which the burdens of climate change are distributed between nations, the requirement that a remedy must be effective calls for collective action at the international level. States' obligations to cooperate internationally to realise human rights indeed entails a duty to cooperate to ensure that those affected by climate change have access to redress. The limitations of the current capacity of the international climate change regime, including its emerging loss and damage component, to provide victims with redress are evident from the analysis in this book. However, these limitations in no way prevent further inquiry into how climate change victims' right to a remedy could be realised through international cooperation. Such an inquiry would need to address questions about international law and governance, including questions about the potential to enhance existing institutional arrangements, finance, and responsibilities and possibilities for creating new ones. Equally important are empirical investigations into the actual needs, interests and wishes of those whose rights are affected by the impacts of climate change. Remedies designed at the international level without direct input from those affected will be neither adequate nor effective. While consultative processes can be built into institutional arrangements aimed at realising the right to a remedy for victims of climate change-related human rights violations, it is not obvious how this can be done. The scale of the challenge is unprecedented. Moreover, those who are at the frontlines of climate change – indigenous peoples; those living on remote low-lying islands; the global poor – are least likely to have easy access to technologies that could be used to connect virtually with people from the usual hubs in Bonn, Geneva or New York. Preliminary insight into what might constitute adequate and effective remedies for different communities would be valuable, as well as broader thinking into how this insight can be obtained and used to shape responses at a larger scale.

A third and related line of inquiry, finally, concerns the effectiveness of rights-based climate litigation as a strategy to address climate change. As noted above, climate change is increasingly being litigated in courts around the world, and human rights law is starting to play an important role in this type of litigation. This book has unpacked a wide range of legal issues that present challenges for litigants in such cases and explained how such challenges may be overcome. Yet on the whole, it remains unclear whether litigation is an effective way of addressing the human rights impact of climate change. There is a specific need for socio-legal investigations into the real-world implications of rights-based climate litigation, paying attention to policy outcomes as well as the implications of litigation for victims. Early results from rights-based climate litigation before domestic courts now make it possible to pursue such investigations, and more case studies will become available over time as this litigation trend unfolds. If and when international-level State responsibility claims for climate change and related human rights violations are actually made, international relations scholars could meaningfully shed light on the drivers and consequences of such claims. Another pressing question that would benefit tremendously from empirical analysis is the relationship between State responsibility claims on the one hand and developments in the international climate change regime on the other.

Whether or not States will actually resort to invoking State responsibility for human rights violations resulting from climate change, this book has demonstrated the potential of existing norms of international law to serve as a basis for such claims. Ascertaining the responsibility of States for the multiple ways in which human rights are affected by climate change naturally stretches the notion of State responsibility. However, this does not need to be a reason for concern: as the International Court of Justice pointed out in its Advisory Opinion on *Reparations for Injuries Suffered in the Service of the United Nations*, the development of international law has been influenced by the requirements of international life throughout its history.[3] Evolving international jurisprudence may provide further clarity on the precise content of the norms discussed in this book. The alternative scenario in which international law fails to respond to the human rights challenge posed by climate change – paralysed by fragmentation, narrow interpretations of the rights concerned or presumed legal obstacles – would imply, to borrow from Judge Aiken's ruling in *Juliana v United States*, that international law 'affords no protection against a government's knowing decision to poison the air its citizens breathe or the water its citizens drink'.[4] International law is just one of many segments of international life pressured to transform in response to a changing climate.

[3] *Reparations for Injuries Suffered in the Service of the United Nations (Advisory Opinion)* [1949] ICJ Rep 174, para 8.

[4] *Juliana v United States*, US District Court for the District of Oregon, Eugene Division, Case No 6: 15-cv-01517-TC, 10 November 2016.

BIBLIOGRAPHY

Books

d'Aspremont, J, *Formalism and the Sources of International Law: A Theory of the Ascertainment of Legal Rules* (Oxford University Press 2011)

Atapattu, A, *Human Rights Approaches to Climate Change: Challenges and Opportunities* (Routledge 2016)

Austin, J, *The Province of Jurisprudence Determined* (WE Rumbleed, Cambridge University Press 1995)

Barnhoorn, LANM and Wellens, KC (eds), *Diversity in Secondary Rules and the Unity of International Law* (Martinus Nijhoff 1995)

Baslar, K, *The Concept of the Common Heritage of Mankind in International Law* (Martinus Nijhoff Publishers 1998)

Bentham, J, *An Introduction to the Principles of Morals and Legislation* (Athlone Press 1970)

Birnlie, P, Boyle, A and Redgwell, C (eds), *International Law and the Environment* (Oxford University Press 2009)

Black, H, *Black's Law Dictionary* (6th edn, Springer 1990)

Brownlie, I, *State Responsibility* (Clarendon Press; Oxford University Press 1983)

——, *Principles of Public International Law* (5th edn, Oxford University Press 1998)

Brundtland, GH and World Commission on the Environment and Development, *Our Common Future: Report of the World Commission on Environment and Development* (Oxford University Press 1987)

Chinkin, C, Freeman, MA and Rudolf, B (eds), *The UN Convention on the Elimination of All Forms of Discrimination Against Women: A Commentary* (Oxford University Press 2012)

Cassese, A, *International Law in a Divided World* (Oxford University Press 1986)

Clapham, A, *Human Rights in the Private Sphere* (Clarendon Press 1993)

Coomans, F and Kamminga, MT, *Extraterritorial Application of Human Rights Treaties* (Intersentia 2004)

Corrin, J and Bamford, DN, *Courts and Civil Procedure in the South Pacific* (2nd edn, Intersentia 2016)

Craven, M, *The International Covenant on Economic, Social, and Cultural Rights: a Perspective on its Development* (Oxford University Press 1995)

Crawford, JR, *The International Law Commission's Articles on State Responsibility: Introduction, Text, Commentaries* (Cambridge University Press 2002)

——, *Brownlie's Principles of Public International Law* (8th edn, Oxford University Press 2012)

——, *State Responsibility: The General Part* (Cambridge University Press 2013)

——, *The Creation of States in International Law* (Oxford University Press 2007)

Crawford, JR, Pellet, A and Olleson, S (eds), *The Law of International Responsibility* (Oxford University Press 2010)

Dernbach, J, *Acting as if Tomorrow Matters: Accelerating the Transition to Sustainability* (Environmental Law Institute 2012)

Doebbler, CFJ, *The Principle of Non-Discrimination in International Law* (CD Publishing 2007)

Dworkin, R, *Taking Rights Seriously* (Harvard University Press 1977)

Feldman, D, *Civil Liberties and Human Rights in England and Wales* (2nd edn, Oxford University Press 2002)

Freestone, D and Streck, C, *Legal Aspects of Implementing the Kyoto Protocol Mechanisms: Making Kyoto Work* (Oxford University Press 2005)

Grant, JP and Barker, CJ (eds), *Encyclopaedic Dictionary of International Law* (3rd edn, Oxford University Press 2009)

Hart, HLA, *The Concept of Law* (PA Bulloch and J Raz (eds) (2nd edn, Clarendon Press 1994)
Higgins, R, *Problems and Process: International Law and How We Use It* (Oxford University Press 1994)
Jayawickrama, N, *The Judicial Application of Human Rights Law: National, Regional and International Jurisprudence* (Cambridge University Press 2002)
Jørgenson, NHB, *The Responsibility of States for International Crimes* (Oxford University Press 2003)
Joseph, S, Schultz, J and Castan, M, *The International Covenant on Civil and Political Rights: Cases, Materials, and Commentary* (2nd edn, Oxford University Press 2005)
Kinley D, *Civilising Globalisation* (Cambridge University Press 2009)
Klabbers, J, *The Concept of Treaty in International Law*, vol 20 (Martinus Nijhoff Publishers 1996)
Koskenniemi, M, *From Apology to Utopia: The Structure of International Legal Argument* (2nd edn, Cambridge University Press 2005)
Matsuda, MK, *Pacific Worlds: A History of Seas, Peoples, and Cultures* (Cambridge University Press 2012)
McAdam, J, *Climate Change, Forced Migration, and International Law* (Oxford University Press 2012)
McGoldrick, D, *The Human Rights Committee* (Oxford University Press 1991)
Meron, T, *Human Rights Law-Making in the United Nations* (Oxford University Press 1986)
Merrills, JG, *The Development of International Law by the European Court of Human Rights* (Manchester University Press 1993)
Milanovic, M, *Extraterritorial Application of Human Rights Treaties* (Oxford University Press 2011)
Mowbray, AR, *The Development of Positive Obligations under the European Convention on Human Rights by the European Court of Human Rights* (Hart Publishing 2004)
Nguyen, D, Daillier, P and Pellet, A, *Droit International Public* (7th edn, LGDJ 2002)
Norgaard, CA, *The Position of the Individual in International Law* (Munksgaard 1962)
Nowak, M, *UN Covenant on Civil and Political Rights: CCPR Commentary* (1st edn, NP Engel Publisher 1993)
——, *Introduction to the International Human Rights Regime* (Martinus Nijhoff 2003)
——, *UN Covenant on Civil and Political Rights: CCPR Commentary* (2nd edn, NP Engel Publisher 2004)
Pond, W, *The Land with All Woods and Water* (Waitangi Tribunal Rangahaua Whanui Series, Waitangi Tribunal, Wellington 1997)
Prost, M, *The Concept of Unity in Public International Law* (Hart Publishing 2012)
Rayfuse, R and Scott, SV (eds), *International Law in the Era of Climate Change* (Edward Elgar 2012)
Salomon, ME, *Global Responsibility for Human Rights: World Poverty and the Development of International Law* (Oxford University Press 2007)
Sands, P, *Principles of International Environmental Law*, vol 2 (Cambridge University Press 2003)
——, *Principles of International Environmental Law*, vol 3 (Cambridge University Press 2012)
de Schutter, O, *International Human Rights Law: Cases, Materials, Commentary* (Cambridge University Press 2010)
Shaw, MN, *International Law* (5th edn, Cambridge University Press 2003)
Shaw, MN, *International Law* (6th edn, Cambridge University Press 2008)
Shelton, D, *Remedies in International Human Rights Law* (2nd edn, Oxford University Press 2010)
Skogly, S, *Beyond National Borders: States' Human Rights Obligations in International Cooperation* (Intersentia 2006)
Steiner, HJ, Alston, P and Goodman, R, *International Human Rights in Context: Law, Politics, Morals* (3rd edn, Oxford University Press 2007)
Tietenberg, TH, *Emissions Trading: Principles and Practice* (RFF Press 2006)
Vattel, *Le Droit des Gens* (1758, Anon trans 1797)
Verheyen, R, *Climate Change Damage and International Law: Prevention Duties and State Responsibility* (Martinus Nijhoff Publishers 2005)
Vizard, P, *Poverty and Human Rights: Sen's Capability Perspective Explored* (Oxford University Press 2006)
Weeramantry, CG, *The Law in Crisis: Bridges of Understanding* (Capemoss 1975)

——, *Universalising International Law* (Martinus Nijhoff Publishers 2004)
Yamin, F and Depledge, J, *The International Climate Change Regime: A Guide to Rules, Institutions and Procedures* (Cambridge University Press 2004)

Contributions in Edited Books

Ahmed, T and French, D, 'Competing Narratives in Climate Change Law' in S Farrall, T Ahmed and d French (eds), *Criminological and Legal Consequences of Climate Change* (Hart Publishing 2012)
Batibasaqa, K, Overton, J and Horsley, P, 'Vanua: Land, People and Culture in Fiji' in J Overton and R Schreyvens (eds), *Strategies for Sustainable Development: Experiences from the Pacific* (Zed Books 1990)
Bernstein, L *et al*, 'Synthesis Report, adopted at IPCC Plenary XXVII, Valencia, Spain, 12–17 November 2007' in *Climate Change 2007* (Intergovernmental Panel on Climate Change 2007)
Blomeryer-Bartenstein, HH, 'Due Diligence' in R Berhardt (ed), *Encyclopedia of Public International Law* (Vol I, Elsevier 1992)
Bodansky, D and Rajamani, L, 'The Evolution and Governance Architecture of the Climate Change Regime' in D Sprinz and U Luterbacher (eds), *International Relations and Global Climate Change* (2nd edn, MIT Press 2013)
Brunnée, J *et al*, 'Policy Considerations' in R Lord *et al* (eds), *Climate Change Liability: Transnational Law and Practice* (Cambridge University Press 2012)
Cameron, J, 'The Status of the Precautionary Principle in International Law' in T O'Riordan and J Cameron (eds), *Interpreting the Precautionary Principle* (Earthscan Publications 1994)
Campbell, J, 'Climate-Induced Community Relocation in the Pacific: The Meaning and Importance of Land' in J McAdam (ed), *Climate Change and Displacement: Multidisciplinary Perspectives* (Hart Publishing 2010)
Campbell-Lendrum, DH, *et al*, 'How Much Disease Could Climate Change Cause?' in AJ McMichael, *et al* (ed), *Climate Change and Human Health* (World Health Organization 2003)
Caney, S, 'Climate Change, Human Rights and Moral Thresholds' in S Humphreys (ed), *Human Rights and Climate Change* (Cambridge University Press 2009)
Cassese, A, 'The Character of the Violated Obligation' in J Crawford, A Pellet and S Olleson (eds), *The Law of International Responsibility* (Oxford University Press 2010)
Charney, JI, 'Third State Remedies for Environmental Damage to the World's Common Spaces' in F Francioni and T Scovazzi (eds), *International Responsibility for Environmental Harm* (Graham & Trotman 1991)
Chowdhury, SR, 'Intergenerational Equity: Substratum of the Right to Sustainable Development' in SR Chowdhury, MGD Erik and JIM Paul (eds), *The Right to Development in International Law* (Martinus Nijhoff 1992)
Daillier, P, 'The Development of the Law of Responsibility Through The Case Law' in J Crawford, A Pellet and S Olleson (eds), *The Law of International Responsibility* (Oxford University Press 2010)
Den Heijer, M and Lawson, R, 'Extraterritorial Human Rights and the Concept of "Jurisdiction"' in M Langford *et al* (eds), *Global Justice, State Duties: The Extraterritorial Scope of Economic, Social and Cultural Rights in International Law* (Cambridge University Press 2012)
Doelle, M, 'Loss and Damage in the UN Climate Regime' in DA Farber and M Peeters (eds), *Elgar Encyclopedia of Environmental Law vol 1: Climate Change Law* (Edward Elgar 2016)
Eide, A, 'Economic, Social and Cultural Rights as Human Rights' in A Eide, C Krause and A Rosas (eds), *Economic, Social and Cultural Rights* (2nd ed edn, Martinus Nijhoff Publishers 2001)
——, 'The Right to an Adequate Standard of Living Including the Right to Food' in A Eide, C Krause and A Rosas (eds), *Eonomic, Social and Cultural Rights* (Martinus Nijhoff Publishers 2001)
Fitzmaurice, M, 'International Responsibility and Liability' in D Bodansky, J Brunnée and E Hey (eds), *The Oxford Handbook of International Environmental Law* (Oxford University Press 2007)
Frey, B, 'Obligations to Protect the Right to Life: Constructing a Rule of Transfer Regarding Small Arms and Light Weapons' in M Gibney and S Skogly (eds), *Universal Human Rights and Extraterritorial Obligations* (University of Pennsylvania Press 2010)

Gormley, WP, 'The Right to Life and the Rule of Non-Derogability: Peremptory Norms of Jus Cogens' in BG Ramcharan (ed), *The Right to Life in International Law* (Martinus Nijhoff 1995)

Humphreys, S, 'Introduction: Human Rights and Climate Change' in S Humphreys (ed), *Human Rights and Climate Change* (Cambridge University Press 2010)

——, 'Conceiving Justice' in S Humphreys (ed), *Human Rights and Climate Change* (Cambridge University Press 2010)

Hunt, PH and Khosla, R, 'Climate Change and the Right to the Highest Attainable Standard of Health' in S Humphreys (ed), *Climate Change and Human Rights* (Cambridge University Press 2009)

Hunter, DB, 'The Implications of Climate Change Litigation' in WCG Burns and HM Osofsky (eds), *Adjudicating Climate Change: State, National, and International Approaches* (Cambridge University Press 2009)

Khan, SA, 'Connecting Human Rights and Short-Lived Climate Pollutants: the Arctic Angle' in S Duyck, S Jodoin and A Johl, *Routledge Handbook of Human Rights and Climate Governance* (Routledge 2018)

Knox, JH, 'Diagonal Environmental Rights' in M Gibney and S Skogly (eds) (University of Pennsylvania Press 2010)

Koskenniemi, M, 'Doctrines of State Responsilbility' in J Crawford, A Pellet and S Olleson (eds), *The Law of International Responsibility* (Oxford University Press 2010)

Kunnemann, R, 'Extraterritorial Application of the International Covenant on Economic, Social and Cultural Rights' in F Coomans and MT Kamminga (eds), *Extraterritorial Application of Human Rights Treaties* (Intersentia 2004)

Lefeber, R, 'Climate Change and State Responsibility' in R Rayfuse and SV Scott (eds), *International Law in the Era of Climate Change* (Elgar 2012)

McCorquodale, R, 'Group Rights' in D Moeckli, S Shah and S Sivakumaran (eds), *International Human Rights Law* (2nd edn, Oxford University Press 2014)

McGoldrick, D, 'State Responsibility and the International Covenant on Civil and Political Rights' in M Fitzmaurice and D Sarooshi (eds), *Issues of State Responsibility Before International Judicial Institutions* (Bloomsbury Publishing 2004)

McInerney-Lankford, S, 'Human Rights and Climate Change' in MB Gerrard and GE Wannier (eds), *Threatened Island Nations: Legal Implications of Rising Seas and a Changing Climate* (Cambridge University Press 2012)

Millar, I, Gascoigne, C and Caldwell, E, 'Making Good the Loss' in MB Gerrard and GE Wannier (eds), *Threatened Island Nations: Legal Implications of Rising Seas and a Changing Climate* (Cambridge University Press 2012)

Ramcharan, BG, 'The Concept and Dimension of the Right to Life' in BG Ramcharan (ed), *The Right to Life in International Law* (Martinus Nijhoff 1985)

Robert, M *et al*, 'Transboundary Climate Challenge to Coal' in MB Gerrard and GE Wannier (eds), *Threatened Island Nations: Legal Implications of Rising Seas and a Changing Climate* (Cambridge University Press 2012)

Rosenne, S, 'Some Reflections Erga Omnes' in A Anghie and G Sturgess (eds), *Legal Visions of the 21st Century: Essays in Honour of Judge Christopher Weeramantry* (Kluwer Law International 1998)

Ryngaert, C, 'Jurisdiction: Towards a Reasonableness Test' in M Langford *et al* (eds), *Global Justice, State Duties The Extraterritorial Scope of Economic, Social and Cultural Rights in International Law* (Cambridge University Press 2012)

Salomon, ME, 'Deprivation, Causation, and the Law of International Cooperation' in M Langford *et al* (eds), *Global Justice, State Duties: The Extraterritorial Scope of Economic, Social and Cultural Rights in International Law* (Cambridge University Press 2012)

Scheinin, M, 'The Right of Self-Determination under the Covenant on Civil and Political Rights' in P Aikio and M Scheinin (eds), *Operationalising the Right of Indigenous Peoples to Self-Determination* (Institute for Human Rights, Abo Akademi University 2000)

——, 'The Right to Enjoy a Distinct Culture: Indigenous and Competing Uses of Land' in TS Orlin, A Rosas and M Scheinin (eds), *The Jurisprudence of Human Rights Law: A Comparative Interpretive Approach* (Institute for Human Rights, Åbo Akademi University 2000)

——, 'Extraterritorial Effect of the International Covenant on Civil and Political Rights' in F Coomans and MT Kamminga (eds), *Extraterritorial Application of Human Rights Treaties* (Intersentia 2004)

——, 'The Human Rights Committee's Pronouncements on the Right to an Effective Remedy: An Illustration of the Legal Nature of the Committee's Work under the Optional Protocol' in N Ando (ed), *Towards Implementing Universal Human Rights* (Martinus Nijhoff Publishers 2004)

——, 'Characteristics of Human Rights Norms' in C Krause and M Scheinin (eds), *International Protection of Human Rights: a Textbook* (Institute for Human Rights, Åbo Akademy University 2009)

——, 'Impact on the Law of Treaties' in MT Kamminga and M Scheinin (eds), *The Impact of Human Rights Law on General International Law* (Oxford University Press 2009)

——, 'Advocating the Right to Development through Complaint Procedures under Human Rights Treaties' in BA Andreassen and SP Marks (eds), *Development as a Human Right: Legal, Political and Economic Dimensions* (Intersentia 2010)

——, 'Just Another Word? Jurisdiction in the Roadmaps of State Responsibility and Human Rights' in M Langford *et al* (eds), *Global Justice, State Duties The Extraterritorial Scope of Economic, Social and Cultural Rights in International Law* (Cambridge University Press 2012)

Shelton, D, 'The Environmental Jurisprudence of International Human Rights Tribunals' in R Picolotti and JD Taillant (eds), *Linking Human Rights and Environment* (University of Arizona Press 2003)

——, 'Remedies and Reparation' in M Langford *et al* (eds), *Global Justice, State Duties: The Extraterritorial Scope of Economic, Social, and Cultural Rights in International Law* (Cambridge University Press 2013)

——, 'Equitable Utilization of the Atmosphere: A Rights-Based Approach to Climate Change' in S Humphreys (ed), *Human Rights and Climate Change* (Cambridge University Press 2010)

Simma, B and Pulkowski, D, 'Leges Speciales and Self-Contained Regimes' in J Crawford, A Pellet and S Olleson (eds), *The Law of International Responsibility* (Oxford University Press 2010)

Singer, P, 'One Atmosphere' in SM Gardiner *et al* (eds), *Climate Ethics: Essential Readings* (Oxford University Press 2010)

Stern, B, 'The Elements of an Internationally Wrongful Act' in J Crawford, A Pellet and S Olleson (eds), *The Law of International Responsibility* (Oxford University Press 2010)

Strauss, A, 'Climate Change Litigation: Opening the Door to the International Court of Justice' in WCG Burns and HM Osofsky (eds), *Adjudicating Climate Change: State, National and International Approaches* (Cambridge University Press 2009)

Thirlway, H, 'The Sources of International Law' in MD Evans (ed), *International Law* (3rd edn, Oxford University Press 2010)

Toebes, B, 'The Right to Health' in A Eide, C Krause and A Rosas (eds) (Martinus Nijhoff Publishers 2001)

Tomuschat, C, 'Reconceptualizing the Debate on Jus Cogens and Obligations Erga Omnes: Concluding Observations' in C Tomuschat and J-M Thouvenin (eds), *The Fundamental Rules of the International Legal Order: Jus Cogens and Obligations Erga Omnes* (Martinus Nijhoff Publishers 2006)

——, 'Global Warming and State Responsibility' in H Hestermeyer *et al* (eds), *Law of the Sea in Dialogue* (Springer 2011)

Werksman, JD, 'Could a Small Island Successfully Sue a Big Emitter? Pursuing a Legal Theory and a Venue for Climate Justice' in MB Gerrard and GE Wannier (eds), *Threatened Island Nations: Legal Implications of Rising Seas and a Changing Climate* (Cambridge University Press 2012)

Wewerinke, M, 'Climate Change: Human Rights Committee, Ad Hoc Conciliation Commission' in M Gibney and W Vandenhole (eds), *Litigating Transnational Human Rights Obligations: Alternative Judgments* (Routledge 2013)

Wewerinke-Singh, M, 'State Responsibility for Human Rights Violations Associated with Climate Change' in Sébastien Jodoin, Sébastien Duyck and Alyssa Johl (eds), Routledge *Handbook of Human Rights and Climate Governance* (Oxford, Routledge, 2018)

——, 'Climate Migrants' Right to Culture' in Avidan Kent and Simon Behrman (eds), *Climate Refugees: Beyond the Legal Impasse?* (Oxford, Routledge, 2018)

Journal Articles

Allen, M *et al*, 'Scientific Challenges in the Attribution of Harm to Human Influence on Climate' (2007) 155 *University of Pennsylvania Law Review* 1353

Allott, P, 'Language, Method and the Nature of International Law' (1971) 45 *British Yearbook of International Law* 79

——, 'State Responsibility and the Unmaking of International Law' (1988) 29 *Harvard International Law Journal* 1

Alston, P, 'Ships Passing in the Night: The Current State of the Human Rights and Development Debate Seen through the Lens of the Millennium Development Goals' (2005) 27 *Human Rights Quarterly* 755

Aminzadeh, SC, 'A Moral Imperative: The Human Rights Implications of Climate Change' (2006) 30 *Hastings International & Comparative Law Review* 231

Anaya, SJ, 'International Human Rights and Indigenous Peoples: the Move Toward the Multicultural State' (2004) 21 *Arizona Journal of International and Comparative Law* 13

Atapattu, S, 'Global Climate Change: Can Human Rights (and Human Beings) Survive this Onslaught?' (2008) 20 *Colorado Journal of International Environmental Law & Policy* 35

Baer, P *et al*, 'The Greenhouse Development Rights Framework: Drawing Attention to Inequality within Nations in the Global Climate Policy Debate' (2009) 40 *Development & Change* 1121

Betsill, M, 'Environmental NGOs meet the Sovereign State: The Kyoto Protocol Negotiations on Global Climate Change' (2002) 13 *Colorado Journal of International Environmental Law & Policy* 49

Biermann, F and Boas, I, 'Preparing for a Warmer World: Towards a Global Governance System to Protect Climate Refugees' (2010) 10 *Global Environmental Politics* 60

Bodansky, D, 'The United Nations Framework Convention on Climate Change: A Commentary' (1993) 18 *Yale Journal of International Law* 451

——, 'Climate Change and Human Rights: Unpacking the Issues' (2010) 38 *Georgia Journal of International and Comparative Law* 511

Bodansky, D and Crook, JR, 'Symposium: The ILC's State Responsibility Articles – Introduction and Overview' (2002) 96 *American Journal of International Law* 773

Brilmayer, L, 'Secession and Self-Determination: a Territorial Interpretation' (1991) 16 *Yale Journal of International Law* 177

Burguenthal, T, 'The Evolving International Human Rights System' (2006) 100 *American Journal of International Law* 783

Cameron, E and Limon, M, 'Restoring the Climate by Realizing Rights: The Role of the International Human Rights System' (2012) 21 *Review of European Community & International Environmental Law* 204

Caron, DD, 'The ILC Articles on State Responsibility: the Paradoxical Relationship Between Form and Authority' (2002) 96 *American Journal of International Law* 857

Cassese, A, 'The Nicaragua and Tadic Tests Revisited in Light of the ICJ Judgment on Genocide in Bosnia' (2007) 18 *European Journal of International Law* 649

Charney, JI, 'Universal International Law' (1993) 87 *American Journal of International Law* 529

Churchill, RR and Ulfstein, G, 'Autonomous Institutional Arrangements in Multilateral Environmental Agreements: A Little-Noticed Phenomenon in International Law' (2000) 94 *American Journal of International Law* 623

Christoff, P, 'The Promissory Note: COP 21 and the Paris Climate Agreement' (2016) 25 *Environmental Politics* 765

Cohen, MA, 'Affirmative Action and the Equality Principle in Human Rights Treaties: United States' Violation of Its International Obligations' (2002) 43 *Virginia Journal of International Law* 249

Comim, F, 'Climate Injustice and Development: A Capability Perspective' (2008) 51 *Development* 344

Cordonier Segger, M-C *et al*, 'Prospects for Principles of International Sustainable Development Law after the WSSD: Common but Differentiated Responsibilities, Precaution and Participation' (2003) 12 *Review of European Community and International Environmental Law* 54

Craven, M, 'Legal Differentiation and the Concept of the Human Rights Treaty in International Law' (2000) 11 *European Journal of International Law* 489

Crawford, JR, 'Revising the Draft Articles on State Responsibility' (1999) 10 *European Journal of International Law* 435

——, 'The ILC's Articles on Responsibility of States for Internationally Wrongful Acts: a Retrospect' (2002) 96 *American Journal of International Law* 874

——, 'Responsibility to the International Community as a Whole' (2001) 8 *Indiana Journal of Global Legal Studies* 303

Crosland, T, Meyer, A and Wewerinke-Singh, M, 'The Paris Agreement Implementation Blueprint: a Practical Guide to Bridging the Ambition Gap (Part 1)' (2017) 25(1) *Environmental Liability* 114

de Schutter, O *et al*, 'Commentary to the Maastricht Principles on Extraterritorial Obligations of States in the Area of Economic, Social and Cultural Rights' (2012) 34 *Human Rights Quarterly* 1084

de Schutter, O *et al*, 'Foreign Direct Investment, Human Development and Human Rights: Framing the Issues' (2009) 3 *Human Rights and International Legal Discourse* 137

Doebbler, C and Bustreo, F, 'Making Health an Imperative of Foreign Policy: The Value of a Human Rights Approach' (2010) 12 *Health and Human Rights Journal* 47

Dudai, R, 'Climate Change and Human Rights Practice: Observations on and around the Report of the Office of the High Commissioner for Human Rights on the Relationship between Climate Change and Human Rights' (2009) 1 *Journal of Human Rights Practice*

Duong, TTV, 'When Islands Drown: The Plight of "Climate Change Refugees" and Recourse to International Human Rights Law' (2010) 31 *University of Pennsylvania Journal of International Law* 1239

Ekwurzel, B *et al*, 'The Rise in Global Atmospheric CO2, Surface Temperature, and Sea Level from Emissions traced to Major Carbon Producers' (2017) 144(4) *Climatic Change* 579

Elzen, MG *et al*, 'Countries' Contributions to Climate Change: Effect of Accounting for All Greenhouse Gases, Recent Trends, Basic Needs and Technological Progress' (2013) 121 *Climatic Change* 397

Fitzmaurice, G, 'Third Report on the Law of Treaties' (1958) II *Yearbook of the International Law Commission* 40

Franck, TM, 'The Emerging Right to Democratic Governance' (1992) 86 *American Journal of International Law* 46

French, D, 'Developing States and International Environmental Law: The Importance of Differentiated Responsibilities' (2000) 49 *International and Comparative Law Quarterly* 35

Gerrard, MB, 'What Litigation of a Climate Nuisance Suit Might Look Like' (2011) 121 *The Yale Law Journal Online* 135

Gewirtz, P, 'Remedies and Resistance' (1983) 92 *Yale Law Journal* 585

Ghandhi, S, 'Human Rights and the International Court of Justice: the Ahmadou Sadio Diallo Case' (2011) 11 *Human Rights Law Review* 527

Gulechha, A, 'Not an Exclusive Sovereign Issue: Advisory Opinion from the International Court of Justice for Global Warming' (2018) *The World Journal on Juristic Polity* 2394

Gupta, J, 'Legal Steps Outside the Climate Convention: Litigation as a Tool to Address Climate Change' (2007) 16 *Review of European Community and International Environmental Law* 76

Hall, MJ and Weiss, DC, 'Avoiding Adaptation Apartheid: Climate Change Adaptation and Human Rights Law' (2012) 37 *Yale Journal of International Law* 309

Harrington, J, 'Climate Change, Human Rights, and the Right to Be Cold' (2007) 18 *Fordham Environmental Law Review* 513

Heede, R, 'Tracing Anthropogenic Carbon Dioxide and Methane Emissions to Fossil Fuel and Cement Producers, 1854–2010' (2013) 122 *Climatic Change* 229

Higgins, R, 'Policy Considerations and the International Judicial Process' (1968) 17 *International and Comparative Law Quarterly* 58

——, 'Derogations Under Human Rights Treaties' (1977) 48 *British Yearbook of International Law* (1976–1977) 281

Hohmann, J, 'Igloo as Icon: a Human Rights Approach to Climate Change for the Inuit?' (2009) 18 *Transnational Law & Contemporary Problems* 295
Hulme, M, 'Climate Refugees: Cause for a New Agreement?' (2008) 50 *Environment* 50
Jacobs, RE, 'Treading Deep Waters: Substantive Law Issues in Tuvalu's Threat to Sue the United States in the International Court of Justice' (2005) 14 *Pacific Rim Law & Policy Journal* 103
Kaplan, M, 'Using Collective Interests to Ensure Human Rights: an Analysis of the Articles of State Responsibility' (2004) 79 *New York University Law Review* 1902
Keith, K, 'The Advisory Jurisdiction of the International Court of Justice: Some Comparative Reflections' (1996) 17 *Australian Yearbook of International Law* 39
Kingsbury, B, 'Sovereignty and Inequality' (1998) 9 *European Journal of International Law* 599
Kinney, ED, 'The International Human Right to Health: What Does This Mean for Our Nation and World?' (2001) 34 *Indiana Law Review* 1457
Kiss, A, 'The Peoples' Right to Self-determination' (1986) 7 *Human Rights Law Journal*
Knox, JH, 'The Myth and Reality of Transboundary Environmental Impact Assessment' (2002) 96 *American Journal of International Law* 291
——, 'Climate Change and Human Rights Law' (2009) 50 *Virginia Journal of International Law*
——, 'Linking Human Rights and Climate Change at the United Nations' (2009) 33 *Harvard Environmental Law Review* 1
Kravchenko, S, 'Procedural Rights as a Crucial Tool to Combat Climate Change' (2010) 38 *Journal of International and Comparative Law* 613
Kysar, DA, 'What Climate Change Can Do About Tort Law' (2012) 42 *Environmental Law Reporter* 10740
Lefeber, R, 'Holding Countries to Account: the Kyoto Protocol's Compliance System Revisted After Four Years of Experience' (2010) 1 *Climate Law* 133
Leroy, SF, 'Can the Human Rights Bodies be Used to Produce Interim Measures to Protect Environment-Related Human Rights?' (2006) 15 *Review of European Community and International Environmental Law* 66
Lillich, RB *et al*, 'Attribution Issues in State Responsibility' (1990) 84 *Proceedings of the Annual Meeting of the American Society of International Law* 51
Limon, M, 'Human Rights and Climate Change: Constructing a Case for Political Action' (2009) 33 *Harvard Environmental Law Journal* 1
Lindroos, A and Mehling, M, 'From Autonomy to Integration? International Law, Free Trade and the Environment' (2008) 77 *Nordic Journal of International Law* 253
Mace, MJ and Verheyen, R, 'Loss, Damage and Responsibility After COP21: All Options Open for the Paris Agreement' (2016) 25 *Review of European Community & International Environmental Law* 197
Mayer, B, 'Climate Change and International Law in the Grim Days' (2013) 24 *European Journal of International Law* 947
McInerney-Lankford, S, 'Fragmentation of International Law Redux: The Case of Strasbourg' (2010) 32 *Oxford Journal of Legal Studies* 609
McNamara, KE and Gibson, C, '"We do not want to leave our land": Pacific Ambassadors at the United Nations Resist the Category of "Climate Refugee"' (2009) 40 *Geoforum* 475
Mekonnen, MM and Hoekstra, AY, 'Four Billion People Facing Severe Water Scarcity' (2016) 2 *Science Advances* 1
Meron, T, 'Extraterritoriality of Human Rights Treaties' (1995) 89 *American Journal of International Law* 78
Middaugh, ME, 'Linking Global Warming to Inuit Human Rights' (2007) 8 *San Diego International Law Journal* 179
Milanovic, M, 'From Compromise to Principle: Clarifying the Concept of State Jurisdiction in Human Rights Treaties' (2008) 8 *Human Rights Law Review* 411
——, 'Al-Skeini and Al-Jedda in Strasbourg' (2012) 23 *European Journal of International Law* 121

Mubangizi, JC 'Know Your Rights: Exploring the Connections Between Human Rights and Poverty Reduction With Specific Reference to South Africa' (2005) 21 *South African Journal on Human Rights* 32
O'Flaherty, M, 'The Concluding Observations of United Nations Human Rights Treaty Bodies' (2006) 6 *Human Rights Law Review*
Orakhelashvili, A, 'Restrictive Interpretation of Human Rights Treaties in the Recent Jurisprudence of the European Court of Human Rights' (2003) 14 *European Journal of International Law* 529
Osofsky, HM, 'The Geography of Climate Change Litigation: Implications for Transnational Regulatory Governance' (2006) 83 *Washington University Law Quarterly* 1789
——, 'The Inuit Petition as a Bridge? Beyond the Dialectics of Climate Change and Indigenous Peoples' Rights' (2005) 31 *American Indian Law Review* 675
——, 'The Continuing Importance of Climate Change Litigation' (2010) *Climate Law* 3
Peel, J, 'Issues in Climate Change Litigation' (2011) 5(1) *Carbon & Climate Law Review* 15
Pogge, T, 'Are We Violating the Human Rights of the Poor?' (2011) 14 *Yale Human Rights and Development Law Journal* 1
——, 'Poverty, Climate Change, and Overpopulation' (2010) 38 *The Georgia Journal of International and Comparative Law* 525
Posner, EA, 'Climate Change and International Human Rights Litigation: A Critical Appraisal' (2007) 155 *University of Pennsylvania Law Review* 1925
Rajamani, L, 'From Berlin to Bali and Beyond: Killing Kyoto Softly?' (2008) 57 *International and Comparative Law Quarterly* 909
——, 'Addressing the "Post-Kyoto" Stress Disorder: Reflections on the Emerging Legal Architecture of the Climate Regime' (2009) 58 *International and Comparative Law Quarterly* 803
——, 'The Increasing Currency and Relevance of Rights-Based Perspectives in the International Negotiations on Climate Change' (2010) 22 *Journal of Environmental Law* 391
——, 'The Durban Platform for Enhanced Action and the Future of the Climate Regime' (2012) 61 *International & Comparative Law Quarterly* 501
——, 'Ambition and Differentiation in the 2015 Paris Agreement: Interpretative Possibilities and Underlying Politics' (2016) 65 *International and Comparative Law Quarterly* 493
Rietiker, D, 'The Principle of "Effectiveness" in the Recent Jurisprudence of the European Court of Human Rights: Its Different Dimensions and Its Consistency with Public International Law – No Need for the Concept of Treaty Sui Generis' (2010) 79 *Nordic Journal of International Law* 245
Roht-Arriaza, N, 'Human Rights in the Climate Change Regime' (2010) 1 *Journal of Human Rights and the Environment* 211
Roht-Arriaza, N and Kravchenko, S, 'Procedural Rights as a Crucial Tool to Combat Climate Change' (2010) 38 *Georgia Journal of International and Comparative Law* 613
Sachs, W, 'Climate Change and Human Rights' (2008) 51 *Development* 332
Salick, J, 'Traditional Peoples and Climate Change' (2009) 19 *Global Environmental Change* 137
Schleussner, C-F *et al*, 'Differential Climate Impacts for Policy-Relevant Limits to Global Warming: the Case of 15°C and 2°C' (2016) 7 *Earth System Dynamics* 327
Scott, J and Rajamani, L, 'EU Climate Change Unilateralism' (2012) 23 *European Journal of International Law* 469
Segger, M-CC and Gehring, MW, 'Precaution, Health and the World Trade Organization: Moving toward Sustainable Devleopment' (2004) 29 *Queen's Law Journal* 139
Shelton, DL, 'Human Rights, Environmental Rights, and the Right to Environment' (1991) 28 *Stanford Journal of International Law* 103
——, 'Protecting Human Rights in a Globalized World' (2002) 25 *Boston College International and Comparative Law Review* 273
——, 'Righting Wrongs: Reparations in the Articles on State Responsibility' (2002) 96 *American Journal of International Law* 833
Simma, B, 'Self-Contained Regimes' (1985) 16 *Netherlands Yearbook of International Law* 111

Simma, B and Alston, P, 'The Sources of Human Rights Law: Custom, Jus Cogens, and General Principles' (1988–89) 12 *Australian Yearbook of International Law*
Simma, B and Pulkowski, D, 'Of Planets and the Universe: Self-Contained Regimes in International Law' (2006) 17 *European Journal of International Law* 483
Singh, S, 'The Potential of International Law: Fragmentation and Ethics' (2011) 24 *Leiden Journal of International Law* 23
Skillington, T, 'Climate Change and the Human Rights Challenge: Extending Justice beyond the Borders of the Nation State' (2012) 16 *The International Journal of Human Rights* 1196
Stott, PA *et al*, 'Human Contribution to the European Heatwave of 2003' (2004) 432 *Nature* 610
Tol, RSJ and Verheyen, R, 'State Responsibility and Compensation for Climate Change Damages: a Legal and Economic Assessment' (2009) 32 *Energy Policy* 1109
van Asselt, H, Sindico, F and Mehling, MA, 'Global Climate Change and the Fragmentation of International Law' (2008) 30(4) *Law and Policy* 423
Vandenbogaerde, A and Vandenhole, W, 'The Optional Protocol to the International Covenant on Economic, Social and Cultural Rights: an Ex Ante Assessment of its Effectiveness in Light of the Drafting Process' (2001) 10 *Human Rights Law Review* 207
Vandenhole, W, 'Is There a Legal Obligation to Cooperate Internationally for Development?' (2009) 23 *International Journal of Children's Rights* 23
Vierdag, EW, 'Some Remarks About Special Features of Human Rights Treaties' (1994) 25 *Netherlands Yearbook of International Law* 119
Voigt, C, 'State Responsibility for Climate Change Damages' (2008) 77 *Nordic Journal of International Law* 1
Weil, P, 'Towards Relative Normativity in International Law?' (1983) 77 *American Journal of International Law* 413
Wellens, KC, 'Diversity in Secondary Rules and the Unity of International Law' (1994) 25 *Netherlands Yearbook of International Law*
Wewerinke, M, 'The Role of the UN Human Rights Council in Addressing Climate Change' (2014) 8 *Human Rights and International Legal Discourse* 10
Wewerinke, M and Doebbler, C, 'Exploring the Legal Basis of a Human Rights Approach to Climate Change' (2011) 10 *Chinese Journal of International Law* 141
Wewerinke-Singh, M and Doebbler, C, 'The Paris Agreement: Some Critical Reflections on Process and Substance' (2016) 39(4) *University of New South Wales Law Journal* 1486
Zaelke, D and Cameron, J, 'Global Warming and Climate Change: An Overview of the International Legal Process' (1990) 5(2) *American University International Law Review* 249

Conference Papers, Working Papers and Scientific Reports

Anton, D, Makgill, A and Payne, C, Advisory Opinion on Responsibility and Liability for International Seabed Mining (ITLOS Case No 17): International Environmental Law in the Seabed Disputes Chamber (ANU College of Law Research Paper no 6, 2011)
Caesens E and Rodriguez MP, Climate Change and the Right to Food: A Comprehensive Study (vol 8, Heinrich Boll Stiftung Publications Series on Ecology 2009)
Castellanos-Jankiewicz L, Causation and International State Responsibility (Amsterdam Centre for International Law, SHARES Series 2012)
Climate Vulnerability Forum, 2nd Climate Vulnerability Monitor: A Guide to the Cold Calculus of a Hot Planet (2012)
Engström, V, 'Who Is Responsible for Corporate Human Rights Violations?' (Åbo Akademi University Institute for Human Rights 2002)
François, A et al, 'The Languages of Vanuatu: Unity and Diversity' (Asia Pacific Linguistics Studies in the Languages of Island Melanesia, College of Asia and the Pacific, Australian National University, 2015)
Frieler, K et al, High Noon for 2 degrees Celsius (Air Pollution & Climate Secretariat Sweden Environmental Fact Sheet 21, 2009)

Humphreys, S, Climate Change and Human Rights: A Rough Guide (International Council on Human Rights Policy 2008)
Intergovernmental Panel on Climate Change, 'Contribution of Working Group I to the IPCC First Assessment Report' in JT Houghton, GJ Jenkins and JJ Ephraums (eds), *Climate Change: The IPCC Scientific Assessment* (Cambridge University Press 1990)
——, 'Contribution of Working Group I to the IPCC Second Assessment Report (1996)' in Houghton, JT et al (eds), *Climate Change 1995: The Science of Climate Change* (Cambridge University Press 1996)
——, 'Contribution of Working Group I to the IPCC Fourth Assessment Report' in S Solomon et al (eds), *Climate Change 2007: The Physical Science Basis* (Cambridge University Press 2007)
——, 'Contribution of Working Group II to the IPCC Fourth Assessment Report' in ML Parry et al (eds), *Climate Change 2007: Impacts, Adaptation and Vulnerability* (Cambridge University Press 2007)
——, 'Contribution of Working Group I to the IPCC Fifth Assessment Report' in TF Stocker et al (eds), *Climate Change 2013: The Physical Science Basis* (Cambridge University Press 2013)
——, 'Contribution of Working Group I to the IPCC Fifth Assessment Report (2013)' in L Alexander, S Allen and NL Bindoff (eds), *Climate Change 2013: The Physical Science Basis* (Cambridge University Press 2013)
——, 'Contribution of Working Group II to the IPCC Fifth Assessment Report' in VR Barros et al (eds), *Climate Change 2014: Impacts, Adaptation and Vulnerability* (Cambridge University Press 2014)
——, 'Contribution of Working Group III to the IPCC Fifth Assessment Report' in O Edenhofer et al (eds), *Climate Change 2014: Mitigation of Climate Change* (Cambridge University Press 2014)
International Energy Agency, World Energy Outlook 2012 (OECD/ IEA, Paris, 2012)
——, World Energy Outlook 2013 (OECD/ IEA, Paris, 2013)
International Organization for Migration, Migration, Climate Change and the Environment: A Complex Nexus (2011)
International Work Group for Indigenous Affairs, Country Technical Notes on Indigenous' Peoples Issues; The United Republic of Tanzania (June 2012)
Kalin, W and Schrepfer, N, Protecting People Crossing Borders in the Context of Climate Change: Normative Gaps and Possible Approaches (UNHCR Division of International Protection, Legal and Protection Policy Research Series PPLA/2012/01, 2012)
Kysar, DA, 'Climate Change and the International Court of Justice' (Public Research Paper No 315, Yale Law School, 2013)
Lambrechts, C et al (eds), 'Vital Forest Graphics' (United Nations Environment Programme (UNEP), Food and Agriculture Organisation (FAO) and United Nations Forum on Forests (UNFF), 2009)
Lifou, Loyalty Islands and New Caledonia, 'Paris 2015: Save Oceania!' (3rd Oceania 21 Summit, 2015)
McInerney-Lankford, S, Darrow, M and Rajamani, L, Human Rights and Climate Change: a Review of the International Legal Dimensions (World Bank Study no 61308, 2011)
McMichael, AJ, et al, 'Global Climate Change' in M Ezzati, AD Lopez,and CJL Murray (eds), *Comparative Quantification of Health Risks: Global and Regional Burden of Disease Attributable to Selected Major Risk Factors* (World Health Organization 2005)
Mustapher, N, Exploring the Potential of Tort-Based Climate Change Litigation in Uganda (2008)
Pratap, A, 'Statement on behalf of Fiji for the review of Australia' (Universal Periodic Review 23rd Session, 2015)
Republic of Vanuatu, 'Statement delivered by the Minister of Climate Change, Adaptation, Geo-Hazard, Environment and Energy, the Honourable Jerome Ludvaune at the High-Level Segment of the 21st Conference of the Parties to the United Nations Framework Convention on Climate Change' (8 December 2015)
Scheinin, M, 'Indigenous Peoples' Land Rights under the International Covenant on Civil and Political Rights' (Orkel Oppsahls minneseminar, Norwegian Centre for Human Rights, University of Oslo, 28 April 2004)

Shelton, DL, An Introduction to the History of International Human Rights Law (GWU Legal Studies Research Paper no 346, 2007)
——, Human Rights, Health & Environmental Protection: Linkages in Law & Practice (Background Paper for the World Health Organization, 2002)
——, 'Litigating a Rights-Based Approach to Climate Change' (International Conference on Human Rights and the Environment, Tehran, 13–14 May 2009)
United Nations Development Programme, Fighting Climate Change: Human Solidarity in a Divided World (Human Development Report 2007/2008)
United Nations Environment Programme, The Status of Climate Change Litigation: a Global Review (2017)
Verheyen, R, Tackling Loss & Damage: A New Role for the Climate Regime? (Loss and Damage in Vulnerable Countries Initiative, 2012)
Watkins, K et al, Human Development Report 2007/2008: Fighting Climate Change: Human Solidarity in a Divided World (United Nations Development Programme, 2007)
Willetts, E, Guadagno, L and Ikkala, N, Addressing Climate Change: Issues and Solutions from Around the World (International Union for the Conservation of Nature, 2010)
World Health Organization, Protecting Health from Climate Change: Connecting Science, Policy and People (2009)
——, World Malaria Report 2011 (2011)
——, Quantitative Risk Assessment of the Effects of Climate Change on Selected Causes of Death, 2030s and 2050s (2014)
World Health Organization and World Meteorological Organization, Atlas of Health and Climate (2012)
Yamamoto, L and Esteban, M, 'Atoll Island States and Climate Change: Sovereignty Implications' (UNU-IAS Working Paper 166, October 2011)

News and Media

Berkes, A, 'A New Extraterritorial Jurisdictional Link Recognised by the IACtHR' (EJIL Talk, 2018)
Bramwell, C, 'Pacific Atolls "could be underwater by 2050"' (Radio NZ, 15 July 2016)
Goering, L, 'Climate Deal Could Bar Poor from Seeking Compensation for Losses' (Reuters, 2015)
Holmes, O, 'Palestine Files Complaint Against Israel under Anti-Racism Treaty' (The Guardian, 23 April 2018)
Laville, S, 'Portuguese Children to Crowdfund European Climate Case' (The Guardian, 25 September 2017)
Office of the Press Secretary, The White House, 'US–China Joint Announcement on Climate Change' (Press Release, 12 November 2014)
Pashley, A, 'Did the Paris Deal Rule Out Climate Compensation?' (Climate Home, 2015)
Republic of the Philippines Commission on Human Rights, 'Press Release: National Inquiry on the Impact of Climate Change on the Human Rights of the Filipino People' (27 March 2018)
Revkin, AC, 'World Briefing Americas: Inuit Climate Change Petition Rejected' (New York Times, 16 December 2006)
United Nations Secretary General, Ban Ki-Moon, 'Address to High-Level Event on Climate Change' (2007)

INDEX

www.ingramcontent.com/pod-product-compliance
Ingram Content Group UK Ltd.
Pitfield, Milton Keynes, MK11 3LW, UK
UKHW020815290926
15470UKWH00003B/1176